THE TRUMAN SCANDALS
AND THE POLITICS OF MORALITY

GIVE 'EM HELL HARRY

Give 'Em Hell Harry Series
Editor, Robert H. Ferrell

Harry S. Truman, the "man from Missouri" who served as the thirty-third president of the United States, has been the subject of many books. Historians, political figures, friends, foes, and family members—all have sought to characterize, understand, and interpret this figure who continues to live in the minds and imaginations of a broad reading public. The Give 'Em Hell Harry Series is designed to keep available in reasonably priced paperback editions the best books that have been written about this remarkable man.

THE TRUMAN SCANDALS
AND THE POLITICS
OF MORALITY

Andrew J. Dunar

University of Missouri Press
Columbia and London

Library of Congress Cataloging in Publication Data

Dunar, Andrew J.
   The Truman Scandals and the Politics of Morality

   Bibliography: p.
   Includes index.
   ISBN 0-8262-1118-6 (alk. paper)
   1. Truman, Harry S., 1884–1972—Personality. 2. Corruption (in politics)—United States—History—20th
century. 3. United States—Politics and government—
1945–1953. I. Title.
E814.D86 1984   973.918′0924   84-2205
ISBN 0–8262–0443–0

∞ ™ This paper meets the requirements of the
American National Standard for Permanence of Paper
for Printed Library Materials, Z39.48, 1984.

To Catherine

ACKNOWLEDGMENTS ▰▰▰▰▰

Many people assisted me at every stage of this project, and I owe them all a full measure of gratitude.

Research was facilitated by grants from the Harry S. Truman Library Institute and the history department of the University of Southern California. The Gerald R. Ford Award, established under the auspices of Dean John A. Schutz of the University of Southern California, provided further assistance.

Dr. Benedict K. Zobrist and his staff at the Truman Library were extremely helpful and accommodating during summer research trips. Dennis Bilger, Harry Clark, Neil Johnson, Philip Lagerquist, Erwin Mueller, Warren Ohrvall, and Pauline Testerman contributed to the study with many suggestions that reflected their familiarity with the holdings of the Truman Library. Librarian Elizabeth Safly helped to solve countless problems and is largely responsible for creating the pleasant atmosphere that led one researcher to refer to the Truman Library as a "family-style research center." The late Mrs. Howard Carvin provided lodging in her home in Independence.

Mr. and Mrs. Howard Post and Steve and Meg Post graciously took me into their homes during research trips to Washington.

I am greatly indebted to two scholars of the Truman era for their professional advice and personal encouragement. Franklin D. Mitchell of the University of Southern California, who originally sparked my interest in the Truman presidency, assisted from the inception of this project, suggesting approaches and leads that were consistently productive. Robert H. Ferrell of Indiana University helped in the revision of the manuscript, suggesting changes in style and substance, teaching me a great deal about writing in the process. Both men have been exceedingly generous with their time and considerable talents, and I am very grateful for their help.

Doyce B. Nunis, Jr., and William W. Lammers of the University of Southern California both offered many useful suggestions.

My wife, Catherine, to whom this book is dedicated, has given me immeasurable support and encouragement. She, my son, James, and my daughter, Kimberly, have given my life an added and rewarding dimension.

A. J. D.
Schenectady
June 1984

CONTENTS

1. A POLITICAL PHILOSOPHY

When Harry S. Truman succeeded Franklin D. Roosevelt as president on 12 April 1945, he was to some Americans an unknown quantity, so it was not uncommon to hear the question, "Who the hell is Harry Truman?" But many Americans did know something about him, and what they knew compounded the question rather than answered it. A confounding duality had manifested itself in the events of previous months, a duality that was to confuse the years of his presidency.

On one side of Truman's reputation was his undoubted competence. On 7 August 1944, shortly after accepting the nomination of his party for the vice-presidency, Senator Truman had addressed the Senate in a statement tendering his resignation as chairman of the committee that had monitored the nation's defense expenditures during the war. Popularly referred to as the Truman committee, the group reportedly had saved taxpayers $15 billion, and leadership of the committee had brought its chairman national prominence, making his selection as vice-presidential nominee feasible. Resignation from the committee's chairmanship was a valedictory event that gave fellow Democrats opportunity to praise his leadership and character. Sen. Carl Hatch, one of his committee colleagues, said that he had been wise, kindly, firm, and courageous. Whatever the committee accomplished, he explained, was a reflection of Truman's integrity, wisdom, and courage.[1]

On the other side of the new president's reputation, however, was a connection with the underside of American politics. The once-powerful boss of the Kansas City Democratic machine, Thomas J. Pendergast, died on 26 January 1945 while on probation from federal prison. Truman never had denied ties to Pendergast and his machine, and the vice-president chose to ignore the political risks and fly back to Kansas City for the funeral. Characteristically, he explained the trip by declaring, "He was my friend and I was his," giving critics opportunity to raise old issues that linked him to a political machine with underworld connections.[2] Throughout his career, Truman faced accusations of having been a Pendergast lackey, indeed, of having gone to Washington in 1935 as "the senator from Pendergast."

To accept either side of the Truman duality was to miss much of the complexity of a man too often viewed by contemporaries as a simple Midwesterner. He had been shaped by many experiences, coming to the presidency at the age of sixty, and was remarkably consistent in his perspectives. He could defend his association with Pendergast with the same conviction that he could boast of accomplishments of the Truman committee. He was part of the machine, but he lived by a strict Baptist morality.[3]

The president's upbringing was traditional, stressing morality and virtue. As a youngster, the eldest of three children, he suffered from an eye defect and from a period of paralysis following diphtheria; both afflictions required maternal attention that established a bond between him and his mother. They were drawn to one another even as his more rugged brother, Vivian, was drawn to his father. Yet the mother was the disciplinarian; as Harry Truman recalled, "We were taught that punishment always followed transgression and my mother saw to it that it did."[4] An Independence resident who knew Truman as a boy wrote aptly, "Here was a boy who never questioned his mother's wisdom or authority and from the beginning always strove in every way to please her. She in turn gave him the watchful care of a mother's kindness and directed him along cultural and intellectual paths."[5]

Martha Ellen Truman was a devout Baptist and schooled her son in the principles so important to her. Truman claimed to have read the Bible twice by the time he was twelve, and he was impressed by the moral codes set out in the twentieth chapter of Exodus and the fifth, sixth, and seventh chapters of Matthew. At eighteen he joined the Baptist church, a membership he was proud to retain for the rest of his long life. Never ostentatious about his beliefs, he thought that religion was "something to live by and not talk about." His grandfather, he liked to explain, "used to say that when he heard his neighbor pray too loudly in public he always went home and locked his smokehouse."[6] Truman's familiarity with the Bible increased after he joined a Masonic lodge in 1909, for Masonic studies delineated what he afterward described as a system of morals based entirely on the Scriptures.[7] What was meaningful in religious studies to the young Truman—in reading the Bible, in Masonry—was a personal moral code. The same theme, honor and integrity, was implicit in a prayer he said daily throughout his adult life: "Help me to be, to think, to act what is right, because it is right; make me truthful, honest and honorable in all things; make me intellectually honest for the sake of right and honor."[8] His mother's moral values affected his personal habits—he did not smoke, he drank in moderation, and he dressed neatly. He was always respectful toward women and considered divorce unthinkable.[9]

In the upbringing that was so important in his public life, his father, John, helped to mold his outlook, guiding him to place a premium on integrity. "My father was a very honorable man," he reflected. "If he guaranteed a horse in a trade that guarantee was as good as a loan. If he agreed to do a day's work for a certain amount of money he'd given good measure on the work."[10] When Harry was twenty-one, his family moved to the family farm near Grandview, a dozen miles from Independence; he joined them there the next year, in 1906, and worked on the farm for eleven years. It was a period he remembered as "the best time I ever had in my life." He grew closer to his father: "We were real partners."[11] When his father died in 1914, he was present in the room; he had gone to sleep, tired in the evening hours, and awoke to find his father dead. When Harry Truman then took over his father's job as township road overseer, he attempted to employ the lessons he had learned: "I was taught that the expenditure of public money is a public trust and I have never changed my opinion on that subject."[12]

A member of the Missouri National Guard for some years after 1905, he saw duty in France during World War I as an artillery officer. Perhaps the most lasting effect of his service came in the friendships he formed with such men as Lt. Harry H. Vaughan, who became his military aide during the White House years, and Sgt. Eddie Jacobson, with whom he ran a canteen at Camp Doniphan in Oklahoma before going to France and with whom he opened a haberdashery in Kansas City after the war.

Before Truman returned to Independence in 1919, he had decided not to resume farming. He had not yet determined what he would do, but after a chance encounter with Jacobson he decided to open the men's furnishing store. The partners established a line of credit and opened for business in November 1919, and for a year and a half the business flourished. Then the recession of 1921 devastated the business, rapidly devaluing the inventory; the partners resisted an opportunity to sell out at inventory price, only to see that value plunge from $35,000 to $10,000 within days.[13] Jacobson later filed for bankruptcy, but Truman refused to follow the same course, resolving to pay off all debts of the haberdashery, which were considerable. Jacobson's bankruptcy statement of 1925 listed his own debts as $10,058.50, of which the principal components were $3,900 owed the owner of the store building for the unexpired portion of the lease and $5,600 owed to the Security Bank of Kansas City. Over the next several years, Truman settled on the best terms he could obtain. Truman's share of the bank loan plagued him; when the Security State Bank failed during the Great Depression, the Continental National Bank took over its assets and obtained a judgment for $8,944.78 for principal and interest; then that bank also failed, and Truman's brother, Vivian, purchased the note from the receiver in early 1935, ending the ordeal.[14]

In later years, Truman's handling of the affairs of the haberdashery provided ammunition for supporters and critics alike. He defended his actions, saying that he and Jacobson "continued to pay and settle our obligations and after about fifteen years cleared them all up honorably. Not one of our creditors, merchandiser or bank, ever accused us of a dishonorable act."[15] Truman lost $28,000 on the haberdashery and could have cut his losses by filing bankruptcy. His supporters pointed to his refusal to go into bankruptcy. The decision not to do so was as much moral as political, to avoid the stigma that likely would have damaged a political career. Discussing another business disappointment just months before the Continental Bank settlement, Truman concluded, "I always did let ethics beat me out of money and I suppose

I always will."[16] Opponents were less charitable. Truman was
not entirely successful in escaping the stigma of bankruptcy,
since Jacobson's action (they said) implicated his partner. As
late as 1951 adversaries also accused Truman of using politics to obtain favorable terms in settling his debts.

Failure of the store opened an opportunity for Truman to
enter politics, and it was at this time that he began his association with the Pendergast machine. In the summer of
1922, while the business was foundering, an army acquaintance, Jim Pendergast, and his father, Michael J. Pendergast,
brother of Boss Tom, walked into the store and asked Truman if he would be interested in seeking the position of
Eastern District county judge, an administrative office in
Jackson County. At the time, the Democratic party was split
into factions, the "Goats" under the Pendergasts and the
"Rabbits" under Joseph B. Shannon, with the Pendergasts
in the ascendancy. Mike Pendergast headed the Goats' operations in the Tenth Ward, the rural, eastern part of Jackson County, which in its western part includes Kansas City.[17]

It might have seemed odd that the Goats would settle on
a thirty-eight-year-old haberdasher as their candidate for
the Eastern District judgeship. In truth, Truman brought
many attractive qualities to the Goat ticket, though it may be
hyperbole to say, as biographer Jonathan Daniels did, that
"Truman had more to offer the Pendergasts than the Pendergasts had to offer him."[18] From an established local family, Truman had friends and relatives throughout the county
district, enabling the machine to avoid the appearance of
forcing a city politician down the throat of country folks. He
was a veteran and could get the veteran vote. As a Baptist
and a Mason, with a Southern heritage, he was a proper
country balance to the Irish Catholic Pendergasts. He had
been a county road overseer and was familiar with local politics. Finally, he was eager to run and proved an indefatigable campaigner.[19]

The combination of these attributes and the support of
the Pendergasts, along with backing from the Shannon faction, brought easy victory, but then came a defeat two years
later. A tactical error by the Pendergasts over the issue of
patronage prompted Shannon to oppose Truman's reelection, the only electoral defeat he ever suffered. In 1926, he

ran for the office of presiding judge of the three-member
county court. By this time, the Pendergast organization had
consolidated its power in Jackson County, and Truman won;
he held the post for the next eight years.[10]

During ten years in county office, until his election to the
U.S. Senate in 1934, Truman established a reputation for
honesty and administrative efficiency that made him a
marked asset to the Pendergast machine. His tenure as presiding judge saw accomplishments that included two new
courthouses and a widely praised system of county roads. In
a brief, handwritten memorandum that recapitulated his
achievements, Truman noted that he had been "responsible
for the expenditure of 50 million dollars over the 8 year
period with no breath of scandal."[21]

Although Truman by the mid-1930s had achieved a reputation for honesty and integrity in county office, association
with the Pendergast machine was not easy to cast aside, and
it would follow him like a shadow throughout his national
political career. A Kansas City reporter, Frank Mason, once
observed that while there was never any evidence that Truman was dishonest when in Pendergast's circle, political enemies could still use the association; nevertheless, "The only
thing they had against him was the emotional shudder that
runs through many people when they hear the name of
Pendergast."[22] The U.S. district attorney who destroyed the
machine in the late thirties said of attempts to dismiss the
Pendergast-Truman alliance, "History is history; the will to
forget a fact cannot totally obscure it."[23] Truman himself
never denied the relationship. After Tom Pendergast had
been rebuked, discredited, and sent to Leavenworth for income-tax evasion, Truman remained loyal and criticized
those who "ran out when the going was rough."[24]

A close relationship between Truman and Pendergast
lasted from the early twenties until the late thirties and gave
Truman opportunity to define his attitude toward corruption. Here it was easy to exaggerate, to draw their relationship as "one of the most bizarre on record" to use the words
of Maurice M. Milligan, the district attorney who sent Pendergast to prison.[25] But it would be difficult to imagine two
men of more diverse backgrounds. The Baptist, bespec-

tacled, erstwhile farm boy and army officer seemed an unlikely ally of the burly Irish Catholic former saloon owner and political operator whose enemies described him as "an overbearing, ruthless, calculating public enemy."[26] Observers who examined the curious association noted that Truman was an anomaly in urban politics—a reformer who adhered to Progressive ideals and yet found himself comfortable within a political machine. The alliance flourished, however, because it was symbiotic. Truman gave Pendergast an honest county administration that solidified machine control over rural Jackson County. Truman gave Pendergast patronage, but not graft. Pendergast in return gave Truman considerable independence—and assistance of the machine's electoral power.[27]

The success and longevity of the relationship owed much to Truman's ability to adapt to a system with which he was not in full agreement. As a party loyalist, he was willing to accept the "lesser evil" argument that sanctioned certain activities in order to keep the party in power. Though he never said so publicly during his Jackson County career, he wrote privately, "I think maybe machines are not so good for the country." Still, he qualified this mild indictment by adding, "There are 'machines' & machines. Tammany, Bill Thompson, Mr. Cox of Cincinnati, Ed Butler, they all have but one end—fool the taxpayer, steal the taxes. The 'people' are dumb." The governance of Kansas City in Truman's view was not as bad as that of other cities, since it had "an extraordinarily clean local government. Chicago, Pittsburgh, San Francisco, Los Angeles make us look like suckers."[28] In Truman's opinion, Kansas City politics were cleaner than those of other machine-controlled cities because of Pendergast's leadership. Boss Tom used all the devices of machine control, but Truman asserted that his ways of employing them were benign. Truman, for example, accepted patronage as the spoils of political battle and never resisted Pendergast's control of the nine hundred positions under jurisdiction of the county court. He endorsed the way in which patronage was administered in Jackson County, saying, "T. J. Pendergast was interested in having as many friends in key positions as possible, but he always took the position that if a man didn't do the job he was supposed to do, fire him and get someone who would. I always followed that policy, and I never had a cross word."[29]

Truman realized that he would always be judged in terms of his relationship with Pendergast. Eager to have his understanding of that association elaborated, he discussed it both in writing and in conversation. His many statements after going to Washington as a senator in 1935 emphasized that Pendergast was a man of his word who gave Truman virtual independence in running Jackson County, in return for control of patronage. Nowhere was there a hint of friction between judge and boss. A literal reading of these accounts would have Judge Truman operating with autonomy, so apart from the Kansas City machine that it left Jackson County unaffected by the unsavory politics of the city. The two organizations appeared as virtually separate, unrelated save for patronage and an occasional meeting between Truman and Pendergast.[30]

Another Truman account demands some reevaluation of this standard version of the Truman-Pendergast alliance. In the early 1930s, Truman wrote a candid autobiographical essay that was inspired with a passion and immediacy missing in later versions of the relationship. On the stationery of Kansas City's Pickwick Hotel, he expounded on his upbringing and early life and made cogent if occasionally cryptic and rambling observations on Jackson County political morality. The notes were dated in only two places, although it appears that portions of what is a long document may have been written at different times. The first date is 3 December 1930—nearly a year into his second four-year term as presiding judge. The second section was written in the early morning hours of 14 May 1934, the day he announced he would seek a Senate seat that fall.[31]

The Pickwick Hotel notes are exceptional in several respects. Foremost, they were written while Truman was associated with Pendergast; he wrote all other accounts after Pendergast died and after he had been in Washington for a decade or more, years in which memory perhaps had screened out the more unpleasant aspects of his Jackson County experience. Perhaps Truman then was more conscious that he was writing for public consumption, or perhaps he succumbed to the human tendency to romanticize. The Pickwick papers are more revealing than others, furthermore, not only for the view they present of the Truman-Pendergast relationship but also for insights into the way in which he coped with corruption while carrying out his responsibilities as presiding judge. These notes show a strain in dealings between Judge Truman and Boss Pendergast that is not apparent in other accounts. Truman wrote years later, in 1952, "Tom Pendergast was a man of his word, and he kept it with me." [32] In the earlier Pickwick papers, he said virtually the same thing—but added, "I am obligated to the Big Boss, a man of his word; but he gives it very seldom and usually on a sure thing." [33]

More revealing are differences in the accounts Truman presented of a meeting with Pendergast and several local contractors seeking favored treatment on road projects. It was a story Truman told on more than one occasion during his years in Washington to demonstrate the support and independence he was granted by Tom Pendergast. According to this tale, which gained credibility as repeated by biographers, Pendergast had summoned Judge Truman to his office to confront some aggrieved local contractors, whom Truman had bypassed when he awarded a road contract for $400,000 to a South Dakota firm. Pendergast loyalists had been accustomed to favored treatment, but Truman stood his ground and insisted that the contracts would go to the lowest bidder. During the meeting Truman refused to budge; Pendergast turned to his friends and admonished them, "I told you he's the contrariest man [or cuss or mule] on earth. Now get out of here." He assured Truman, "You carry out your commitment to the voters." [34] In Truman's account in the Pickwick papers the confrontation over road contracts was much more acrimonious:

> The Boss wanted me to give a lot of crooked contractors the inside and I couldn't. He got awful angry at me but decided that my way was best for the public and the party. But I had to compromise with him. . . . This sweet associate of mine, my friend, who was supposed to back me had already made a deal with a former crooked contractor, a friend of the Boss's who had robbed Jackson County. . . . I had to compromise in order to get the voted road system carried out all because of my associate. I

had to let a former saloon keeper and murderer, a friend of the
Big Boss, steal about $10,000 . . . from the general revenues of
the County to satisfy my ideal associate and keep the crooks
from getting a million or more out of the bond issue. Was I right
or did I compound a felony? I don't know. . . . The Boss tells
me that in Kansas City they doctor every bid so that the inside
gentlemen get the contract.[35]

Clearly there was more pressure on Judge Truman than
he later was willing to admit. Pendergast was not as magnan-
imous, nor Truman as independent, as later accounts indicated. Nor was the confrontation with the contractors an
isolated incident. Politics-as-usual did not cease when Truman became presiding judge, however much he may have
resisted. According to the Pickwick papers Truman believed
that, altogether, "I was able to expend $7,000,000.00 for the
taxpayers' benefit. At the same time I gave away about a
million in general revenue to satisfy the politicians. But if I
hadn't done that the crooks would have had half the seven
million." The arrangement clearly bothered him. "I wonder
if I did right to put a lot of no account sons of bitches on the
payroll and pay other sons of bitches more money for supplies than they were worth in order to satisfy the political
powers and save $3,500,000.00. I believe I did do right.
Anyway, I'm not a partner of any of them and I'll go out
poorer in every way than when I came into office."[36]

There are indications that Truman bowed to machine
pressure in other ways as well. In November 1930, while the
two other county judges were absent from the court, he
made two appointments to justice of the peace courts in Kaw
Township, even though the Missouri legislature had eliminated the positions. Truman had been informed earlier by
counsel that the appointments would be illegal, but he proceeded anyway. He said later that the law eliminating the
positions had been poorly written and that he only had
meant to force a clarification of the statute. Pendergast of
course wanted the positions and had written Gov. Guy Park
in October 1933, "We are in great need of additional Justices
of the Peace in Kaw township," adding a handwritten note
at the bottom of the letter: "Dear Governor: I am very much
interested in this. TJP"[37]

As realities of politics clashed with Truman's moral code

and forced him to concessions, he understandably became discouraged. On one occasion, he wrote an introspective note to himself: "It was my opinion . . . that most men had a sense of honor. Now I don't know. 'The Boss' says that instead most of them are not when they are put into a position where they can get away with crookedness. I guess I've been wrong in my premise that 92% are not thieves but it is a certainty that 92% are not ethically honest." Still, he refused to succumb to temptations that were paraded before him. He refused to participate in the graft around him and could rightly contemplate later that "We've spent $7,000,000.00 in revenue in my administration. I could have had $1,500,000.00. I haven't $150.00. Am I a fool or an ethical giant? I don't know."[38] Truman never considered himself a fool, but he did work throughout his Jackson County days to retain his reputation for integrity. His efforts often went far beyond what was legally necessary, as if he were compensating for the corruption around him. When a county road project intersected his mother's farm, he refused to pay her county funds to compensate for the loss of eleven acres that he conceded were worth $11,000. Margaret Truman observed that her grandmother "complained about this super-honesty for years."[39]

Both at the time and later, Truman's reflections on a trip to select a consulting architect for Jackson County civic and community buildings reveal a man seeking to insure that his actions would be beyond reproach. "I took my private automobile, not a County one" to travel from city to city, he remarked pointedly.[40] "I'm still an idealist," he wrote, "and I still believe that Jehovah will reward the righteous and punish the wrongdoers."[41] He later expressed pride that when state and federal grand juries and the FBI investigated the county programs during his tenure, "They could give me only a clean bill of health."[42]

Even Truman's speeches during his days on the county court reflected preoccupation with political morality. His addresses attacked corrupt officials at all levels of government as he called for honor and morality in public and personal conduct. Targets of his attacks ranged from the Harding administration ("the rottenest administration in all the history of the United States") to a local attorney who attempted to profit by forcing the sale of his land to the county ("There is a blot on Mr. Scaritt and his law firm").[43] He excoriated "rotten, putrid bribe taking rulers" and state officials charged with graft.[44] To counter corruption he urged a rebirth of honor: "We must get back to the old ideals of honor in government, honor in our personal dealings and a reliance on ourselves."[45] When chosen to speak at a Washington's Birthday banquet in February 1925, as representative of his class at Kansas City Law School (which he attended desultorily from 1923 to 1925 while Eastern District judge), he chose as his subject honor and government. While presiding judge, his speeches defended the court: "We have expanded the county's bond funds honestly and efficiently."[46] To young people, he emphasized moral behavior, not to "go to excess in anything," closing with a familiar appeal—"let's prepare to live normal honorable and proper lives as God intended we should."[47] These speeches were not rhetoric; they were the sentiments of a man fighting to maintain moral independence from machine politics.

From the time he left the Jackson County courthouse at the end of his second term as presiding judge in 1935 until he returned to Independence nearly two decades later, Truman often would be charged with his Pendergast connections. In fact, he honed his political skills during his Jackson County days, but lessons from that experience were seldom those his critics supposed. He had recognized corruption and dealt with it in a way that left him his reputation. Some of his faith in human nature had been shaken; he was now convinced there would always be people who would seek public positions for private gain. Yet he was equally convinced one could survive in the midst of corruption, and even stop some of it.

Jackson County taught Truman strategies that a leader could employ to counter corruption. It was essential to be honest and forthright. It was necessary to get trustworthy subordinates into key positions; he recalled N. T. Veatch and Col. E. M. Stayton, the engineers who designed and carried out the Jackson County road plan, and noted that "if Veatch and Stayton had been crooks my career as a public official would have been the usual scandal." Truman learned to avoid corruption by working around people who were responsible for it, as he circumvented the two judges on the court during part of his term as presiding judge: "When I wanted something done I'd let Baer and Vrooman start a crap game and then introduce a long and technical order. Neither of them would have time to read it and over it would go. I got a lot of good legislation for Jackson Co. over while they shot craps. Both of them thought that public office is a means of personal enrichment."[48]

Another of his lessons in county government was the need to take issues to the people, who would vindicate an honest and well-reasoned position even if it ran counter to conventional political wisdom. When he sought a bond issue for roads, he recalled, "Pendergast told me that a County bond issue would not carry. I told him that if I told the voters how I would handle it, it would carry. I went to the people . . . and [the] bond issue carried by a three-fourths majority instead of the required two-thirds."[49]

Finally, Truman had learned of the enmity of the press. Pendergast's administration had long been a target of Kansas City journalists, and Truman considered much of the criticism unwarranted: "What chance is there for a clean honest administration of the city and county when a bunch of vultures sit on the side lines and puke on the field. The *Star* does as much puking as the rest."[50]

Having learned these lessons and employed these tactics in Jackson County, he would do so again as president. They would not always serve him in the presidency—in part because he occasionally misapplied them. Trusting subordinates could mean failing to check on them; integrity meant less when one bore responsibility for people who had none; going to the public was risky when one's adversaries could make an equal or better claim to virtue. Leaving Jackson County politics, moreover, did not allow Truman to step out of the shadow of Pendergast. It was Pendergast who chose Truman to seek the Democratic nomination for the Senate in 1934. It was Pendergast who provided much of Truman's backing in the campaign. And it was Pendergast who was a major issue. In a three-way primary race between Truman, Rep. Jacob L. ("Tuck") Milligan, and Rep. John J. Cochran, Truman tried to counter charges of machine connections by pointing out that both his opponents had sought Pendergast support in 1932 when all Missouri congressional races were contested on an at-large basis because the state legislature had failed to redistrict. He accused them of being controlled candidates—Cochran by the St. Louis organization and Milligan by Sen. Bennett Clark.[51]

Truman's victory in the primary in 1934 assured his election and demonstrated the statewide influence of the Pendergast organization. Indeed, charges of voting headstones and of other chicanery necessary to obtain 93 percent of the Jackson County vote tarnished the victory and added to Truman's image as a Pendergast stooge. "If he had the Pendergast support," Jonathan Daniels observed years later in a friendly biography, "he had the Pendergast smear at his heels all the time."[52]

In his subsequent service in the Senate, Truman proved unwilling to break with the Kansas City machine yet chafed at the notion that he was "the senator from Pendergast." It was his county court experience all over again. While he recognized his debt to the machine, he yearned to be regarded as his own man. He sought to take the same approach he had used in Jackson County—Pendergast would receive the patronage Truman saw as the Boss's due, but the senator would seek an independent role in national affairs. Pendergast, alas, gained more than he lost in the exchange, for control of federal patronage, particularly Works Progress Administration jobs, enabled him to expand his influence throughout the state. But Truman's quest for independence was fraught with hazards because he had to seek to demonstrate that he was the puppet of neither Pendergast nor President Franklin D. Roosevelt while remaining loyal to both men. When a battle developed over the post of Senate majority leader in 1936, Truman seized the opportunity to make a gesture of independence from both of his supposed masters. President Roosevelt, channeling his desires through Pendergast, apparently told the chairman of the Democratic National Committee, James A. Farley, to press Truman to support Alben Barkley of Kentucky; Farley telephoned Pendergast who telephoned Truman. Truman already had promised to back Pat Harrison of Mississippi and was rankled that the president had not approached him directly; he refused to go back on his pledge to Harrison.

Pendergast pressed no further. According to Truman, it was the only time the Kansas City boss ever attempted to influence him in the Senate.[53] Midway through Truman's first Senate term, Boss Pendergast's fortunes suffered an astonishingly rapid reversal. He suffered a heart attack in 1936 and a short time later underwent a serious cancer operation. Physically weakened, he could not counter effectively an assault by political opponents. The U.S. district attorney, Maurice Milligan—whose brother Truman had defeated in the 1934 primary—initiated an investigation of vote frauds in the 1936 Kansas City primary. The headlines garnered by the probe prompted Missouri's ambitious and opportunistic Gov. Lloyd Stark, who had won office with Pendergast support, to assist Milligan in seeking a broadened investigation of the Kansas City machine. Assisted by agents from the Treasury and the FBI, the district attorney demolished Pendergast. In the end, the Boss was the victim of his own excesses. A predilection for gambling had led him to betting on virtually every horse race in the United States, a habit he could sustain only through obtaining even larger sums of money. A group of insurance companies gave him $600,000, hoping to obtain a favorable ruling from the state's insurance commission, which he controlled, and Pendergast failed to report the money on his income tax. Indeed, he had underreported his taxes since 1927, and in 1939 the ill and vanquished Boss was convicted and imprisoned for evading $1 million in income taxes. The Kansas City machine passed nominally into the less capable hands of the Boss's nephew Jim; in reality, it virtually disappeared with the demise of the man Truman had called the Big Boss.[54]

Truman refused to disassociate himself from the Pendergast machine even as corruption engulfed the organization that had helped his political career. He considered Stark's joining the anti-Pendergast forces to be an act of rank political expediency and duplicity. Truman simply was not going to walk out on Pendergast. When Milligan's term as U.S. district attorney expired in 1938, President Roosevelt decided to reappoint him over Truman's objection. For Truman it was a no-win situation. If he opposed Milligan, he was Pendergast's lackey; if he did not, he was a turncoat deserting a friend in trouble. Truman chose not to exercise his senatorial prerogative to block the appointment, but he did rise in the Senate to denounce Milligan. The speech provided grist for gleeful opponents, one of whom described it as "the speech of a man nominated by ghost votes, elected with ghost votes, and whose speech was probably written by a ghost writer."[55]

The final months of Truman's first term in the Senate were a low point, with the continued loyalty to Pendergast apparently signaling the end of his career. As Margaret later recalled, "Never before or since can I recall my father being so gloomy as he was in those last months of 1939."[56] Close friends and advisers suggested that it would be foolish to seek reelection in 1940; his career seemed in shambles. His pet legislative proposal, a transportation bill, was bogged down in committee. Roosevelt backed Stark in what soon became a campaign for Truman's Senate seat. Ironically, the actions of Democratic adversaries enabled Truman to win the 1940 primary. While most observers expected the Pendergast affair to destroy Truman, Stark's campaigning proved inept. Milligan then joined the race and siphoned off enough of Stark's anti-Pendergast support to enable Truman to win the Democratic nomination, edging Stark by a plurality of less than eight thousand votes.[57]

The general election for Missouri's Senate seat in 1940 was not the foregone conclusion it had been in 1934. The Republicans nominated Manvel Davis, a Kansas City lawyer and an opponent of Pendergast, and challenged Truman not only on the basis of association with the Kansas City machine but on two peripheral matters as well. The first involved a foreclosure on the Truman family farm in Grandview. A substantial mortgage had encumbered the farm since the death of Truman's maternal grandmother, Louisa Young, in 1909. His mother and his uncle Harrison (for whom he was named) had inherited the farm, but they had been forced to mortgage the property to settle rival claims when the will was contested by the other Young children. During the intervening years, no progress was made in reducing the principal on the mortgage, as family finances were restricted by Truman's business debts and by years of unproductive farming during the Depression. In 1938, Truman's mother refinanced the mortgage, borrowing $35,000 from the Jackson County school fund. During the 1940 senatorial campaign, the presiding judge of Jackson County engineered a foreclosure, and Truman's political enemies charged that he had misused the school fund. Truman was embittered, claiming that he was not given a second chance to refinance the loan and blaming the county for forcing his elderly mother to a strange house in Grandview where she fell down the stairs and broke her hip.[58] Truman's integrity also was questioned that year when he was chosen Grand Master of the Masons of Missouri. He was assailed as unfit for the post, although even Republican gubernatorial candidate Forrest C. Donnell, also a Mason, acknowledged that Truman was worthy of it. So the Republican smear had been discredited, and in spite of a vigorous campaign by candidate Davis, Truman won a forty-thousand-vote victory.[59]

Although the Pendergast association dominated Senator Truman's public image, many of his Senate colleagues recognized that his performance during his first term was not that of a mere machine operative. His perseverance and attention to detail earned respect. Under the tutelage of Sen. Burton K. Wheeler of Montana, he had worked diligently on the Interstate Commerce Committee, eventually cosponsoring the bill that became the Transportation Act of 1940.[60]

In his second Senate term, Truman distinguished himself not only for independent judgment but also as a man capable of becoming a national leader. Having at last overcome the Pendergast association, he began his second term exuding confidence. He established a reputation as a man to be trusted. He recalled an occasion on which he arbitrated a dispute between colleagues, as he happened to have information that was needed to settle the argument, after which Sen. Arthur H. Vandenberg of Michigan said, "When the Senator from Missouri makes a statement like that, we can take it for the truth."[61]

Truman was of course not a national figure when he was sworn in for his second term in January 1941, but that was to change dramatically within the next two years. The work that brought him national prominence was for the Special Committee to Investigate the Defense Program, popularly known as the Truman committee. Chairmanship of that committee changed his image from that of machine accomplice to that of crusader for honesty and efficiency in expenditure of public funds.

Truman was alerted to problems in the military establishment by letters from constituents complaining of waste at Fort Leonard Wood in Missouri. Bothered by the persistence of these reports, he set out on a national tour of war camps, defense plants, and other projects related to the war effort. After driving his own automobile on a trip that took him to sites throughout the eastern half of the country, he returned to Washington convinced of the immediate need for attention to a grave situation. In a broadly worded resolution, he asked the Senate for authority to establish a five-member committee to investigate the national defense program and requested a modest initial appropriation of $25,000.

At the outset of his committee work he almost met with defeat—and here again, if such were needed, was evidence both of his political shrewdness and of the manner in which his career in politics had a way of moving upward through all obstacles. James F. Byrnes, a powerful man in the Senate, acting perhaps on advice from the president, awarded Truman's committee an initial appropriation of $15,000, a ridiculously small amount to investigate a war program that was costing tens of billions. Byrnes and Roosevelt probably did not want any serious investigation of what were some very loose expenditures of federal funds. Schooled, however, in the Pendergast experience, Truman took this petty appropriation and gave almost all of it to a skilled investigator and lawyer, Hugh Fulton, and proceeded to establish a record as chairman of a marvelously efficient committee; before Byrnes and Roosevelt could congratulate each other on how they had outwitted the junior senator from Missouri, Truman showed such tact, and such sheer ability, as chairman of the committee that the Roosevelt administration had to go along with his investigation. Indeed, the president eventually realized—as had Boss Tom years before—that he needed Truman more than he had thought. As the committee met with success and demonstrated its impartiality in an unbroken string of unanimous reports, it was accorded increasing newspaper and magazine attention and was able to command a realistic budget. Over the next three and a half years, Truman estimated that the committee saved the taxpayers $15 billion in return for operating expenses of $400,000.[62]

The committee's success was not due to Truman's efforts alone, of course. Members of the committee were, with exception of Texas's Tom Connally, younger senators eager to establish reputations in Congress. They proved a courageous group, willing to risk criticism of their respective parties and of the people who had elected them. Among the strengths of the committee, Truman numbered the fact that its members had "no preconceived notions, no partisan views to promote, no beliefs to prove."[63]

Preeminent among the members of the staff was its chief counsel, Fulton, who had been recommended by Attorney General Robert H. Jackson. Fulton's contribution was so important that one of the members of the staff later remarked, "There is no telling what course history might have followed, in my opinion, if Truman had not found Fulton."[64] Vigorous, self-assured, and competent, Fulton was a brilliant organizer who originated many of the committee programs. Truman and Fulton, both country boys with a love for reading, were well matched. Early risers, they met regularly at the start of the day in Truman's office where they mapped strategy for the committee's operations. Although Truman selected the rest of the committee's staff on the basis of ability rather than politics, he did bring old Missouri associates to the staff. Fred Canfil, a political aide, served capably as an investigator. William M. Boyle, future national chairman of the Democratic party, was assistant counsel.

Truman directed the inquiry with unfailing care and tact. Aware that a similar committee during the Civil War, the Committee on the Conduct of the War, was ineffective because of involvement in political issues and military strategy, he set forth procedures that would avoid pitfalls. He insisted that the committee offer constructive criticism and seek to eliminate corruption. He refused to become involved in military decisions, to dictate to government agencies, or to be distracted by politics. His nonpartisan approach won support of senators whom Truman once had considered prima donnas, enabling the committee to generate the unanimous reports that added force to its findings. His devotion and dedication to the committee, along with his tenacity, won the loyalty of his associates. Outwardly modest in a disarming manner, which won affection of the press, Truman privately was delighted with the attention he received and wrote a friend: "I am working night and day—still standing the boys on their heads and getting more favorable publicity in the papers than all the rest of the Senators put together."[65] Years later, his pride in the committee had not diminished. It was, he reflected, a "very successful committee. It was not partisan, and it was always fair."[66] Even the usually critical *Kansas City Star* granted a grudging accolade: "The Truman case proved one of those rare exceptions where a boss-chosen candidate showed exceptional capacity for development under responsibility."[67]

Without the national attention afforded by the success of the committee, it is inconceivable that President Roosevelt would have chosen Truman as his running mate in 1944. The vice-presidency was of immense importance, for Roosevelt's deteriorating health made it unlikely that he would live to complete a fourth term. The end came within months of the 1945 inauguration. In April, Truman became the nation's thirty-third president as an apparent contradiction in terms: a product of machine politics who had won a national reputation as a crusader against corruption. With this unusual background, Truman seemed well suited to deal with any threat of scandal that might touch his administration. With a strong sense of morality and a jealously guarded reputation for integrity, he had witnessed at firsthand what corruption could do to public officials. Any naïveté he had regarding the inherently honorable nature of his fellow men had been shaken by twenty years of officeholding in Jackson County and Washington.

2. EARLY ██████████████████████████
ALLEGATIONS ███████████████████████████

President Harry S. Truman began to put his mark on the high office during his first year in the White House, and the character of his appointments gave indications of the course he set for his administration. Contemporaries who sought to judge the new administration on the basis of appointments were presented with a combination that made analysis difficult. While some reflected the deliberation of a statesman, others seemed touched by politics, raising the charges of cronyism and Pendergast politics that shadowed Truman's presidency until he left office in 1953.

Of statesmanlike appointments, selection of Gen. Omar N. Bradley to head the Veterans Administration presented an intriguing example. Years before, during the Harding administration, the Veterans Bureau had been plagued by corruption. With his acute sense of history, Truman seemed determined to avoid a recurrence. Appointment of a national hero of impeccable credentials seemed designed to do just that.

Yet other appointments epitomized what critics saw as the cronyism of the administration. The first was James (Jake) Vardaman, whom Truman had known since the two had been officers in the National Guard at Fort Riley, Kansas. Truman chose Vardaman as his naval aide (Vardaman had been in the naval reserves since 1939) shortly after assuming the presidency. Vardaman's head swelled with what Margaret Truman later described as "an acute case of Potomac fever."[1] Intruding into areas that were beyond the largely ceremonial position of a naval aide, Vardaman quickly produced enough ill will to convince Truman that he had to be removed. Rather than dismiss an old friend, however, the president decided to "kick him upstairs" and nominated him to a position on the Board of Governors of the Federal Reserve Board. There was vigorous opposition to the nomination in the Senate. Vardaman's banking career in St. Louis was found wanting, and his close relation to the president lent itself to accusation of cronyism. Nevertheless, the nomination was approved in April 1946.[2]

Another ill-considered nomination proposed the affable George E. Allen as one of the five directors of the Reconstruction Finance Corporation (RFC). As secretary of the Democratic National Committee, Allen had helped secure the vice-presidential nomination for Truman in 1944. In the early months of Truman's presidency, Allen performed several tasks, including surveying war agencies to determine which should be liquidated and acting as a liaison to Congress. Allen also was an enjoyable fellow to take down the Potomac on a boat trip. He was a student of "the art of probabilities," which was the president's public description of the game of poker; he was a funny fellow, full of good jokes, almost as competent in that department of life as was the president's old friend Harry Vaughan, who had become his military aide. As for ability at finance, that was something else. Truman nonetheless nominated Allen to an RFC directorship, supposedly because of his business experience. Opposition developed immediately to what Interior Secretary Harold L. Ickes later branded "the worst appointment so far made by President Truman, and that is adding fragrance to a skunk cabbage."[3] Allen's reputation as one who ingratiated himself with the powerful in order to enhance his position had aggravated many of those who were skeptical of the nomination. Some did not take the nomination seriously; they saw Allen as a backslapper or a court clown, unqualified for a responsible position on the RFC board. Critics of the nomination, including influential Republican Sen. Robert A. Taft, raised the issue of cronyism but pointed to the more substantive charge of a possible conflict of interest. Allen suggested that he could retain his private directorships and still maintain independent judgment as a director of the RFC. If a conflict were to arise, he would resign the private directorships. The appointment cleared the Banking and Currency Committee and finally won Senate approval, but not without contributing to Truman's reputation as a machine-bred politician.[4]

A third nomination early in the president's first term generated even more controversy and brought the administration to the brink of scandal, for it provided the first serious challenge to President Truman's personal creed of loyalty. In January 1946, Truman forwarded the nomination of California oil executive Edwin W. Pauley to be under secretary of the navy. Like Allen, Pauley had played an important role in the selection of Truman as Roosevelt's running mate in 1944. Although Pauley was a staunch party man and an effective Democratic fund-raiser, the contention over his nomination was not solely because of party politics. The most vociferous opposition came from within Truman's cabinet; Secretary Ickes envisioned another Teapot Dome if an oil man received control over naval oil reserves.

Unlike the Vardaman appointment, Truman had ample reason for nomination of Pauley; he had demonstrated that he could handle difficult assignments with dispatch. His fund-raising ability had attracted the attention of President Roosevelt, who had made him treasurer of the Democratic National Committee in 1942. Within two years, he liquidated the party's $750,000 debt. Shortly after assuming the presidency, Truman assigned him as American representative on the Allied Reparations Commission, a difficult post, but he proved a tough bargainer who understood the president's positions well and argued them forcefully with Soviet negotiators. Pauley kept the president well informed of the progress of negotiations, and Truman considered Pauley's final report a masterpiece and was very pleased with his performance.[5]

There was another compelling reason for appointing him under secretary of the navy. Roosevelt, with the concurrence of his secretary of the navy, James V. Forrestal, had planned to appoint Pauley to the post upon resignation of its incumbent, Ralph Bard. Although the appointment had not been made at that time, Forrestal remained behind Pauley. Forrestal was considering resignation, and both he and Truman saw Pauley as a likely successor to his own post. In fact, Margaret Truman later asserted that the president had even larger plans for Pauley, as secretary of defense when the plan for unification of the armed services was approved.[6]

When Bard's successor as under secretary, Artemus L. Gates, indicated late in 1945 that he planned to resign, Forrestal again suggested that Pauley might be appointed. Truman was receptive and persuaded an initially reluctant Pauley to take the position. Truman was aware that there might be a fight over the nomination, but he was convinced that Pauley would stand up to any challenge in confirmation hearings. Nevertheless, even as the nomination was submitted, there were undercurrents of skepticism on the president's staff about the wisdom of the appointment and trepidation about the Senate. At the time, few observers would have suspected that the most ardent opposition would come from within the cabinet. By the middle of the summer of 1945, Truman had restructured the cabinet he had inherited from his predecessor, and Roosevelt appointees remained in only two domestic cabinet positions. Both of them—Ickes and Henry Wallace—would oppose Truman on crucial issues that led to their resignations. Ickes's issue turned out to be the Pauley nomination.

Ickes was a man of notorious independence and enormous self-confidence who had held his post for nearly thirteen years, longer than any cabinet member in history. Truman professed fondness for Ickes and respected his disavowal of special economic interests, but the president had reservations about him and considered him to be a headliner seeker. Truman later wrote, "'Honest' Harold Ickes, who was never for anyone but Harold, would have cut F.D.R.'s throat—or mine—for his 'high-minded' ideas of a headline—and did."[8] Ickes appeared responsible for leaks of information at cabinet meetings, leaks to columnists and reporters critical of the administration. Cabinet members were reluctant to speak in front of him, suspecting that their words might appear in a Drew Pearson column. When a planted story that had been given only to Ickes appeared in the press the next day, suspicion was confirmed.[9]

The issue that divided Ickes and Pauley was whether the states or federal government should control tidelands oil. Although the term *tidelands* literally applied only to the strip of land between high- and low-water marks, the term had been generalized to include all submerged lands extending three miles from the coast. Well into the 1930s, the Department of the Interior—and Ickes—interpreted tidelands as within the purview of the states and thus turned down applications for federal leases. Inquiries of several attorneys prompted Ickes in 1937 to review department policy; he concluded that the federal government might have a claim to the tidelands and began to hold in abeyance applications for tidelands leases pending outcome of lawsuits directed toward resolving the sensitive issue. Ickes urged Roosevelt to have Attorney General Francis Biddle file suit against the state of California in order to settle the question in the Supreme Court. Suit was filed shortly before Roosevelt's death, but contrary to Ickes's wishes it was filed in a district court against an oil company. After Roosevelt's death and Biddle's resignation, Ickes had to begin once again with Truman and Attorney General Tom Clark, who resisted Ickes's arguments, claiming unconvincingly that he did not want to disturb the action of a predecessor. Ickes finally persuaded a reluctant Truman, and the president ordered Clark to drop the lower court case and file against California.[10]

Pauley was the head of the Petrol Corporation and a stockholder in Standard Oil of California, and he was interested in production of California tidelands oil. He had discussed the issue with Roosevelt and other officials. Although he denied pressure on behalf of his point of view, Pauley admitted doing everything within his power to retain the states' titles to the tidelands. He had been one of the leading advocates of 1945 quitclaim legislation under which the federal government would have forfeited claims to tidelands oil. Truman vetoed the quitclaim bill in August 1945 on the ground that the issue was before the Supreme Court.[11]

Ickes and Pauley were not strangers, and in spite of their sharply contrasting perspectives on the tidelands question, their dealings had not been acrimonious. Pauley initially had impressed Ickes as energetic and resourceful. Pauley ironically had advocated that federal control of the oil industry during World War II should reside in the Department of the Interior rather than with the navy. He had helped plan the wartime Petroleum Administration, and during the war he had traveled to London to discuss the Russian oil situation with the British—as a representative of Ickes, the petroleum administrator.[12]

Ickes's reservations about Pauley were formed long before Pauley's nomination to be under secretary of the navy, and Ickes ruminated in his diary during 1945 about the pressures that Pauley had brought to bear on behalf of private interest. "I could just about ruin him," he mused, reflecting on the consequences if he were to disclose those pressures.[13] In his conversations with the president, Ickes was more guarded, and Truman recalled the substance of their exchanges: "The conversation got around to Pauley and Mr. Ickes expressed high admiration for him and said that Mr. Pauley had been very helpful to him as petroleum administrator. Mr. Ickes seemed very much relieved that I was not considering Pauley for Sec. of the Interior. . . . Mr. Ickes seemed very happy and very cooperative in the Cabinet. A few weeks ago he was talking to me about other matters and again expressed a high regard for Mr. Pauley."[14] Even after he learned of Truman's intention to appoint Pauley, Ickes did not indicate any inclination to oppose Pauley. At a luncheon meeting with Secretary Forrestal, Ickes indicated he would not speak out, but if summoned to appear at the confirmation hearings he would be compelled to tell the truth.[15]

While Ickes was potentially the most damaging opponent of the Pauley nomination, he was not alone in his reservations. *Time* correspondent Frank McNaughton reported that Senate and party leaders and friends had informed Truman that the Pauley nomination would be extremely difficult. Truman balked at the suggestion that he drop it, according to McNaughton, and Pauley spurned the notion that he ought to convince the president not to submit the nomination. Actually, Pauley had spoken to Truman but had given in at the insistence of the president and Forrestal.[16]

Opposition to the Pauley nomination developed quickly, the attack led in the Senate by Republicans Charles W. Tobey of New Hampshire and Raymond E. Willis of Indiana, ranking minority members of the Naval Affairs Committee, which was charged with examining the nomination. Tobey insisted that it was improper to have an oil magnate overseeing the nation's reserves. He indignantly charged that he was being subjected to pressure on behalf of large capital interests, pressure that exceeded anything he had experienced during his thirty-year career. The tense atmosphere of the hearings was described by a contemporary who sketched the roles of prominent senators: "Each Senator knew his own political future had become mixed up somehow in the hearings. During the long hours of constant, almost monotonous questions, Senator Tobey, the chief interrogator, became a changed man. The bald, pink-faced New Englander became taut, excitable, and furiously angry. He clashed constantly with Senator Tydings, the lean, precise, sarcastic Democrat from Maryland. Tydings had taken over the defense of Pauley and protested what he called 'the oral lynching.'"[17]

The climax of the hearings was the testimony of Ickes, who after receiving his summons met twice with Truman prior to his scheduled 1 February 1946 appearance. In their first meeting, on 30 January, Ickes assured the president he did not plan to attack Pauley but that he would answer any questions posed. The second meeting between Truman and Ickes was more crucial to the later development of the case because it inspired an accusation by Ickes tantamount to an allegation that he had been asked to commit perjury on behalf of Pauley. After a cabinet meeting on the morning of his scheduled appearance, Ickes conferred briefly with Truman. In light of later accusations, their respective recollections of what was said at the time do seem to be in agreement. Ickes noted in his diary that Truman told him "that of course I must tell the truth but he hoped I would be as gentle with Pauley as possible. I told him that this was my intention."[18] Truman's version was nearly identical: "I told him to tell the truth but be as kind as possible to Mr. Pauley."[19]

On the opening day of testimony, a confident Pauley told the committee, "I have publicly, privately and repeatedly stated it to be my firm conviction that ownership in the tidelands rests with the states."[20] Responding to questions from Tobey, Pauley admitted having discussed the issue frequently but denied having attempted to influence either the tidelands suit or quitclaim legislation. He claimed that he had not presented his viewpoint on the tidelands issue to President Roosevelt, Attorney General Biddle, or Ickes.

When Ickes testified on 1 February, he contradicted much of Pauley's testimony, claiming that Pauley not only had expressed interest in the tidelands suit but had tried to stop it as well. He had, Ickes claimed, promised to raise several thousand dollars from California oil men for the Democratic party if the suit would not be filed. Ickes's testimony received support from Norman Littell, a former assistant attorney general, who had chaired a committee that had recommended to Roosevelt in 1939 that the federal government file suit to gain title to the tidelands. Littell recounted a meeting in which Pauley allegedly told him that while no one wanted to do anything improper, oil men had contributed sizable sums to the Democrats and expected a return on their investment.[21] Pauley responded to those charges the following Monday and reiterated that he had never sought to press anyone regarding tidelands suits or legislation. He suggested that Littell may have "read into . . . expressions of my views some sinister purposes which were not intended"; Pauley claimed he regretted that "any misunderstanding should have arisen in Secretary Ickes' mind." He categorically stated, "I never solicited, never received and would never take a contingent political contribution of any kind or character."[22]

Pauley's contention was challenged in return by Ickes the next day, in the most dramatic session of the hearings. Recalled by Tobey, Ickes returned armed with memos written at the time of several meetings with Pauley and proceeded to tick off a devastating series of charges against the president's nominee. McNaughton described the scene as Ickes acidly read his memos into the record: "Sitting less than 6 feet behind, Pauley turned ashy pale, his face sagged and grew almost haggard in a space of minutes. Big beads of sweat popped out, and Pauley mopped his brow with a handkerchief. The audience craned to get a better look at the man who was being butchered. It was butchery, and Ickes wielded the knife with the finesse of an expert meatcutter. His tones at times were heavy with disgust, again sharp with irony and outraged honesty."[23]

The case built by Ickes's memoranda gave Pauley reason for discomfiture. Ickes testified that he had warned Roosevelt that having an oil man as treasurer of the Democratic National Committee was risky; his private interests might conflict with the government, creating potential for scandal. In 1944, according to Ickes's record, Pauley had expressed apprehension that the government might bring suit regarding title to the tidelands and twice urged Ickes not to do it. One of these occasions had seemed particularly insensitive, occurring on the train returning from the interment of

President Roosevelt in Hyde Park.[24] The most damaging and controversial incident described by Ickes was a meeting that allegedly took place on 6 September 1944—a meeting that produced what Ickes described as "the rawest proposition that has ever been made to me."[25] On this occasion, Pauley and Paul Porter of the national committee had joined the national committee chairman, Robert F. Hannegan, and Ickes in the latter's office to discuss radio campaign presentations. When the discussion ended, Pauley asked to stay. Hannegan and Porter departed, leaving in the office Pauley, Ickes, and Abe Fortas, whom Ickes had summoned in the interim. Pauley then allegedly told Ickes that three hundred thousand dollars in campaign contributions could be raised from oil men in California if they could be assured that the government would not attempt to assert title to the tidelands. Ickes responded that if title rightfully rested with California, no harm would be done by the suit; if title rightfully rested with the United States, dropping the suit would result in a scandal entrapping not only Ickes and Pauley but the president as well. Pauley denied ever raising the two issues in one conversation, refusing to admit having made such a contingency offer. Fortas's testimony did not clarify the issue, although it seemed to look toward Ickes's version. Fortas recalled the circumstances of the meeting and Ickes's anger after Pauley's departure, and he confirmed that Pauley had raised both issues in the same conversation. He was not certain that a contingency offer was made, however.

After Ickes's ravaging performance, things did not augur well for Pauley. There were inconsistencies in his testimony: on the first day of the hearings, he claimed he had done nothing to hasten quitclaim legislation pending in Congress; on 4 February 1946 he said he had done all he could do to further that legislation.[26] An Interior Department internal memo underscored other inconsistencies implicit in his testimony: "It is not clear . . . how one can promote [quitclaim legislation] and yet stay almost entirely clear of the lawsuit it is designed to prevent. Nor is it easy to see how the Treasurer of the Democratic National Committee could present his views on every possible occasion and yet avoid making a request of or influencing anyone."[27]

Although the preponderance of opinion—in press, public, and Senate—was against the Pauley appointment, the White House held out hope for confirmation. Truman gave no indication of backing down. His appointments secretary, Matthew J. Connelly, claimed he heard there was a fifty-fifty chance the nomination might be reported out by the Naval Affairs Committee.[28]

In a White House press conference on 7 February, President Truman stood behind the nomination, asserting that Pauley was an honest man in whom he had utmost confidence. Asked if he had been told in advance of Ickes's testimony, Truman claimed he had not discussed it with the secretary. Asked about his relationship with Secretary Ickes, Truman replied, "Mr. Ickes can very well be mistaken, the same as the rest of us."[29]

With the president having declared himself in Pauley's corner, Ickes determined he had no alternative but to resign. In a lengthy letter submitted to the White House on the afternoon of 12 February, the secretary of the interior traced the events that led to his decision and reiterated his concern about the mixture of politics and oil. Alluding to the Teapot Dome scandal of the Harding era, he issued a warning to the president: "The forces that ruined Secretary Fall will always be playing upon anyone who is Secretary of the Interior. It is not now certain that other departments will be immune to similar pressures." Ickes challenged Truman's press conference remarks, accusing the president of having "prejudged this case without giving me a chance to be heard." The president's alignment with Pauley, Ickes argued, made his continued presence in the cabinet untenable. He offered to resign as of 31 March 1946.[30]

Not content to let a two thousand–word letter of resignation state his case, Ickes elaborated his criticism of Truman in a press conference the next day. Referring to the president's comment to him before his initial testimony, Ickes remarked, "I wonder whether the President was speaking in a Pickwickian sense when he told me to tell the truth." Then Ickes added a statement calculated to enrage Truman by the gravity of its implication: "Things have come to a pretty pass when men are urged to testify under oath to what is not true."[31]

White House reaction to Ickes's invective was restrained,

although Truman confided to his staff his feelings about the events of the preceding two weeks. On 13 February, he instructed his correspondence secretary, William D. Hassett, to draft an innocuous letter, without rancor, accepting Ickes's resignation effective 15 February rather than 31 March, the date that Ickes had suggested. In his staff conference, Truman commented that Ickes could now compete with Secretary of Commerce Wallace, who was seeking the support of the liberal wing of the Democratic party, for the constituency of the liberal CIO Political Action Committee, adding parenthetically that the PAC had nowhere to go but to the Democratic party anyway. In a more serious tone, he explained that he was not sure whether Pauley had said the things Ickes alleged. He was sure that Pauley had never had asked him, Truman, for anything for anyone and that he had not asked for the job for which the president had nominated him. Then, as assistant press secretary Eben Ayers recalled, Truman revealed the depth of his rage: "The President, referring to all the attacks and many problems now, said this is war. He added that it is worse than a shooting war—he said he had been in both—and in a shooting war you could shoot back."[32] Then, in a statement that would become a refrain throughout his administration, Truman said the criticism of Pauley (and others in the administration) was really an attack on the president.

The next morning, the fourteenth, Truman told his staff he had written a statement of facts about the Ickes-Pauley controversy. The memorandum, as it was read to the staff, was surprisingly moderate and contained words of praise for the service Ickes had rendered to the cabinet. Staff members nevertheless recommended that it would be prudent not to make the statement public; doing so would give Ickes still another chance for rejoinder.

The most inflammatory sections of Truman's memorandum referred to events of the previous two weeks, particularly to Ickes's testimony and press conference. In this concluding part, the president's rage was evident in sentences he later reconsidered and crossed out. As read to his staff, the memorandum thus was considerably more moderate: "In his statement at his press conference he made it appear that I had asked him to perjure himself. Quite the contrary

I told him to tell the truth." From that point, an expurgated section of the memorandum continued: "and I don't think he told it. I am reliably informed that he and Sen. Tobey rehearsed his appearance before the committee and edited his memo so as to take out the favorable statements in it about Mr. Pauley." Truman preserved the next sentence, "In his statement he left out my admonition to him to tell the truth," and crossed out a bitter evaluation of Ickes: "Ickes is an honest public servant in his actions, but he is not intellectually honest about himself, or anyone else if it makes him a hero to distort the truth." The memorandum aptly concluded with the president's perspective on the controversy: "I regret the necessity to make this statement—but I want the record straight. Mr. Ickes has tried to ruin an able public servant in Mr. Pauley and I have had to dispense with the services of another able public servant in Mr. Ickes."[33]

Truman's memorandum, read in conjunction with Ickes's letter of resignation and press conference comments, reveals how quickly a relatively amicable and productive working relationship had degenerated into one of distrust and suspicion during a two-week period in which there had been no personal contact between the president and his Interior secretary. Truman's accusation of rehearsed testimony was ill founded, but neither had Ickes been forthright in making a pledge not to initiate attacks on Pauley. After his first day before the committee, Ickes had used reporter Edwin A. Harris of the *St. Louis Post-Dispatch* as an intermediary to inform Senator Tobey that a more convincing case against Pauley could be generated by posing more direct questions and by requesting Ickes to read relevant memoranda before the committee.[34]

At his press conference the next day, 15 February, President Truman once again expressed support for Pauley and spoke of the earlier intention of Secretary Forrestal and President Roosevelt to appoint Pauley. Truman explained his understanding of the controversial conversation with Ickes on 1 February; when challenged with Ickes's press conference remarks, the president shot back, "I never speak in a Pickwickian sense." He spoke out in behalf of the Pauley nomination again the following week, telling reporters,

"When I get behind a man, I usually stay behind him."[35] True to his word, Truman refused to modify his position in succeeding weeks, although chances for the nomination appeared virtually nonexistent. Columnist Walter Lippmann suggested that Truman had a choice: withdraw the nomination or give up the battle and allow the Senate to defeat the nomination.[36] A Navy Department survey of editorial opinion suggested that the nation's press continued to be anti-Pauley and that Forrestal's increasing coolness and lack of enthusiasm for the appointment seemed another "indication of the need for a black-ball."[37]

Finally, on 13 March 1946, Pauley eased the president out of his predicament by asking him to withdraw the nomination. Truman accepted, praising Pauley's honor and integrity and assuring him that "the disclosure of all the evidence has vindicated my confidence in you."[38]

The protracted battle of political wills was a costly encounter for the president. By his own reckoning he had lost the services of two able public servants. Moreover, the incident raised questions of his political judgment. A political scientist, Harold Gosnell, later put it simply: "Truman was loyal to the wrong man."[39] To others, the affair demonstrated once again that Pendergast politics ruled the White House—that party loyalty meant more than talent and ability and that campaign coffers had to be filled even if ethics were sacrificed.

While Ickes was instrumental in killing the Pauley nomination, he did not emerge from the fray unscathed. Sen. Millard Tydings, Pauley's defender during the hearings, had put Ickes on the defensive several times. The *Chicago Tribune* pointed out that Ickes "sat on his story of what, by his own interpretation, was an attempt at criminal bribery, for nearly two years, during which Pauley was given another position of public trust."[40] Ickes's cantankerous personality had made enemies in Washington, so there was no large sadness over his departure. Federal Trade Commissioner Edwin L. Davis told Truman, "I have all along anticipated that he would double-cross you." Truman responded, "I find a lot of people are not shedding any tears over the departure of Mr. Ickes."[41] In commenting on the loss of Pauley and Ickes, the

Chicago Tribune expressed a minority opinion, but one not unheard elsewhere: "The public is well served in both respects."[42]

In the end, Truman did not suffer inordinately from the controversy. Although he did lose the services of Ickes, it is unlikely that the two men could have worked together much longer under ordinary circumstances. Years later Truman wrote, "I had to accept the resignation of Harold Ickes because he wanted me to be a Franklin Roosevelt—and I could not be."[43] While it is true that the image of the Truman administration as one staffed with cronies enlarged, what with the Pauley nomination stacked atop those of Allen and Vardaman, many observers found something attractive and harmless in Truman's insistence on staying with Pauley in spite of the barrage of criticism that accompanied his nomination. An editorial in the *Washington Daily News* declared, "None of Truman's mistakes has been fatal. They have been small and human errors, reflecting the trustful qualities of the man who is loyal to his friends and has faith in the good intent of others."[44]

And so the Ickes-Pauley confrontation disappeared into history, but not quite, for there were consequences. Ickes, for example, had a feeling that, after all, he had not shown good judgment—and within weeks he tempered his criticism of Truman. In 1948, when the president was running for his political life against a Republican party that felt its nominee, Thomas E. Dewey, could hardly lose, Ickes supported Truman and used his newspaper column—by that time he was a columnist—to barb and shaft the innocuous Republican candidate, in ways that made Truman look good by comparison. Pauley would be in the public eye again a year and a half later, when the distinction between his private affairs and public office would again be challenged.

Cronyism was not the only charge that critics used against President Truman late in 1946, as aspersions of Pendergast politics came up once again, this time when charges of irregularities in a Kansas City primary election offered a more direct link with Jackson County corruption. In the 6 August Democratic primary in Missouri's Fifth Congressional District, President Truman had endorsed Enos Axtell over the incumbent, Roger Slaughter, and another challenger, Jerome Walsh. Axtell took the nomination, but his victory was tarnished by allegations of fraud that prompted an immediate reportorial investigation by the *Kansas City Star*. A grand jury concluded that fraud had deprived Slaughter of victory, and Truman's involvement focused significant national attention on the investigation.[45]

At the outset, the Department of Justice was slow to respond to charges against what was left of the Kansas City Democratic political machine. Although reports were received on 14 August, the department did not initiate an FBI investigation until two months later, well after the *Kansas City Star* published its findings. Then, in accord with department policy, the FBI conducted a preliminary investigation, basing most of it on the work completed by the staff of the *Star*. After reviewing the FBI report and conferring with Peyton Ford, special assistant to the attorney general, Assistant Attorney General T. Lamar Caudle, head of the Criminal Division, recommended that the case be closed because of questionable federal jurisdiction.

But the case did not end, for Republican Sen. James P. Kem of Missouri began agitating to reopen it. Sworn to office in January 1947, the freshman senator challenged the attorney general to use the prerogatives of his office: "In 1946, Boss Pendergast, the second, again said in effect to the people: 'So long as I count the ballots, what are you going to do about it.' The answer of the law enforcement officers of the United States in 1946 and since has been inaction—total and utter inaction. They have done nothing."[46] Kem charged that the FBI was deferring to Boss Tom's nephew Jim and that the investigation had been so drawn as to render it useless. Kem's persistence convinced the Senate Judiciary Committee to open hearings.

On the eve of the hearings, at the end of May 1947, the case took two more bizarre twists. Attorney General Tom Clark, after going over the case with Caudle, took the latter off the case by naming him as head of the Justice Department's Tax Division. A 1953 investigation of the Department questioned whether this move was prompted by Caudle's competence or by Clark's fear of "Caudle's naive honesty as a liability in other ways."[47] Then, astoundingly, someone broke into the Kansas City courthouse and stole several boxes of impounded ballots from the 1946 primary. While no one ever demonstrated that President Truman had even a marginal involvement in the case, it was easy for critics to draw that conclusion. Rep. Albert L. Reeves, who had defeated Axtell in the general election that followed the controversial primary, did just that, charging that "the man who called for the purge of Roger Slaughter in that primary election is the same man who, in 1940, while a member of the other body, bitterly opposed the reappointment as district attorney in Kansas City of Maurice M. Milligan, whose courageous devotion to the duties of his office had resulted in the indictment and conviction of a small army of election crooks."[48] By coincidence Truman was in Kansas City at the time of the ballot theft, another circumstance that delighted critics. Even after Truman left office questions remained. A 1953 panel that investigated the Department of Justice pointed out that despite investigatory expenditures of nearly $250,000 only four minor figures were ever punished and that "Department of Justice officials who became involved in it fared unusually well in their subsequent careers."[49] Truman, however, simply refused to be drawn into the fray. When questioned about the investigation at a press conference during the subsequent hearings, he responded that the "Kansas City vote fraud investigation should be carried through to its logical conclusion. No one wants to condone vote frauds. It is the worst thing that can happen in a democracy."[50]

Unlike either the Ickes-Pauley controversy or several of the scandals that later encroached upon the reputation of his administration, Truman emerged from the Kansas City vote fraud investigation with little political damage. In spite of his involvement in the primary campaign, his opponents could make only a vague and circumstantial argument for any Truman link to the irregularities. The case had appeared in the headlines in the autumn of 1946 and flared again when hearings were held in the spring of 1947, but otherwise it remained in the Justice Department, well away from public awareness. Criticism of Attorney General Clark's conduct of the investigation drew most of the criticism that otherwise might have found its way into the White House.

In another incident that appeared at the end of 1947, the president was not so fortunate and once again was compelled to support close associates whose actions embarrassed the administration. Ironically, Pauley appeared to be entwined in this controversy, accompanied by an unlikely suspect for political controversy, the president's personal physician, Brig. Gen. Wallace H. Graham. As part of a food conservation program to help stave off a shortage in Europe, President Truman addressed a television and radio audience from the White House on the evening of 5 October 1947 and attributed part of the problem of high food prices to commodity speculation. "Grain prices naturally responded to the law of supply and demand," he explained, "but they should not be subject to the greed of speculators who gamble on what may lie ahead in our commodity markets."[51] The administration emphasized its intent to curb speculation, instituting a one-third margin requirement on commodity trades.[52] At a press conference on 17 October, Truman was more explicit in condemnation of speculating: "Gambling on those commodity exchanges . . . is what causes high prices principally in the food products."[53]

This was the beginning of trouble. Early in December, what had been an economic and trade issue suddenly became political when Harold R. Stassen, who was emerging as one of the contenders for the Republican presidential nomination, charged Pauley as being a grain speculator. Assistant to Secretary of the Army Kenneth Royall at the time, Pauley was accused of taking substantial profits on the basis of inside information. Senate Appropriations Committee Chairman M. Styles Bridges, a New Hampshire Republican, quickly appointed a subcommittee to investigate. Pauley in three years had made $932,703 in commodity speculation and was again at the center of controversy. During the hearings, Stassen maintained that Pauley's consistent record of profits was an indication that he had traded on information. Sen. Theodore Green of Rhode Island defended Pauley, for many of his transactions ran counter to what insiders would have been likely to do. Pauley insisted that he was innocent but resigned from the Department of the Army on 11 January 1948. Again, a Pauley resignation ended embarrassment for the administration.[54]

Compared to Pauley, Graham was a mere dabbler in the market. Responding to congressional pressure and the allegations of Stassen and Bridges, the president ordered the Commodity Exchange Authority and Secretary of Agriculture Clinton P. Anderson to release names of individuals who had speculated in grain futures. Graham's name appeared. The son of Truman's family physician in Missouri, he had been serving as the president's personal physician since joining Truman at the Potsdam Conference. Until now he had been involved in politics as an observer; suddenly he was at the center.

Graham's lack of political savvy was immediately apparent, for he not only failed to heed the advice of White House staff members but also tried to bluff his way out of the political thicket with a series of quickly demolished lies. He prepared a statement that was reviewed by the president's press secretary, Charles Ross, and special counsel, Clark Clifford; in it he claimed to have spoken to his broker on 7 October, two days after Truman's initial criticism of grain speculation. Upon learning he had small holdings of grain, Graham said he had ordered his holdings liquidated, even if at a loss. While releasing his statement, he compounded his problems by ignoring admonitions of the White House staff and the president and discussed his already tenuous situation with reporters. He denied knowledge of the trades by his broker, even as the brokerage house was insisting it had informed Graham of all trades. Truman defended him at a 31 December press conference, and when asked if he considered that Graham had done anything wrong, the president replied he had not.[55]

Early in January, Graham again became entangled in the web of deceit he had spun so clumsily. Bache and Company, the brokerage house with which he had dealt, submitted a report to the Department of Justice that belied much of what he had said. When Truman made his 5 October speech criticizing speculators, Graham held contracts for twenty thousand bushels of wheat and sixty thousand pounds of cottonseed oil. He sold half his wheat contracts on 6 October but retained the balance until late November, contrary to what he said in his press conference. He then invested in cotton futures and did not liquidate his account until 18 December 1947, the day the Senate passed a resolution authorizing release of speculators' names. Graham's post-October commodity transactions had netted less than fifteen hundred dollars.

Truman continued to insist that Graham had done nothing wrong, as with Pauley. In a 19 January 1948 staff conference, the president discussed privately the cases of Graham and Pauley. Neither, in his view, had done anything wrong. He suspected that Pauley had been in league with speculators but did not think he had inside information. The president did allow that Pauley should have closed his commodity account when he entered government service.[57]

Incidents involving grain speculation did not affect Truman's relationship with either man. Graham continued to serve as the president's physician throughout the last years of the administration and remained close to the Truman family after the president returned to Missouri in 1953. Pauley's public service was at an end, but he too remained a friend of the president in the years of retirement.

By early 1948, the administration had not been involved in anything that one could consider a major scandal, but several incidents had embarrassed the administration and hurt the reputation of its president. Questionable appointments of Allen and Vardaman and uncompromising loyalty demonstrated toward Pauley and Graham seemed to confirm the notion that Truman had instituted government by crony, practicing Pendergast politics on a national scale.

3. THE CASE OF
GENERAL VAUGHAN

More than any other person, Harry Hawkins Vaughan provided a test of President Truman's reputedly fierce loyalty. He was the subject of a series of embarrassing incidents that unfolded episodically throughout the early years of the Truman administration. The president's military aide and long-term friend later emerged as a central figure in the "five percenter" inquiry that investigated Washington influence peddlers who allegedly accepted a percentage of government contracts they arranged for private business. Truman acknowledged Vaughan's nuisance-making capabilities in private but unflinchingly defended the general in public.

Truman's relationship with Vaughan antedated his acquaintance with any other member of his administration. The two men had met in 1917 when they were artillery officers at Fort Sill. Ironically, at their first encounter it was Vaughan who rescued Truman, a situation reversed in later years. Lieutenant Truman was receiving a thorough dressing-down from the brigade commander when a tardy Vaughan burst noisily into the room, diverting attention and relaxing the situation. The two officers talked briefly after the incident, initiating what was to be a life-long friendship.[1]

Although Vaughan and Truman saw little of each other in Europe during World War I, they renewed their friendship while serving as officers in the National Guard at Fort Riley after the war. During the next several years, while Truman was beginning his political career, Vaughan moved from job to job and city to city, working as an engineer, a railroad-tie company manager, a railroad inspector, and a salesman. In 1927 he married Margaret Lisle Pilcher, who was to be a loyal companion during the stormy events that lay ahead.

When Truman began campaigning for his second Senate term in 1940, Vaughan served as treasurer for the campaign. For a short time in 1941, he was the senator's executive assistant. During World War II, Vaughan served as provost marshal in Brisbane, Australia. When a broken back suffered in a plane crash curtailed his activities, he returned to Washington and went on limited duty. Assignment as the army liaison to the Truman committee again brought him into regular contact with the Missouri senator, and from that point on Vaughan's wagon was hitched securely to Truman's star. When Truman assumed the vice-presidency in 1945, he created the position of military aide to the vice-president in order to bring Vaughan with him. When President Roosevelt died, Vaughan became military aide to the new president.[2]

The relationship between Vaughan and Truman was thoroughly understandable. To Vaughan it was "a friendship which I believe I value above all others."[3] Vaughan was unstintingly loyal. Brig. Gen. Cornelius J. Mara, Vaughan's assistant later, said, "There was nothing that General Vaughan could do to assist the president that he would not do. And the president knew that."[4] When Vaughan's actions embarrassed Truman, it was not because of lack of loyalty but because of his failure to recognize the consequences of words and actions. Vaughan was angered over any disloyalty. A Truman aide who described Vaughan as "fiercely loyal" once overheard the general ask the president how he could be "so nice and friendly to those s.o.b.s who have treated you so badly." Truman replied, "Harry, I got to be president, and you didn't!"[5]

Truman enjoyed Vaughan's sense of humor. Although Vaughan was often ridiculed as the administration's court jester, Truman valued his aide's ability to ease tense situations with a comment or story. Vaughan was a marvelous storyteller, as was the president, and a tale from one would inspire a story from the other. From some quarters, Vaughan was criticized for what one presidential assistant called "a sort of outhouse wit"[6]; a reporter who observed Key West poker games disagreed, finding Vaughan's wordplay "biting, brilliant, riotously funny, and singularly free from the senseless profanity which frequently dominates the sound effects of a stag poker game."[7] Truman could relax and let down his guard with Vaughan, and in return he knew that Vaughan would not pay him undue deference. As Mara noted, "The president realized that Vaughan would bring *anything* to his attention that needed to be brought to his attention. I don't think anyone in the White House had that close rapport."[8]

General Vaughan's closeness to the president made him an inviting target but Truman readily dismissed press barbs, believing that "there is always jealousy of the people who have an entrance to the White House."[9] He reassured his military aide that such attacks were really aimed at the president.[10] And it was that personal association, rather than the nature of Vaughan's responsibilities, that was at the root of his notoriety. As military aide, Vaughan was the president's liaison to the army. He also served as coordinator of veterans' affairs and liaison with J. Edgar Hoover of the FBI. Several of Truman's former staff members have commented on Vaughan's slight effect on policy, so the criticism of Vaughan seems out of proportion to his influence. Vaughan even referred to himself and to the other uniformed armed services aides as "scenery." Critics labeled this disclaimer a smokescreen, however, saying that it was "the carefully cultivated practice around the White House to picture Vaughan as nothing more than a playtime companion, with no influence with the president on big issues." They argued that Vaughan's daily contact with Truman, particularly at vulnerable and reflective moments, gave his views importance.[11] Moreover, Vaughan's character, attitude, and manner seemed to solicit criticism. In appearance he was once described as an "unmade bed." Robert L. Dennison, who had been Truman's naval aide, claimed that the general "looked as if he had a perpetual hangover" despite the fact that he seldom drank.[12] He was considered brusque, "a rough tough sort of blustery kind of chap,"[13] a man whose outspokenness often got him in trouble. As Mara noted, "He doesn't hold anything."[14]

Generosity was another of Vaughan's attributes, but generosity can be a liability for a presidential aide. Cmdr. William M. Rigdon, assistant naval aide, considered this trait to have been the factor that caused Vaughan most of his problems—many people were eager to take advantage of it. Vaughan relished his image as someone who could cut through the bureaucracy, and he was an easy mark for men who chose to prey on his generosity. His role as "untitled administrative troubleshooter" was the source of embarrassing difficulties.[15]

Vaughan's status as a reserve officer increased his vulnerability. Mara noted that many regular officers were jealous, but Dennison argued that the problem was of Vaughan's making: "He was disliked intensely by some professional Army people, mainly because he disliked them, which may have been some kind of a complex with him."[16] Vaughan believed that his reserve status was one of the reasons he was so frequently criticized; he noted that his post previously had been "sacred" to regular officers.

His close relationship with the president, his manner and attitude, and his lack of political savvy combined to make Vaughan an object of press derision, ridicule, and criticism. The first attack came early. Ironically, Vaughan, who was an elder in the Presbyterian Church and whom Mara considered "one of the most genuinely religious men that I have ever known," was thrust into a controversy over the quality of Protestant chaplains in the army.[17] Speaking to the women's auxiliary group at his own church in Alexandria in early September 1945, the general commented: "I don't know why a minister can't be a regular guy, but unfortunately some of them are not. You have to give the Roman Church credit. When the War Department requests a bishop to supply 20 priests for chaplains, he looks over his diocese and picks out the 20 best men. But it is different in the Protestant Church. Frequently a Protestant [minister] does not have a church at the moment or is willing to go on vacation for three years."[18]

Vaughan was acquainted with most of those present at the informal gathering, and his guard was down. Unfortunately for Vaughan, one of the church members was a reporter for the *Washington Post*, and the private remarks were soon in the public domain. *Time* magazine ran the story under the heading "Uncensored Dope." Hundreds of letters to the White House blamed Vaughan for an ill-considered and unworthy disparagement of Protestant chaplains.

The most indignant and vociferous reaction to Vaughan's remarks came from the General Commission on Army and Navy Chaplains, an organization representing Protestant denominations. Truman's first reaction came in a letter responding to Bishop Angus Dun of the Episcopal Diocese of Washington, a member of the commission, who wrote independently to the president. Truman apologized for the disturbance, but in regard to Vaughan's statement said simply, "I am very sure he didn't make it."[19] But Vaughan did make the statement, and when Bishop Henry Knox Sherrill, the commission's chairman, wrote the president, Vaughan was told to reply. His explanation did not satisfy Sherrill, who asked the general to get *Time* magazine to issue a retraction. Vaughan demurred, uncertain of how he could influence *Time* to do anything.[20]

The silly contretemps, once stated, went on and on. The commission waited a decent interval, then stepped up pressure on Truman and his military aide. A resolution was sent to Truman on 18 October describing Vaughan's remarks as "highly offensive" and asking for a repudiation of them. The president's reply displayed more tact than his earlier attempt, but he refused to back down, noting that Vaughan's pastor, Cliff R. Johnson, claimed he had said nothing derogatory. Truman did avow that the remarks "whether authentic or unauthentic in nowise represent my views."[21]

Vaughan did not learn from his experience. Nearly a decade later he reflected, "I did not speak as Military Aide to the President, nor even as an officer in the army, but entirely as a member of my church participating in a meeting and discussion with other members."[22] He never realized that he could not have the luxury of setting aside his role as military aide. As aide to a senator, or even to a vice-president, he could escape public scrutiny, but his old army buddy was now president of the United States. Truman in the early months of his presidency was adjusting. Vaughan was not. One of the reasons the president liked Vaughan was that he did not change, that he was not in awe of his friend's new status. Their relationship remained much as before.

The fray over the chaplains revealed a flaw and demonstrated that the press would make the most of lapses. Throughout Truman's presidency Vaughan was pursued—in his view persecuted—by the press to an extent that he claimed, "The press has largely forsaken its moral obligation to truth, and . . . has descended to depths of bias, concealment, distortion and untruth."[23] Drew Pearson became his particular bête noire. A muckraker in the classic mold, Pearson had a national audience through his widely syndicated column, "The Washington Merry-Go-Round," and a weekly radio broadcast. He had an instinct for the jugular unmatched in the Washington press corps, and Vaughan became one of his favorite subjects. The contempt with which Pearson treated Vaughan was reciprocated; the general considered the columnist a "perennial liar."

Pearson spread an offensive against Vaughan in a series of columns and broadcasts early in 1947 and continued until after Truman had left office. Many of the charges in the five-percenter inquiry in the summer of 1949 were first leveled by Pearson. The charges eventually encompassed several tangential issues, but the central topic and the source from which other charges emanated was Vaughan's friendship with a former bootblack from Kansas City named John F. Maragon.

Vaughan's first contact with Maragon had been in 1941, when Vaughan was serving as Senator Truman's secretary and Maragon was a passenger agent for the Baltimore and Ohio Railroad. Maragon's official responsibilities included getting tickets and reservations for senators and congressmen, and he did favors and ran errands in order to ingratiate himself with the powerful. Vaughan later remembered him as an "eager beaver" who behaved "like a friendly pup if you had on a Palm Beach suit." "Johnny" Maragon was "eternally underfoot" and continually tried to do more than he was asked. Once Vaughan gave him a twenty dollar bill to get six small turkeys for a church function, intending to have several women from the church prepare them at home. Maragon, believing more was better, returned with six turkeys that were too large for at-home preparation.

Through the favors he performed, Maragon worked himself into the good graces of General Vaughan, but what Vaughan did not know, or was unable to recognize, was that Maragon was exploiting the friendship. He represented himself as an intimate of the president's military aide, often making and receiving phone calls in Vaughan's White House office. Vaughan's open, trusting style was a perfect foil for Maragon's flattery and maneuvering; as Vaughan later recalled, "It was a matter of several years before I realized, in the case of Maragon, that he was misrepresenting his relationship to me." Even then, Vaughan never did believe that Maragon had done anything illegal, though it was surely a case of damning with faint praise when the general explained, "I don't think Maragon ever did anything dishonest. He was always too busy doing something stupid."

While Vaughan was taken by Maragon's charms, others in the White House were not. Well before Pearson began hammering at the Vaughan-Maragon relationship, other staff members, and Truman himself, had grown weary of the ubiquitous Maragon's activities. Maragon procured a temporary White House pass the day after President Roosevelt died and a permanent pass five weeks later. Although Truman late in 1945 ordered the pass revoked, Maragon was able to hold it until 4 April 1946. In the intervening months, with Vaughan's cooperation, he wangled his way onto a mission to Greece to supervise elections there. When it became known on 9 January 1946 that his name was on the mission list, Truman ordered it removed immediately.[24]

A mere presidential order was of little consequence to Maragon, however. Eben Ayers, Charles Ross's assistant press secretary, was visited by a representative of the Overseas News Agency on 26 February. The New York office of the agency had received a cablegram from its Athens agent:

> Please try to get some dope on John Maragon. He is in Athens with the United States election mission. Greek born. He says he has been living in Washington. I have never heard of him. He is getting VIP—very important person—treatment. He has an unimportant job with the commission which, I am sure, is a cover for something else. He claims he is an old chum of Truman's and has pictures to prove it and that he once lived in Missouri. Have a hunch he may be from F.B.I. or Secret Service. In Athens he is snooping around and terrorizing mission members by talking with correspondents. Possibly you can get something from State Department sources. Like to know for example precisely what kind of job Maragon has with commission.[25]

Such was Maragon's tenacity. When Ross brought the Athens matter to Truman's attention at a conference the next morning, the president responded that he thought he had ordered Maragon off the mission. Vaughan remarked only that it was not necessarily true. But Vaughan had intervened, perhaps with appointments secretary Matthew Connelly's blessing, to allow Maragon's name to stay on the mission list. Vaughan later claimed that this was the only assignment he had ever gotten for Maragon, and he remembered only giving Maragon responsibility for handling travel accommodations and baggage transfers.[26]

Maragon seemed to have a talent for raising suspicions among those with whom he came in contact. Only Vaughan continued to have implicit trust in him. The reporter's query regarding Maragon's FBI connections may have been more than a blind hunch, for Maragon claimed to have worked for several months in 1923 in the Bureau of Investigation of the Department of Justice, the forerunner of the FBI. Ironically, he claimed to have landed the job as a result of a favor he had done for a midwestern senator—taking the rap for a prohibition violation[27]—curious background for such a close "friend" of the administration. In any case, Vaughan's continued faith in Maragon was like a time bomb waiting to explode in the press. It was impossible to control a man as presumptuous as Maragon, who continued to trade on his contacts in the White House and made a special point of his access to Vaughan, aggravating a situation that already beckoned to critics of the administration.

Pearson's first denunciation of Vaughan was a veiled sally that mentioned neither the general nor Maragon by name. In a radio broadcast on 26 January 1947, Pearson addressed himself to the president, remarking, "If your military aide chooses to lie down with dogs, he can't complain about getting fleas."[28] Two days later, his column featured a charge that Vaughan had told a reporter that the president would as soon place Mickey Mouse in control of war assets as Donald Nelson or Leon Henderson.[29]

Vaughan soon found an opportunity to retaliate. Although he later asserted that he blocked the columnist's attempt to send Washington lawyer George C. Vournas as a member of an economic mission to Greece, Vaughan's action was precipitated by a call from the Greek chargé d'affaires, who strongly opposed Vournas's inclusion on the mission. Because Vournas admitted that his brother was with the Communist guerillas against the Greek government and because Vournas desired to get in touch with Yugoslavia's Communist President Tito and was not an official member of the mission, Vaughan recommended that Truman withdraw Vournas's name. Truman concurred, and the State Department was notified. When Pearson learned of Vournas's exclusion, he sent one of his associates, David Karr, to press secretary Charles Ross with an ultimatum. Karr claimed that Pearson had assembled a complete record on Maragon and intimated that his shadowy background included a murder inquiry. Karr then threatened that if Vournas was not reinstated, Pearson would blast Vaughan in his Sunday night broadcast. Ross phoned Vaughan while Karr was in his office. Vaughan told Karr he would not reverse his position and that he would be listening to his radio that Sunday night.[30]

The threatened attack did not come that Sunday night, but it was not long in coming. To cross Pearson was to pique his combative spirit. Jack Anderson, who was to inherit the "Merry-Go-Round," later wrote about his mentor: "He was, I came to believe, one of that tenacious breed for whom nothing produces so much exhilaration, zest for life, and all-round gratification as a protracted vendetta that rages for years and exhausts both sides, often bringing one to ruin."[31] The Pearson-Vaughan dispute became a vendetta in Pearson's columns and broadcasts and drew the president into direct involvement in an effort to defend his military aide from what he considered unjust attacks.

Truman needed little persuasion to be convinced of Pearson's intentions. He had a run-in with the columnist a year earlier, which destroyed the possibility of friendly relations between the two. On 8 January 1946, Pearson delivered to Truman a stack of petitions from soldiers demanding to come home from overseas. The president took the opportunity to chastise Pearson for a recent broadcast in which he had incorrectly charged that Mrs. Truman and Margaret had received special consideration on a rail trip to Independence. Poking his finger into Pearson's abdomen, the president threatened to punch him in the nose the next time he told a falsehood about Mrs. Truman; Truman then declared, "Ninety-nine percent of your statements are falsehoods." Later that day during a cabinet meeting, Truman branded Pearson a liar.[32]

Vaughan was fortunate to have the president in his corner, for Pearson launched an offensive on 16 March. Listeners to ABC at 7:00 P.M. that Sunday heard Pearson exploit the Vaughan-Maragon relationship and hint at further revelations: "Attention Senator Vandenberg: As you know, Senator, if we are to have a united foreign policy it is important that there be no Greek favorites around the White House throne. Therefore, I respectfully suggest that you investigate the very close friendship between General Harry Vaughan, the White House Military Aide, and one John Maragon, formerly of Kansas City, an ardent supporter of the King of Greece. I suggest that you probe the amount of liquor which the Greek-born Maragon supplies to General Vaughan, the amount of money that certain Greeks contributed through Vaughan to Truman's personal candidate for Congress in Kansas City, Enos Axtell, and especially please investigate how General Vaughan reached right into the files of the Washington police and pulled out the police record of his friend Maragon. A very interesting story, Senator, and if you don't have time to investigate it, I'll try to write it."[33] The bombardment continued in "Washington Merry-Go-Round" for the next two days. The first column fired at Maragon's relationship with Greek Archbishop Athenagoras and an American Catholic priest, the Reverend Thomas Daniels, both of whom had visited Truman and both of whom Pearson considered Greek Royalists, a scathing epithet in the Pearson lexicon. The second column attacked Maragon's ties to Vaughan and charged that Maragon had accompanied Truman to Potsdam.[34]

After only a brief respite Pearson resumed the attack. His 1 April column charged that when Brig. Gen. William L. Lee struck Maragon in the face in an encounter in Rome, Maragon used his influence with Vaughan to have Lee demoted and relieved. "John could dictate to the army through his pal, the President's Military Aide," Pearson charged. A few days later, on 7 April, Pearson lengthened his indictment, reciting old charges and adding new ones. He claimed that Vaughan had sold wristwatches on the Russian black market, turned loose a pig in J. Edgar Hoover's office, and told the D.C. district attorney whom to prosecute and whom not. Most of the article was devoted to a charge that Vaughan had attempted to persuade Secretary of Agriculture Clinton P. Anderson not to reduce the quotas of grain allocated to distillers.[36]

Vaughan considered many of the charges libelous and was unsure how to respond. Some of the charges were clearly inflammatory, since they had been aired in the press earlier. The charge that Vaughan sold watches on the Russian black market stemmed from the 1945 church gathering at which Vaughan made his statement regarding selection of Protestant chaplains. Vaughan then had said that while in Potsdam he had sold his fifty-five-dollar American watch to a Russian officer for five hundred dollars. Other charges were distortions. The story about the pig in Hoover's office was lifted from one of George Dixon's old columns: Vaughan admitted he had brought a pig to Hoover's office, but he claimed it was destined for Hoover's farm and was crated when he left the office.[37]

Considering the extent of Vaughan's outrage, a libel suit may have seemed a likely recourse, but Vaughan never did file a suit directly against Pearson. He later explained that it would have sapped any financial resources he had and brought unfavorable publicity to the administration. The first of these explanations is without merit; Vaughan later said that several attorneys offered to handle his case without fee. In fact, at the time of the allegations he made an exploratory investigation. William H. Neblett, an attorney and friend who later became a subject of the five-percenter inquiry, checked into several of the Maragon-related charges and turned up evidence refuting Pearson's allegation that Vaughan had pulled Maragon's police record. After the initial investigations, Vaughan thought he had a case and even broached the subject with the attorney general.[38]

Vaughan had another chance for indirect retaliation several weeks later when Madeline Karr, the wife of David Karr, applied for a position in the G-2 Division of the War Department. Employed at the time by the *Greek National Herald* of New York, Mrs. Karr was described by Eben Ayers as "a pleasant, rather pretty little girl" who has never caused any difficulty.[39] A letter concerning her application was inadvertently sent to a Greek newspaper in Washington, the *Greek News*, and Maragon's contacts there promptly informed him of the application. He told Vaughan, asserting that Pearson and the "Communist" *Greek National Herald* were trying to infiltrate the War Department.[40] Vaughan needed no further prodding. He promptly sent a letter to Brig. Gen. C. B. Ferenbaugh, commanding general of the Military District of Washington, recommending against employing Mrs. Karr in "any position where confidential or secret information would be available."[41] He did not stop there. He got in touch with a friend who was a stockholder in the *National Herald* and pressed him to have Mrs. Karr fired. The paper released her, supposedly because of economic necessity.[42]

Meanwhile, members of the White House staff feared that someone might be leaking information to Pearson. It was well known that Attorney General Tom Clark was a friend of the columnist. Speculation also ran to a deputy in Sen. J. Howard McGrath's office, and Vaughan suspected a Trans-Radio correspondent named Gene Davis. Vaughan had a contact in the Pearson organization who was of limited value—a man whom Mara had once helped to find a house and who occasionally stopped by to chat with Mara.[43]

As intrigue increased, Vaughan found he had an ally in the press: Pearson's columns often would be countered by responses from Westbrook Pegler, who was no supporter of Vaughan but a staunch opponent of Pearson. Pegler's biographer later observed, "It became almost axiomatic that anybody exposed by Pearson could find comfort in Pegler." Cementing this union of mutual disdain for Pearson was Pegler's memory of his days in baseball training camps in the South with his old friend—John Maragon.[44]

All the while, rumor circulated about more sycophants seeking favors through Vaughan. A man named John Crane used Vaughan to gain entry to the White House to prepare guidebooks he planned to market. Other friends sought the release of excess materials to complete construction of a racetrack, and there were stories about a Col. James V. Hunt who could get things done in Washington—for a fee. (These last two cases are recorded in Chapter 4, "The Five Percenters.") Eben Ayers described in his diary the worries of the staff as Vaughan stories continued. On 24 October 1947 he wrote: "I think there is a general feeling among the staff—Ross, Connelly and Hassett certainly, as well as myself—that sooner or later Vaughan and his associates are going to cause a great deal of trouble. No one goes so far as to intimate that Vaughan is dishonest or grafting himself but there is grave suspicion of some of his friends." The feeling persisted, and a month later Ayers wrote: "Connelly fears, as I do, that Vaughan may do something or something may develop out of some of the activities of these friends of Vaughan's that will cause embarrassment. Connelly asked what could be done. There is no job, he said, that Vaughan could be given, that would be commensurate with his rank as major general, he said. Vaughan isn't capable enough."[45]

In February 1948, an incident gave Ross and Connelly a chance to check Vaughan, however temporarily. At the conclusion of the regular morning staff conference on 6 February, Vaughan gave a typed announcement to Truman, who handed it to his press secretary, Charles Ross. The announcement, designated for the *Congressional Directory*, would have made Vaughan senior armed services aide, in effect demoting the naval aide, Captain Dennison, and the newly appointed air aide, Col. Robert Landry. Ross sensed the possible repercussions of placing senior navy and air force officers under the command of an army officer and he corralled Connelly: the two went in to see Truman before his cabinet meeting. They warned that the new arrangement would "raise *particular* hell" and urged him to reconsider. Ross at his press conference announced only Landry's appointment, Vaughan's impending promotion held in abeyance.[46]

When Vaughan learned of the omission he challenged Ross, who excused the delay by explaining that the *Directory* would not be published until March or April. Vaughan passed through the lobby as he left Ross's office and was accosted by newsmen who asked him to clarify the aide situation. The general held what amounted to his own news conference, announcing his role as senior armed services aide.

When Ross heard of Vaughan's action he was livid. Conferring with Connelly again he muttered, "Oh, that damn Vaughan has done it again."[47] He felt that Vaughan was undercutting his authority as press secretary. By this time Dennison and Landry had contributed their vehemently negative opinions of the new arrangement. Connelly told Ross that he would speak to the president. When Truman was informed that there was a problem with Vaughan, he erupted, "What in the hell did he do now?" At Connelly's request, the president summoned Ross and angrily called Vaughan, ordering him to get over to his office "on the double." Truman assured Connelly and Ross that the aide situation would remain unchanged and authorized Ross to inform the press. Vaughan received a dressing down and left quickly, passing through Connelly's office "with his tail between his legs."[48]

Actually, Vaughan had not behaved as badly as had appeared. When the story was aired in the press it seemed as if Vaughan had initiated his own promotion, but that was not the case. Vaughan later asserted that John Steelman, who held the title of The Assistant to the President, had originated the plan as part of the armed forces unification plans then in progress. Truman himself had broached the subject with Secretary of Defense James V. Forrestal four months before the incident and had told Ross that he had been trying to find another place for Vaughan for a long time. Whatever the origin of the plan, Vaughan brought about its abrupt termination. He seemed to have a political death wish. He recognized the press as his opponent, yet he could not refrain from talking to reporters. He had an opportunity for greater authority, yet undercut it. His own postmortem on the incident was that "it's as much of a misdemeanor to be premature as it is to be inaccurate."[49]

Publicly, Vaughan took the turn of events in stride, telling reporters that he "was not sore at anybody," and at the morning staff meeting the next day he acted as if nothing had happened.[50] Privately, however, he was deeply wounded, not so much for the loss of face or failure of the senior aide position to materialize as for the admonishment he received from the president. Vaughan's pastor and close friend, Cliff R. Johnson, said Vaughan was "hurt and confused" over the incident. Johnson was so moved by his friend's depression that he wrote to Truman, asking him to do something to restore Vaughan's feeling of security in their relationship.[51] Truman was content to let his aide squirm this time. He considered the flap to be entirely of Vaughan's making and made no public statements exonerating the general or mitigating the impression that Vaughan had tried to promote himself. Replying to Johnson, he reaffirmed the strength of his relationship with Vaughan but added, "The recent event . . . was due entirely to Harry's talking out of turn."[52] And there, to Vaughan's chagrin, the matter rested.

For the next several months, the election campaign of 1948 took Vaughan off the front page—if not out of the "Washington Merry-Go-Round." Pearson's charges during this period, however, were either relatively minor or rehashes of previous allegations. But Pearson suspected he was being wiretapped at Vaughan's instigation, though he was to wait over a year before leveling that charge.[53]

The next sensational story—the kind of story Pearson loved—was unearthed by another reporter for whom the president had low regard, Walter Winchell. Truman once had written in his sporadically kept diary: "Pearson's no good. He, Fulton Lewis + Walter (Winchellistic) are pathological liars par excellence. It's too bad."[54] Now Winchell and Pearson in concert were to create an issue that again would embarrass Vaughan and provoke Truman. Winchell learned in December 1948 that Vaughan had been chosen to receive a medal from the dictatorial government of Col. Juan Perón of Argentina. Pearson waited to see if the president and State Department would approve of the award. When it became clear that Vaughan would accept it, Pearson eagerly joined the fray, telling his radio audience, "Next Friday, when [the award ceremony] takes place, I am going to be at the door of the Argentine Embassy and will publish the names of those who go to see Harry Vaughan receive his dictatorial decoration."[55] Despite some second thoughts, Pearson made good on his threat. His display engendered a mixed response. Pearson claimed that Truman's physician, Brig. Gen. Wallace Graham, "ducked in the door as if he was running from Satan."[56] But Gen. Hoyt Vandenberg gave Pearson his card to be sure his name was included. In retrospect, Pearson was not proud of the affair: "I made something of an ass of myself."[57]

The incident did not end there. Truman, his antipathy toward Pearson piqued by the most recent round of the columnist's shenanigans, rallied to his military aide. Demands for Vaughan's scalp had exasperated the president. On 22 February 1949, at a Reserve Officers Association dinner at which Vaughan was honored as "Minute Man of 1949," the president exploded. "I want you to distinctly understand," he began, "that any s.o.b. who thinks he can cause any one of these people to be discharged by me by some smart aleck statement over the air or in the paper, has another think coming."[58] Pearson in his next broadcast and in a later column proposed that the initials s.o.b. might as well designate a "Servant of Brotherhood," and he began to dispense other such awards. Truman had been bested, and realized it, but two months later he blamed Pearson for harassing former Secretary of Defense Forrestal to the brink of suicide. According to one of Pearson's White House sources, Truman erupted, "That son of a bitch Pearson got the best of me on the SOB thing but I'm going to get the best of him on the Forrestal suicide. I'm going to rub it in until the public never forgets."[59] The incident did neither Pearson nor the president any great credit.

While Truman could display rage over Vaughan's treatment by the press, he could demonstrate a sense of humor, as he did a few months later. In July 1949, when Vaughan and his family, together with Mara and a few other friends, returned from a vacation in Central America, they were greeted at Union Station by a small group of reporters who asked how the trip had been financed. Vaughan, who later claimed to have paid his own way, considered the question impudent and let loose a tirade. Hearing of the encounter, Truman decided that his beleaguered aide should be decorated again. He had a White House plumber fashion a metal out of tin and hid it inscribed:

Operation Union Station
July 6, 1949
Major General Harry H. Vaughan
from
President Harry S. Truman

The award was presented in a "solemn" ceremony at the close of a staff meeting a few days later.[60]

Truman's capacity to make light of Vaughan's problems

was a counterpoint to what lay immediately ahead. A month after Vaughan was decorated for Operation Union Station, Sen. Clyde R. Hoey of North Carolina dropped the gavel to open the five-percenter investigation. Allegations that had plagued Vaughan since 1945 were to be the focus, and Vaughan's testimony proved to be the climax of the hearings.

Truman's attitude toward his aide and the allegations that filled the "Washington Merry-Go-Round" and other columns had formed well before the five-percenter investigation. Vaughan was Truman's blind spot, the president blinded by his faith in Vaughan's loyalty and by lack of respect for Pearson and to a lesser degree for Winchell and other columnists. He had reason for each of these feelings. Harry Vaughan was loyal; his problems resulted from poor judgment but never from disloyalty. Truman had been victimized by Pearson in cases when the columnist had used unverified information.

Instances in which the president reprimanded the general—directly or by implication as a result of his decision not to comment publicly on an incident—were always cases in which Vaughan spoke out of turn. The chaplain incident and that of the senior armed services aide reflected this attitude. Other allegations were potentially serious, but Truman discounted them. Even when he did recognize a problem, as with the Vaughan-Maragon relationship, he attempted to solve it by barring Maragon from the White House and from executive commissions rather than by criticizing Vaughan. And Truman recognized Vaughan's chronic foot-in-mouth disease. Often accused of being a dullard, Vaughan emphatically was not. Ayers noted: "For a person with as quick a wit as Vaughan, it seems strange that he should have so little appreciation of the effect of the things that he says. He is one of those persons who cannot keep still."[61]

Truman, nevertheless, was wrong in seeing Vaughan's problem as solely one of talking out of turn. After the senior armed services aide incident, the president wrote to Vaughan's pastor, Cliff R. Johnson, that Vaughan had "only one difficulty and that is to keep from saying things to newspapermen."[62] Vaughan's problem was more serious, and by the time Truman wrote Reverend Johnson he should have realized it. Vaughan's associations, however innocent, created embarrassing situations, magnified by publicity from the Hoey committee in 1949. Vaughan, moreover, was beginning to play a dangerous game with Pearson, and when he used his influence to hurt Mrs. Karr he was fortunate that Pearson did not find out.

Compounding the situation, Truman's staff realized that internal criticism of Vaughan was a forbidden subject. When Pearson accused the general of using influence on behalf of Maragon and Archbishop Athenagoras, Ayers noted, "This is something I had been expecting to break for more than a year and on every possible occasion I have tried as much as I dared, to sound a warning. I know that Ross has also felt concerned about it, but it has been difficult to get him to take any action."[63]

Truman's last press secretary, Roger Tubby, described a meeting with Truman after returning from a trip to Vermont, during which he had discussed the president's accomplishments with some Republican friends. Although his friends had agreed with Truman on many points, "There was a refrain, I said, and the refrain was, 'But what about Harry Vaughan?' When I got started on this and I sort of realized, I sort of naturally sensed, that I was getting into some very dangerous ground. Yet, I felt, you know, maybe this kind of comment ought to get back to him, from somebody whom he was fairly close to, not just a gollywhopper of a Republican writing for Republican newspapers, but somebody on his own staff. As I recall, he stood up and walked over to one of the long windows and looked out towards the Washington Monument with his hands behind his back, and I knew I was dismissed."[64]

4. THE FIVE PERCENTERS

Charges leveled by an obscure furniture maker in Massachusetts accomplished something that years of Pearson columns were unable to do—make the president's military aide the centerpiece of a congressional inquiry. Throughout the summer of 1949, Vaughan was headline and editorial material for the nation's press, cited daily as a source of high-level influence for John Maragon and others. During the weeks leading to the hearings and the month of the inquiry, Vaughan weathered the crisis of his career, and not once during the ordeal did the president waver in support.

The story began to unfold when Paul Grindle, the head of a Framingham, Massachusetts, furniture factory and a former *New York Herald Tribune* reporter, told one of his old newspaper friends of dealings with an influence peddler named James V. Hunt. Grindle claimed that when he visited Washington to seek government contracts in May 1949, Hunt dazzled him with stories of his ability to cut through bureaucratic tangle by using contacts in high places. Among people Hunt claimed to know were the Army quartermaster general, Maj. Gen. Herman Feldman; former War Assets Administrator Jess Larson; and his "closest and dearest friend," Maj. Gen. Harry H. Vaughan. Hunt's fee for wielding influence on Grindle's behalf: $1,000 down, $500 a month for expenses, and 5 percent of any contract.

As shock waves of the *Herald Tribune* story reverberated in Washington and across the country, the term *five percenter* became part of the national vocabulary. Feldman denied that Hunt influenced either Larson or him. The War Assets Administration and the House Armed Services Committee promised to investigate. The Senate Committee on Expenditures in the Executive Departments charged its Investigations Subcommittee, chaired by Senator Hoey, with responsibility for hearings to probe the five-percenter problem. The work of this subcommittee became the focal point of charges against Vaughan and others accused of using positions to aid friends in getting favors from the Washington bureaucracy.[1]

The similarity between the new allegations of a Hunt-Vaughan relationship and Pearson's refrain of a Maragon-Vaughan connection immediately thrust the general into the limelight. The day before the Hunt story appeared, Bert Andrews of the Washington bureau of the *Herald Tribune* sent a radiogram to Vaughan aboard a cruise ship, returning from a Central American vacation. Andrews asked Vaughan to comment on his relationship with Hunt. Vaughan wired back that he had seen Hunt socially but had no business dealings, since Hunt a few years earlier had left his job as deputy to the quartermaster general. The reporters awaiting Vaughan's return—Operation Union Station—were inspired by the five-percenter story. Vaughan's blast at reporters included an intemperate remark that delighted his adversaries. "What is all the excitement about Hunt?" he queried. "There must be 300 people in Washington in the same business."[3] The inference was that Vaughan knew 300 five percenters.

Vaughan's comment initiated a change in the nature of his problems. Previous attacks against him had been restricted to the "opposition press"; the *New York Herald Tribune*, for example, which broke the Hunt story, was among several papers the administration considered sympathetic to Republican causes. Republican legislators had delighted in Vaughan's difficulties, but they had not attacked him directly. Now Republican congressmen attempted to exploit the situation. Rep. Kenneth R. Keating of New York demanded that Vaughan provide names, dates, and figures to substantiate his "300 five percenters" statement. Political heat intensified when Quartermaster General Feldman and Maj. Gen. Alden H. Waitt, chief of the Chemical Corps, were suspended pending a probe into the Hunt allegations. Rep. Paul W. Shafer of Michigan called for Vaughan's suspension, raising the specter of "Pendergastism . . . on a national scale."[4] The agitation led one press wag to comment that it was "two down and Vaughan to go."[5] Pearson jumped in, reporting that Shafer's comment had produced a White House threat: the congressman had better "lay off" Vaughan or risk being deprived of favors to his district.

Shafer denied the allegation in a statement that took the
sting out of both Pearson's column and his own previous
remarks, saying he had always assumed Vaughan to be of
high character and that his previous statement "contained
no charges by me of any misconduct by General Vaughan."[6]
As the weeks crept by, the White House was reduced to a
position of responding to events beyond its control. Rumors,
Pearson's columns, leaks from the Hoey committee's initial
closed hearings, and a continuing *Herald Tribune* series kept
the story before the public in the interim before open hearings began on 8 August. It was rumored that Truman would
not allow Vaughan to testify; even the president's assertion
to the contrary did not silence the report. Vaughan's "300
five percenters" remark refused to go away. Truman was
asked about it at his 31 July news conference and dismissed
it with a curt "I don't know anything about it."[7]

Truman was low-key in public, but behind the scenes his
actions demonstrated that he placed high priority on staff
unity against an attack from the outside. While he wanted
to be kept abreast of developments, he was willing to sacrifice information at risk of creating an impression of panic,
or even excessive concern, which might have developed had
he begun his own administrative probe. When it was reported that he had ordered Defense Secretary Johnson to
conduct an "all-out inquiry" he denied it, saying, "There
were no particular instructions to anybody."[8] Twice in staff
meetings during the week before the Hoey subcommittee
began open hearings, the president took pains to support
Vaughan, once assuring him that the entire staff was behind
him, telling him not to think they were going back on him.
While this may have comforted Vaughan, it was not entirely
accurate. Out of loyalty to Truman the staff never opposed
Vaughan openly, but there were rumblings as the affair continued. After one staff meeting, Ross, the press secretary,
and Ayers, his assistant, discussed the developing situation, and Ayers recorded their conclusions: "We are agreed
that Vaughan is entirely to blame for his troubles and
the troubles he has brought on the president and other
people."[9]

Although Truman hesitated to launch anything resembling an internal investigation, his staff performed rear-guard activities in conjunction with the impending in-quiry—some at the president's instigation, others inde-pendently. When it was learned that Hoey had possession of a thousand-page diary in which Hunt had recorded names, dates, times, and places of meetings along with other details, the president apparently directed Clark Clifford to check into the matter. Clifford obtained a copy of the diary, and Vaughan assembled a listing of all entries that referred to himself, his secretary, Mara, Dr. Graham, Steelman, and oth-ers, but nothing was incriminating. Mara urged Ross to re-lease the diary, feeling that it cleared Vaughan, but Ross and others believed that the frequency of Hunt's White House contacts would be more detrimental than beneficial.[10]

Moreover, the Maragon connection continued to be of concern, especially when the Senate subcommittee began holding closed-door sessions with him at the end of July. Ayers checked with the Secret Service to learn what he could about Maragon's White House access.

On the other side, Vaughan received a pair of unsolicited affidavits that bolstered his case, and he planned to present them to the subcommittee if he were called to testify. Signed by Col. Hubert F. Julian and a friend, Frederick S. Weaver, the affidavits swore that an investigator for the subcommit-tee who had identified himself as a Mr. Alderman had ap-proached Julian and offered $75,000 to implicate Vaughan for soliciting a bribe in an influence scheme. Although Ju-lian felt he had been treated unfairly by General Feldman while attempting to put together a deal to sell cigarettes in Europe, he insisted that Feldman never had suggested a payoff. Moreover, Vaughan "had never asked me for a nickel and I had never given him a cent."[11]

Vaughan claimed to have received affadavits from three other individuals who stated that they had been offered bribes to testify; one of these men was working for the in-vestigators in the case. Vaughan considered his collection of affadavits his ace in the hole and was eager to play it when opportunity arose. A sense of loyalty, however, dictated that he clear it with the president. To the general's disappoint-ment, Truman suggested, "Don't use it, Harry, unless you have to. Senator Hoey is an old man, and it would destroy him, and they would tear the people who have given you these statements to shreds."[12]

After a month and a half of speculation, conjecture, and accusations following the initial *Herald Tribune* story, the Investigations Subcommittee of the Committee on Expenditures in the Executive Departments (later renamed the Government Operations Committee) began open hearings. The four Democrats and three Republicans were chaired by the seventy-one-year-old Hoey, the Democrat whose attire of a "frock coat, high shoes, wing collar and red boutonniere" had become his trademark.[13] He was too conservative for Truman's taste, but he had refused to participate in the 1948 Dixiecrat revolt. Observers considered his handling of the hearings to be dignified, an accolade in light of the political overtones that cast a shadow over the inquiry. Democrats on the subcommittee were conspicuous by their absence from most sessions of the inquiry and had little effect on the proceedings. A. Willis Robertson of Virginia occasionally objected to the questioning by Republican senators at the few sessions he attended, but Republicans usually had a free hand, although they were sometimes interrupted by the elderly Hoey.[14]

Subcommittee Republicans Joseph R. McCarthy of Wisconsin and Karl E. Mundt of South Dakota used the hearings to hone methods that became familiar to the public after McCarthy assumed chair of the Government Operations Committee in 1953. Margaret Chase Smith of Maine, the third subcommittee Republican, participated fully in the inquiry but was dominated by her two male colleagues. The subcommittee's chief counsel, William P. Rogers, had the confidence of Hoey and won high marks from the press for conduct of the investigation. Vaughan, however, believed that he was treated unfairly not only by McCarthy and Mundt but also by Rogers, another Republican. "Before the McCarthys, the Mundts and the Rogers you are presumed guilty and given no chance to prove your innocence," he later complained.[15] Mara coordinated Vaughan's side of the case, visited Rogers's office on several occasions, claimed that Pearson was frequently in the office, and implied that Rogers was a conduit to the columnist.[16]

By the time Senator Hoey called to order the initial open session of the subcommittee, there was much public interest in the hearings. Many people who had lined up hoping to attend the spectacle were turned away. The small room in the Senate Office Building was packed with spectators and members of the press, and Hoey barred television and newsreels in an attempt to diminish the theatrical aspect of the inquiry.[17] "I am sure that I speak for the whole committee," he proclaimed, "in saying that the purpose of this investigation is not to embarrass or humiliate anyone."[18] But it was a hollow gesture, for the inquiry increasingly centered on General Vaughan. In the fifteen days of hearings, not a single day passed without reference to Vaughan's role. Speculation as to whether the general would testify became a preoccupation of the press. When Vaughan did appear, his testimony was the climax of the hearings.

During the three-week interval between the opening of the hearings and Vaughan's appearance, the White House maintained a careful silence. The president held three press conferences and at each one declined to comment, remarking only that nothing had changed his opinion about Vaughan. Truman's only other comment relative to the hearings proved an embarrassment to the president and a setback to Vaughan. Before the 18 August 1949 press conference, Truman was given a statement by Ross; the president read it, asking the media to suspend judgment until after Vaughan's testimony. The statement included a pledge by the president not to answer questions regarding the hearings, but after repeating it at the request of a reporter, Truman offered an additional comment: "The principal reason for [the refusal to answer questions] is that all these committee hearings have been behind closed doors, and everything that has come out has been leaks."[19] Eight open sessions already had been held, and several reporters at the press conference had attended them. A couple of reporters attempted to give the president a chance to wriggle off the hook later in the press conference, but it was too late. Compounding Truman's error was an offer by the committee earlier in the week to release transcripts of its executive sessions. Vaughan had requested the transcripts, and the committee agreed on condition that they be made public.

Vaughan demurred, and the office of the special counsel, Clark Clifford, agreed. Following Truman's comment, however, the committee reconsidered and agreed unanimously to release the transcripts, after which it became clear why Vaughan had objected to their release. Among other damaging evidence was testimony contrary to Vaughan's claim that the controversial freezers that he and others had received as gifts in 1945 were factory rejects.[20]

With newspaper charges appearing daily and editorials calling for Vaughan's dismissal, the general decided to offer his resignation. He told Truman that while he did not want to run from a fight, he did want to do what he could to take the heat off the president. Truman would not hear of it. He rose, walked around his desk, put his arm around his old friend, and told him, "Harry, we have been together for a long time. We understand each other. You and I came into the White House together, and we will go out together, and don't let me hear any more of this damn foolishness about you wanting to resign."[21]

Such support was a great comfort to his military aide. For Vaughan, the entire period since his return from Central America had been an ordeal. The president tried to lighten the mood on one occasion by fashioning another "medal," this one from a Truman campaign button and a 1949 inaugural badge. It was inscribed:

Harry Vaughan
Whipping Boy First Class

Vaughan thought the appellation so appropriate that he later used it as the title of an unpublished memoir.

When the time arrived for Vaughan to appear before the Hoey committee, it was again President Truman who gave him last-minute encouragement. Shortly before Vaughan left the White House on the morning of 30 August to testify, Truman reassured him: "Harry, this investigation is entirely political, trying to embarrass me by discrediting you. You have nothing to hide. Go up there and tell the committee anything they want to know. You have been conducting your office in the way I want you to conduct it. When I want it conducted differently, I'll tell you so."[22]

When Vaughan reached the Hill that August morning, he

faced a constellation of allegations that had accumulated in three years of Pearson columns and other newspaper stories and in three weeks of public hearings and the preceding executive sessions. The issue that received the most public attention, and that was destined to become a symbol of corruption, was a gift of deep freezers to Vaughan and others in the administration. Harry Hoffman, a Milwaukee advertising agent and a friend, had been in the White House in 1945 while Vaughan was involved in a phone conversation concerning Mrs. Truman's desire to procure a freezer. Hoffman phoned David Bennett, president of Albert Verley & Company, a perfume manufacturer whose account he handled, and told him of the conversation. The wealthy Bennett concurred with Hoffman's suggestion to send freezers to Mrs. Truman, Vaughan, and several others. (Freezers were eventually sent to Fred Vinson, Secretary of the Treasury at that time; Truman's first personally selected naval aide, Commodore James K. Vardaman; Director of the Office of War Mobilization and Reconversion John W. Snyder; and presidential appointments secretary Connelly.) When the freezer arrived at Vaughan's house in Alexandria, the general was with Truman's party at the Potsdam Conference, and he did not find out about the gift until his return. At that point he was still unaware of Bennett's involvement, attested by his note of thanks to the manufacturer, in which he mentioned Hoffman, not Bennett.[23]

That the deep freezer became such a cause célèbre was due in part to clumsy efforts to explain it away. In a 13 August public statement written for him by Ross and Clifford, Vaughan claimed that the freezers were of no commercial value, either factory rejects or experimental models. He later said he may have been in error, either because of the time lapse or the frequent repairs and nonstandard parts on the appliances. Vaughan had good reason for his negative memories of the notorious freezer; he paid $74.65 for six repair calls in a year and a half. Mara said Vaughan's deep freezer was the worst of the lot, describing it as "of plywood, painted with ordinary paint," with a separate little section for the compressor.[24] Even Bennett described the celebrated appliances as "crappy."[25] Vaughan eventually had to pay $5.00 to have a trash service haul his freezer away.

The 13 August statement created the impression that additional freezers distributed by Bennett had been sent at Vaughan's request. The general denied foreknowledge of any freezers being shipped and claimed that misunderstanding had resulted because his statement had been written hastily to prevent causing embarrassment to Mrs. Truman.[26]

The deep freezer issue was not an isolated charge. During the inquiry, Republican senators, especially Mundt, attempted to connect the freezers with a payoff to Bennett, Hoffman, or Bennett's seemingly omnipresent employee, the notorious Maragon. The subcommittee entered into evidence several letters from Vaughan on behalf of Maragon and Bennett—letters of introduction to American officials in Europe and requests to the Passport Bureau to expedite passports or to arrange visits with American military authorities in Europe. The link was never established, though Mundt left no doubt of his certainty that such a connection existed. Hoffman in executive session emphatically denied any payoff, solicited or delivered. Vaughan claimed he did nothing for Bennett or Maragon that he would not have done for anyone he knew and that the one "favor" he did for Bennett—arranging a flight to Norfolk atop sacks of mail in a mail plane when Bennett was taken ill in the Azores—he would have done for any American citizen.[27]

Mundt failed to implicate Vaughan as an influence peddler, but he was successful in furthering the general's reputation for poor judgment. Vaughan's faith in Maragon had been demonstrated to have been misplaced in several instances, yet Vaughan continued to extend courtesies to him. "Honest John" (as reporters referred to Maragon) performed unsatisfactorily on a mission to Greece, was caught smuggling oils essential for perfume into the country, and continued to use Vaughan's White House office as a base of operations after being ordered to stop. Nevertheless, none of these incidents had been enough to destroy Vaughan's confidence in Maragon, for even as he offered testimony to the committee he expressed some confidence in his friend, allowing only that "he does not reprimand easy."[28]

Vaughan came under fire on another issue that involved Hunt and Maragon, who were accused of using influence to divert scarce building materials, needed for housing for returning veterans, to a friend who had interest in Tanforan Race Track near San Francisco, which had been taken over by the government in 1942 and then used as a Japanese-American relocation camp and by the navy during the war. It was returned to its owners in April 1946, although not in its original condition as required by the wartime agreement. Application was made with the Civilian Production Administration to restore the track to its original condition. After a series of rulings and reversals, which granted limited construction authority, a stop order was issued, followed by an injunction forbidding further work. The injunction was defied, and track officials were convicted, sentenced to prison, and fined.[29]

The Tanforan affair was nothing if not complicated. An acquaintance of Vaughan, William Helis, Jr. (Vaughan had known his father in connection with work on the Greek Relief Fund), acquired interest in the track, and in October 1947, he and his associates sent three men, including Maragon, to see the federal housing expediter, Frank Creedon, in a meeting arranged by Vaughan; they hoped to get building materials released to the track. After the meeting, Helis phoned Vaughan and complained of shoddy treatment at the hands of Creedon's lieutenants. Vaughan complained to Hunt, a friend of Creedon, in a meeting described in one of Hunt's files that later came into the committee's hands: "General Vaughan, while talking to me about other subjects, remarked with vehemence that 'your friend Creedon is a fine guy,' meaning the opposite."[30] Not one to miss an opportunity to demonstrate his influence, Hunt assumed the role of peacemaker and met with representatives of the Office of the Housing Expediter three days later.

Tighe Woods succeeded Creedon as housing expediter on 1 November 1947, and within his first week in office he signed two letters to the Justice Department stating that his office would not object to modification of the injunction against Tanforan on the basis of the change in ownership. Although Woods had not reviewed the case, he testified that as the law was written even "Al Capone from Alcatraz Prison" would have been entitled to a modification. Woods met with his staff and counsel on 5 January 1948 to discuss

Tanforan. They decided to issue a permit for $54,000 worth of building materials under "hardship" provisions of the law. On 9 January, Vaughan talked to Woods for the first time, when Woods, in the White House for a conference with Steelman, stopped in to see Vaughan. The general urged Woods not to be prejudiced because the case dealt with a racetrack. He said that friends of his were involved, and he wanted to be sure they received fair treatment. Woods testified that he considered Vaughan's role to be similar to that of a senator or congressman making a request, not an exertion of pressure from the White House. Three days later, Vaughan visited Woods with a representative of Tanforan and asked Woods to hurry a decision on the permit because there was a possibility that the Tanforan group might lose its franchise with the California State Racing Commission. The permit was issued the next day.[31]

The Tanforan issue provided fodder for the columns of Pearson and Bob Considine long after the hearings ended, and it appeared as a case of White House influence in return for campaign contributions. Helis had given Vaughan a sizable amount of money in 1946, which Vaughan turned over to the Democratic party chairman of Missouri. Had Vaughan exerted undue influence on behalf of Helis? Both principals in the case—Vaughan and Woods—testified that his actions were routine requests on behalf of constituents and that the decision to act favorably on the Tanforan permit had been made on the basis of operative law before Vaughan saw Woods.[32] Technically, Vaughan's influence only could have expedited the decision; his sole actions were to make an appointment for Helis with the housing expediter and to utter indiscreet remarks to Hunt (whose subsequent actions were independent). On the question of the expedited decision, Vaughan claimed that "an interesting bit of skulduggery" had altered testimony to show him in a less favorable light. The mimeographed transcript of Woods's testimony, prepared immediately from the official stenographer's record, contained the following version:

> Senator McCarthy: In other words, he asked you to please hurry and issue a permit?
> Mr. Woods: No, just to hurry.

The official version of the hearings released later read:

Senator McCarthy: By please hurry up he did not mean please hurry up and refuse a permit but please hurry up and grant the permit.

Mr. Woods: Yes, sir.[33]

This small bit of testimony became crucial to Vaughan's argument in assessing his culpability in the case. His argument that the decision had been made before his first contact with Woods was not convincing. It was an excuse framed in retrospect, after he had a chance to read Woods's testimony. In January 1948, when Vaughan met twice in four days with the housing expediter on Tanforan, he had no way of knowing that the decision to grant the permit had been made. Vaughan's testimony demonstrates that he tried to have the decision expedited. Whether he tried to do more than that, and use influence to obtain a favorable decision, rested with Woods's perception of Vaughan's intent, and Woods, in the original transcript, substantiated Vaughan's claim of innocence. Yet even Woods's testimony did not excuse Vaughan's indiscretion; when a presidential aide made two personal contacts within a four-day period while a final decision seemingly hung in the balance, it was hard to avoid the impression of White House pressure. For indiscretion, then, Vaughan again received the derision of the press. The attacks were unnecessarily severe before the hearings and clearly unjust after. There is no evidence to support the charge that he "diverted scarce materials," yet the allegation was repeated on several occasions by Pearson and Considine after the hearings and reechoed in articles of other reporters.[34]

President Truman never expressed his opinion on Tanforan publicly. The matter was discussed at length at a staff meeting, however. The 5 August 1949 discussion was prompted by Pearson's column that morning—four days before Woods spoke to the Hoey committee. Vaughan offered his explanation. The president endorsed it and branded Pearson's column as false. Thus, even before the evidence was in, Vaughan's most consistent critic and his most ardent supporter had formed their opinions, and neither would be swayed by what was to transpire before the committee.[35]

Of all the allegations that Vaughan faced during the five-percenter investigation, the most incriminating charge of misused influence was by Herbert C. Hathorn, an attorney who had been employed by the Department of Agriculture. Hathorn stated that in November 1946, while he was administering the rationing-control program for edible syrups and molasses, he received a call from Vaughan, who pressed him to release molasses to the Allied Molasses Company to avoid embarrassment to the White House. Vaughan allegedly said he had met the president of Allied, a Mr. Ross, at a football game. In the course of a conversation in which Ross complained about his difficulties, the general mistakenly told him molasses would be decontrolled. On that information Ross contracted for a large order. Hathorn alleged that Vaughan told him, "We Democrats have to stick together." Hathorn added that Vaughan reminded him of his ability to have Hathorn removed from his job or to be helpful in getting him a better job. Hathorn refused to go along; Allied had been a serious violator of the rationing program and deserved no special consideration.

The next person to testify was the assistant director of the sugar branch in the Department of Agriculture, Joseph T. Elvove. He said that Vaughan had phoned on 19 November 1946 and requested release to Allied of a tank car of molasses contracted for but held in demurrage. That was the only time Vaughan contacted Elvove, but over the next two months Elvove had three visits from Maragon and ten phone conversations on the Allied problem. Maragon implied he was representing Vaughan and at least one of the calls originated from Vaughan's White House office.[36]

Hathorn and Elvove both had been forthright and informative in testimony. When Vaughan had opportunity to respond, he labeled Hathorn's statement "an out-and-out fantasy insofar as it relates to me." He had no recollection of having met Ross. Nor could he recall having talked to Hathorn or Elvove, though he admitted he may have done so.[37] In concluding his testimony on the molasses issue, Vaughan offered an explanation for his usual course of action in cases in which he called a department for a petitioner: "My duty, as I see it, and as the President has seen it for the many years I have worked for him, I do these people the courtesy of putting them in contact with the person with whom they can tell their story to. I do not hold a brief for them, because I don't know enough about the facts. And where the depart-

ment head tells me that these people are all wet, we can do
nothing for them, I have done what I set out to do."[38]

It was a policy that would have put any government official
beyond reproach. It was when Vaughan went beyond refer-
ral that his trouble started, which is exactly what happened
in the Tanforan case (although Vaughan denied it) and in
the Allied molasses case (although Vaughan could not recall
it). The thin line between reference and advocacy was one
that the impulsive general could cross almost without real-
izing, and certainly without recognizing the consequences.

Another charge against the president's military aide was
the allegation that the FBI had investigated him for accepting a bribe, in the form of a campaign contribution, for
intervening in the income tax–evasion case of W. T. Burton,
a prominent New Orleans oil man and a friend of Helis.
Pearson had referred to the case in his column and made
his only appearance before the committee on this issue. He
claimed to have been in the office of Assistant Attorney General James P. McGranery in 1946 when Vaughan phoned to
ask for intervention in the Burton case. (When McGranery
promptly denied Pearson's story, the columnist speculated
in his diary that the denial came because McGranery was
angling for appointment to the Supreme Court to replace
the dying Justice Rutledge.) Mara appeared prior to Pearson
and testified that he had visited Peyton Ford at the Justice
Department to see if Vaughan had been implicated in the
investigation. Mara had not seen the file, but Ford assured
him that Vaughan had been cleared. (Pearson claimed
Vaughan was cleared because the FBI did not pursue the
matter of contributions.) Long after the hearings, Vaughan
asserted that Pearson had initiated the FBI probe through
Attorney General Clark, claiming that Hoover had informed him of Clark's role. Hoover had refused to initiate
an investigation until he received a written memorandum
from Clark, and Vaughan claimed to have been shown the
memo by the FBI director.[39]

The deep freezer case (and related charges concerning
travel priorities), the Tanforan issue, the Allied molasses
matter, and the Burton tax case formed the main allegations
against Vaughan at the five-percenter investigation. There
were other charges, but they echoed the main ones or were

of less substance. In a matter with remarkable parallels to both the Tanforan and molasses cases, Vaughan was accused of pressing the Department of Agriculture to increase the allocation of grain to distillers at the expense of food needs. Vaughan concurred that there were calls to the White House requesting that the distillers' quota not be reduced. He said that his only involvement, however, had been to make an inquiry to the Department of Agriculture at the request of the president.[40]

There were accusations related to campaign contributions, including one that Vaughan had taken money in return for parole of a man who sold liquor on the black market.[41] Another charge alleged that Vaughan had bought a car for resale on the black market, but Hoey called it "chicken feed."[42] In these cases and a few others, the Republican senators were trying to draw up a catalog of indictments against the general.

When Vaughan went to Capitol Hill on the morning of 30 August 1949, he was well prepared, thanks to Mara's assistance. Mara had studied several of the cases that he and Vaughan knew would come up. He had served as Vaughan's liaison to the committee counsel. Aware of Vaughan's temper and his attitude toward Republicans on the committee, he coached the general on behavior during the hearings, advising him to answer everything calmly and not to get excited. Aware of the dismal attendance records of committee Democrats at the hearings, Mara called them and urged them to attend the sessions when Vaughan testified. The 30 August session was the first since the opening session three weeks earlier at which all members of the subcommittee were present.[43]

Attired in full dress military uniform, Vaughan arrived at Room 357 in the Senate Office Building some seven minutes before the scheduled 10:00 A.M. start of the session, accompanied by his attorney, Col. Carl Ristine, and by Mara. Hoey had refused to change the hearing to a larger room in a futile effort to treat Vaughan's testimony as an ordinary session. Newsmen and photographers crowded into every space in the small room. Hoey allowed five minutes of picture taking before beginning.[44]

Once the hearing was underway, Vaughan presented a

prepared statement in which he addressed each of the anticipated allegations, denying any wrongdoing. During questioning, Senator McCarthy went out of his way to project a
deprecating attitude toward Vaughan. Time and again he
addressed the general as "Mr." Vaughan, on one occasion
called him "colonel," and on another, "Mr. Maragon."[45] At
one point McCarthy made a cryptic remark loaded with innuendo, a statement he never explained: "I have said all
along I have had the feeling that General Vaughan did not
profit financially personally because of these various deals.
Then I added the statement that that was still my opinion. I
am going to ask that the last half of that statement be striken
from the record, that part in which I said that still was my
opinion."[46]

Mundt joined McCarthy in dominating the interrogation,
just as the two men had dominated previous sessions. Senator Robertson attempted to serve as a buffer but was at a
disadvantage because he had missed so much of the testimony—which McCarthy was not reluctant to point out.
Nonetheless, Robertson did counter McCarthy and Mundt
when they were misconstruing Vaughan's remarks.

Vaughan fared relatively well in his appearance. After the
first of two days of testifying, he returned to the White
House in a buoyant mood and described his experience to
staff members in Connelly's office. Mara had been at
Vaughan's side throughout the ordeal and later said that
Vaughan had done "marvelously."[47] Even critics were impressed by Vaughan's performance. Frank McNaughton of
Time, who had described the general as "a big mud-brained
jerk throwing his weight around for small favors," admitted
he was "a pretty cool character," although he considered the
committee partly responsible for the general's showing. "It
is apparent that the committee lacks incisive, sharp cross-
examiners. They try hard, but they couldn't even bring
Vaughan up to boiling, or get him boxed in a corner. Old
Fatty at this point had the confidence of a pug who never
expected to last the first round, and suddenly finds himself
knocking away in the tenth, going strong."[48]

Vaughan's satisfaction did not erase his bitterness over the
inquiry, and four years later, after Truman had left office,
he still was resentful, claiming he had been the victim of

"rigged justice" by political opportunists and a malicious press. Describing his experiences, Vaughan wrote: "It is not what you have done, but what distortion, insinuation or lie that can be built around your action. . . . Your constitutional rights are a mockery. You can answer only such questions as are put to you, and they are so loaded that they do not seek to reveal the truth. You face a battery of prosecutors and may not produce a defense. You have no recourse whereby you may protect yourself against perjured testimony, as I have discovered."[49]

Truman refused to get into any public discussion concerning the five-percenter hearings. At his press conference on 1 September, the president abruptly cut off questioning, saying, "The committee hearing was held up at the Capitol. We will not continue it up here." He reaffirmed that he would not fire Vaughan. Six weeks later, at his 13 October press conference, Truman opened up slightly. Asked if he approved of the committee having ended its hearings, the president responded, "I don't think they ever had an intelligent investigation, so there was no sense continuing it."[50]

The five-percenter question drifted from the public consciousness for a few months, but when the committee released its report in January 1950 it was again revived. The report reserved its harshest criticism for Maragon and Hunt, but Vaughan received his share of fire, particularly for his association with Maragon. "There is no doubt," the report concluded, "that Maragon's friendship with Gen. Harry H. Vaughan made his activities in his dealings with the Federal Government possible." Vaughan also was criticized for making calls to departments on matters pending before them, since this implied a White House sanction that often did not exist.[51]

Although Vaughan fared somewhat better than Hunt and Maragon in the report, the general had been at the center of the five-percenter investigation since its inception. The focus of the inquiry on Vaughan was unfortunate. When the inquiry took this direction, it diminished the possibility that the committee might change the negotiation process of government contracts. It became political. Republican senators on the committee lost sight of remedying the problem of the five percenters and set their sights instead on Vaughan.

Democratic senators, with the exception of Hoey, the chairman, became nominal participants. Hoey retained a sense of the committee's purpose, but he was ineffective in his effort to steer the committee.

The "get Vaughan" attitude of the committee dictated to President Truman his relation with the committee. For the president, as well as for the committee, the question was not how to eliminate operators like Maragon from the Washington scene but whether Vaughan would stay. Nowhere was this better demonstrated than at the president's press conferences, at which the recurring question of the "status of the military aide" overshadowed other references to the hearings. It became a political game, with McCarthy and Mundt writing the rules. Truman had little choice but to resist unless the committee unearthed conclusive evidence, which it was unable to do.

While Vaughan was never proven to have done anything illegal—there was no indication that he had received a payoff and only inconclusive evidence regarding his use of influence—there were examples of what can leniently be described as improprieties. Vaughan pinpointed his problems during testimony: "My duties at the White House . . . were a continuance of my duties, the same duties, practically the same duties as I had here in Senator Truman's office. . . . I was performing according to the President's instructions previously given by the President. He had never had occasion to change them. I would just continue to operate in the same way, and I felt sure he would be the first to tell me if he wanted a change."[52] Vaughan had continued to function as he had in Senator Truman's office, where it had been his responsibility to do favors for constituents. When Truman became president, Vaughan acted under the assumption that the United States was the constituency of the president.[53]

To equate the role of a senator's secretary with that of a presidential aide is naive. It is a justification that overlooks the power of the presidency. If Vaughan did not recognize this fact, another Truman aide, Stephen Spingarn, did: "When Harry Vaughan moved to the White House I don't think he quite made in his own mind the change he should have made. I think he still regarded himself as a senator's secretary, and the constituents came around and he would introduce them at the agencies, and he didn't realize perhaps the impact, the different impact it had when the introduction came from the senator's secretary."[54] Senators' secretaries have not only a right but a responsibility to expedite matters for their constituents. When a presidential aide takes the same action, however, he invites criticism. A senator or congressman is expected to advance the interests of his state, even if it may at times mean a loss to other states. Yet because a president's position includes the entire nation, he no longer has the luxury of advancing the interests of a single group without suffering political repercussions.[55]

Truman never tempered Vaughan, so he had to absorb the political repercussions of his military aide's indiscretions. He did so willingly and never backed down in his support of the general. Even after he left office, Truman would say, "Harry Vaughan did an excellent job as Military Aide to me. He knew his duty and he carried it out."[56]

Truman's attitude toward the five-percenter investigation was shaped long before the hearings began: it was a continuation of the press attacks on Vaughan. The only difference was that the chief adversaries were now McCarthy and Mundt instead of Pearson and Winchell. Truman already had decided that the committee had no case; he did not keep informed fully on its day-to-day progress and blundered into the unfortunate press conference reference to closed hearings. His preconceptions also prevented any coordinated effort to counter committee revelations. When the staff did take action, it was in a haphazard manner that clouded issues rather than clarifying them. Such was the case when Ross and Clifford wrote Vaughan's 13 August statement on the deep freezers. The hastily drawn statement created the impression that Vaughan had lied about the freezers, that he had been responsible for the distribution of other freezers; both impressions lingered. When Truman did discuss the inquiry with his staff, it was to bemoan the committee's handling of the matter or to bolster Vaughan's morale and rally the staff.

The five-percenter investigation was a missed opportunity. The committee's mission paralleled that of the World War II Truman committee. Had the president and the committee worked to correct the government procurement system, the combination of presidential and committee authority could have produced reform. As it was, the accomplishments were meager. The Department of Defense made a few cosmetic modifications in procedure, and the General Services Administration developed a new form for federal procurement. The committee's report recommended no new legislation. It was nearly three years after the hearings before the committee recommended legislation to punish influence peddlers.[57] Part of the blame for the failure of the hearings must rest with the committee. The "get Vaughan" approach guaranteed Truman's reaction. The adversary relationship, however, was aided and abetted by the president's judgment of the issue. Because the adversary approach doomed the proceedings, there were no winners and many losers—including the American public.

5. SENATOR FULBRIGHT ■■■■■■
AND THE RFC ■■■■■■■■■■■■■

When the Reconstruction Finance Corporation (RFC) was established under President Herbert Hoover in January 1932, it was intended to bolster smaller banks, insurance companies, and railroads that could assist the recovery of business, industry, and agriculture from the ravages of the Depression. During the years of the Roosevelt presidency, the RFC was a flexible organization that adapted to changing economic conditions under the capable, moderating leadership of Jesse Jones, a banker from Texas. After 1934, businesses received direct aid; by the end of the 1930s, half a billion dollars had gone out in nine thousand loans.[1] The Second World War prompted further adaptation within the RFC. The agency bore eonormous responsibilities in gathering and stockpiling materials and in assisting wartime industry. Subsidiary agencies—the Defense Supplies Corporation, the Rubber Reserve Company, the Defense Plants Corporation, and the Metals Reserve Company—executed the wartime functions of the corporation, which at its peak employed twelve thousand people.

The RFC that Truman inherited in April 1945 had a reputation for having served the nation well during depression and war. While Truman occupied the Oval Office, however, the corporation deteriorated into a scandal-ridden, poorly administered bureaucracy with a hazy sense of purpose. By the time he left office, it was a lame-duck organization, simply taking care of business during the transition to its institutional successor, the Small Business Administration. But to blame Truman for the decline of the RFC would be grossly unfair. Political, bureaucratic, and economic forces contributed to the demise of the agency. It was his misfortune that during his era the corporation was tarnished by allegations of an influence ring with White House ties, and Truman again found himself squabbling with prominent senators of his own party over administration of the RFC when the so-called RFC scandals erupted during his second

term. Hearings conducted by a subcommittee of the Senate
Banking and Currency Committee developed into a political
confrontation with Truman reminiscent of Senator Hoey's
five-percenter investigation. As during the five-percenter investigation, many of the issues were obscured by the process.
The problems that plagued the RFC in the last years of
the Truman presidency had begun well before the Missour-
ian moved into the White House. The productivity of the
wartime RFC was like a glossy coat of paint that covered
fissures in the corporation. By April 1945, the RFC already
had given evidence of fundamental weaknesses in its loan
and personnel policies, its administration, its sense of purpose. Problems went unnoticed until exacerbated by economic uncertainties of the postwar years.

Weaknesses in both loans and personnel were exposed in
the hearings before the Committee on Banking and Currency. New Hampshire Democrat Charles W. Tobey, an
alumnus of the Truman committee, began investigating the
RFC in 1945 while reviewing a proposal to extend the charter of the corporation. Hearings continued intermittently
over the next several years and focused on one of the RFC's
largest borrowers, the Baltimore and Ohio Railroad. The
B & O first had made application for a loan in the early
months of the corporation and eventually accumulated an
indebtedness in excess of $80 million. In 1944, the railroad
received a twenty-year extension that Jesse Jones asserted
kept the railroad out of receivership.[2] Senator Tobey, described by a reporter who covered portions of his investigation as a "lean, whip-tongued . . . man of considerable
charm, and at times considerable heat," led an attack on the
corporation's loan policy in general and the B & O loan in
particular.[3] He accused the RFC of preferential treatment to
the B & O, granting a long-term frozen loan—contrary to
agency policy of temporary loans—and intimated that it was
done to benefit Jones's protégés working with the railroad.
The corporation, he said, did not have authority to extend
a loan beyond January 1955 and had attempted to make it
appear legal by describing it as a purchase of bonds rather
than as an extension. Jones countered that the "charges
were without foundation and undoubtedly were inspired by
some selfish or vindictive motive."[4]

The B & O affair touched on personnel policy as it related to borrowers. Under Jones, former employees often took positions in private industry—in many cases with companies that had loans. In the case of the B & O, three former RFC employees obtained positions prior to the hearings. While one had not cleared his acceptance with Jones, his was a singular case. Jones generally approved employment of subordinates with RFC borrowers and in fact pointed with pride to their record in industry. During Jones's chairmanship the policy had never been questioned.[5]

That weak administration was a fundamental problem of the RFC became clear during the Fulbright hearings, but again it was a difficulty that antedated the Truman administration. Jones had the confidence of Congress and was widely regarded as a strong administrator. President Roosevelt nonetheless had determined to replace Jones as secretary of Commerce, removing him at the same time from his conjunctive position as Federal Loan Administrator, a position that included responsibility over the RFC. Undoubtedly, the dismissal of Jones began several years of less able leadership. But the General Accounting Office (GAO) had found RFC accounting procedures so poor that it was not possible to complete a satisfactory audit for the period that included the last months of Jones's tenure. The GAO said that the RFC had "not developed an adequate concept of the control of financial and operating responsibilities through accounting."[6]

Loss of a clear purpose, a final symptom of incipient RFC illness, was in part the result of the departure of Jones, but it became a serious matter in the years that followed. The RFC was to have been a temporary agency, with an expected life of ten years. As the threat of war loomed in the summer of 1940, Congress took a step toward making the RFC a permanent part of the bureaucracy, giving it greatly enhanced power.[7] As the war drew to a close, however, there was no reevaluation of whether a continuing need for the "temporary" agency existed.[8]

When a Senate review of the RFC functions began in the spring of 1947, it was conducted in an atmosphere of apparently contradictory economic crosscurrents. The administration faced problems that dictated restraint of credit; in deed, credit controls were imposed before the year was out. At the same time, the fear of a recession had not been quelled. The RFC was caught in the middle.[9] As the review began, opinion was that RFC powers accumulated under Jones had to be curbed. Critics suggested that the corporation had outlived its usefulness. Former President Hoover, in a letter that foreshadowed the criticism the Hoover Commission would make about the RFC, suggested that it ought to get out of the lending business except in the case of emergency. Directors J. D. Goodloe and Henry T. Bodman agreed. Goodloe favored extension but argued against institutionalization. The bill that emerged after the 1947 Senate hearings gave the RFC a one-year lease on life.[10] In the following year, the Banking and Currency Committee refused to endorse the RFC but recognized that economic conditions might again make it useful. The committee recommended extension. The organization had its charter extended for eight years.

The RFC limped through Truman's first term under a cloud of uncertainty—the B & O loan, an unsettled economy, and an undetermined future. As Truman prepared to move into his second term, the 1948 law that was to clarify the corporation's purpose and stabilize the institution under congressional guidance was misinterpreted into ineffectuality.

The instrument of the RFC's collapse was the same subcommittee of the Senate Banking and Currency Committee that earlier had probed the loan to the B & O. Chairmanship of the subcommittee had passed to Arkansas's junior senator, J. William Fulbright. The president again found his administration under attack by a senator of his own party, as during the five-percenter investigation. Moreover, he had a strained personal relationship with Fulbright that dated back to a remark the latter made on the eve of the Republican sweep of the 1946 off-year elections. Fulbright had suggested that for the sake of national leadership Truman ought to appoint a Republican secretary of state (who, because the vice-presidency was vacant, would be next in line to the presidency) and then resign. Truman had described such a notion as "utterly fantastic" and was wont to refer to the freshman senator as "an overeducated Oxford SOB."[11]

Fulbright's inquiry began innocently enough. Conducting a routine examination of RFC operations in June 1949, the subcommittee was troubled by a loan to the Waltham Watch Company. The head of the RFC agency in Boston, John J. Hagerty, had endorsed the loan enthusiastically after initially recommending disapproval. A short time later, he accepted a position with Waltham at three times his RFC salary. The committee suspected that the loan had bailed out several of Waltham's creditors among New England banks.[12]

Another loan that caught the attention of the subcommittee went to the Lustron Corporation, an Ohio-based manufacturer of prefabricated houses made of enameled steel, which had applied for $52 million in 1946. Despite ardent support of the housing expediter, Wilson Wyatt, who saw prefabricated houses as a way out of the housing shortage, Lustron had been rejected by RFC director George Allen, who cited lack of performance and a paltry $36,000 in assets. Wyatt resigned in protest. But Lustron persisted, and although its corporate structure was virtually unchanged, the company received a series of installment credits that reached $32.5 million by the time of the Fulbright hearings. In what was becoming a pattern, RFC examiner E. Merl Young took a position with Lustron within days after approval of a $10 million installment and soon was earning two and a half times his RFC salary. In June 1949, when the Fulbright committee took the Lustron loan request under consideration, factory production of Lustron houses was at a level of twenty units per day—a fifth of earlier projections—and the company was losing $1 million each month.[13]

The Waltham and Lustron loans led the committee to suspect, at the very least, poor RFC management, and Fulbright sought a broader inquiry into the corporation. A senate resolution in February 1950 granted the request.

On the eve of the renewed hearings, the committee's critical attitude toward the RFC received an endorsement of sorts from an unlikely source, the former head of the corporation, Jones. Fulbright had solicited Jones's views, and Jones went beyond criticism and suggested that the RFC "should be given a decent burial, lock stock and barrel." He based his recommendations on the altered economic conditions since the halcyon days of his leadership, as well as what he called the prostitution of the organization through such loans as those to Waltham and Lustron.[14]

The subcommittee opened its investigation with a probe of a $15 million loan to the Texmass Petroleum Company of Dallas, which RFC directors had authorized the previous September. In 1944, a Dallas oil entrepreneur, Homer A. Snowdon, had convinced an impressive group of Boston-area individual and institutional investors to back him in development of oil properties he owned. The company failed to produce any return and was reorganized several times, emerging as Texmass in October 1946. In debt from the outset, Texmass was rescued the following year by an $8 million loan from two Boston insurance companies, John Hancock Mutual and Massachusetts Mutual. It applied to the RFC in March 1949. The company's many creditors were among the supporters of the loan—not surprising since they were slated to receive four-fifths of the money. An indignant Fulbright condemned the loan as a bailout that did not meet the public-interest test of the 1948 RFC recommendations. The chairman of the RFC, Harley Hise, defended the Texmass cash distribution as a way to get creditors to release liens on the corporation's property and to convert short-term indebtedness to long term. But even RFC Director Walter L. Dunham was unable to avoid referring to the loan as a bailout when he testified before the committee. When the loan was approved, only two of the five directors actually voted in favor; a third was ill, Hise disqualified himself, and one director opposed. One of the two favorable votes, that of Harvey J. Gunderson, was cast primarily because Gunderson believed the development of oil reserves was in the national interest. A similar perspective was a factor in Dunham's favorable vote.

The committee alleged that the RFC directors had given only superficial consideration to the Texmass loan, on which the directors had divided. Recommendations changed at different levels of the loan review, but at the time of the loan the directors had negative recommendations from the Dallas loan agency, the Washington loan examiner, and the Washington review committee, while a midlevel review committee recommended approval. Property offered by Texmass as collateral had been examined three times by petroleum engineers and geologists. Even the most charitable assessment—on which the RFC based approval—concluded that company indebtedness was too large. After the committee released its report on the Texmass loan, Hise attacked the committee for "misrepresentations of facts and nonfactual data."[15] He accused committee staff director, Theodore Herz, of prejudice.

President Truman had two possibilities for response, neither of which was attractive. He could have cooperated with the committee to rectify the problems of the RFC, but his poor relationship with the committee's chairman precluded such a course. The alternative, treating the committee as a political forum, gave little latitude for maneuvering but perhaps was preferable to entering an enterprise with Fulbright. In choosing to counter Fulbright, Truman had few cards to play. He could appoint directors of the corporation, and he had authority (under the 1949 Reorganization Act) to alter the RFC's institutional framework. The president quickly played both cards.

Truman's actions in regard to reorganization were less overtly political than his decisions concerning the board, but there were undeniable political ramifications in both moves. On 9 May 1950, he transmitted to Congress three new reorganization plans for the RFC. The first two were not controversial, proposing to transfer the Federal National Mortgage Association and the lending authority related to prefabricated housing from the RFC to the Housing and Home Finance Agency. Both suggestions won easy approval. The third plan proposed placing the RFC under the secretary of commerce and immediately met opposition. The Citizens Committee on the Hoover Report, a watchdog group that attempted to oversee the implementation of recommendations of the commission chaired by former President Hoover, objected that the report had suggested transfer of the RFC to the Treasury Department, although a Hoover Commission minority opinion had favored Commerce. Fulbright objected on different grounds, that transfer of the RFC to any executive department would place a layer of insulation between Congress and the corporation. In this first skirmish of an increasingly politicized battle over the RFC, Fulbright scored on Truman. On 6 July the transfer to

Commerce lost, without even the formality of a roll call in the Senate. Appointments secretary Connelly informed the president that the bill had been turned back by a voice vote.[16]

Truman's second course, changing the directors, resulted in a protracted struggle that led to the agency's demise. Despite its supposedly nonpartisan structure, the RFC board of directors was a highly politicized group. Two years earlier, for example, director Henry Bodman testified before a Senate committee in a vein that implied that Truman had approved of the Lustron loan; a staff memo to the president suggested that Bodman be eased out in favor of Dunham.[17] Bodman resigned within months and Dunham took his place. But by April 1950, the board had divided along lines that defied party allegiance. Dunham, a Republican, and William E. Willett, a Democrat, composed one faction; Hise, a Democrat, and Gunderson, a Republican, made up the other, with the fifth seat vacant after the resignation of Henry A. Mulligan. The terms of all directors were to expire on 30 June, so Truman had an uncommon opportunity to use his appointment authority.

Both factions on the board were well aware of the sensitivity of the appointment issue. The Dunham-Willett faction had a powerful White House ally, the president's assistant for personnel matters, Donald S. Dawson, an energetic and persuasive man who had worked in the RFC and risen rapidly to the position of personnel director before being chosen by Truman to take a similar position on the White House staff. Dawson's experience and access to the president gave him the opportunity to help to shape RFC policy, but it left him open to criticism. He apparently had recommended Dunham and was not hesitant to give advice on RFC matters. In mid-April, when Hise was scheduled to meet with the president, Dawson assumed that the discussion might center on the appointment issue and accused Hise of "duplicity when he last made a recommendation." He urged Truman to "defer consideration of his recommendation for the time being until we have a chance to look at it."[18]

Truman at this point received advice from an anonymous source familiar with RFC operations, in a memo that was directed to "the President Only, and no member of his staff," presumably to avoid Dawson's scrutiny. The writer had little regard for Hise's rival directors: "Dunham's contribution to R.F.C. is zero and Willett's is minus something like 100." Ironically, the source suggested that if Dunham and Willett were to be reappointed, they "might well be called to the president's office and be given a few words about cooperation." He named three possibilities for expiring directorships and claimed that Willett was already trying to undermine one of them, a "Mr. Haggarty" (probably John J. Hagerty, the RFC loan examiner who had taken a position with Waltham Watch).[19]

If there had been any doubt in Truman's mind as to which RFC faction he should support, it was dispelled as hearings on the RFC reorganization plan unfolded on the Hill. There had been rumblings that RFC officials opposed the reorganization plan, and White House staffers feared that opposition would come out in the hearings. Gunderson thereupon testified before Fulbright's committee and opposed the plan. At a cabinet meeting on 16 June 1950, Secretary of Commerce Charles Sawyer discussed his own appearance before the committee and Gunderson's negative testimony. Before the cabinet meeting adjourned, Truman began to formulate his counterattack and suggested that instead of sending RFC board appointments to Congress at the time of their expiration on 30 June, Congress might allow a sixty-day delay until transfer of the RFC to Commerce.[20]

Gunderson's testimony, coupled with Truman's unfavorable opinion of Hise, clinched the issue for the president.[21] On 9 August, when he forwarded his nominations for the RFC board of directors, he did not name Hise and Gunderson. He nominated their political adversaries on the board, Dunham and Willett. Remaining slots on the board went to C. Edward Rowe (whom Willett had supported), W. Elmer Harber, and Walter E. Cosgriff.

Fulbright was taken aback by the president's actions. Dunham and Willett had been criticized on more than one occasion during the hearings, and their reappointment seemed overtly political. In September, the senator told the White House of the committee's initial findings, urging a fundamental reorganization of top-level RFC administration. By December no action had been taken. Fulbright, unwilling to initiate an open intraparty squabble, sought a meeting with the president. An appointment was scheduled for 12 December 1950.

When Dawson heard of the scheduled meeting, he anticipated points that Fulbright might raise and attempted to counter them. In Dawson's view, the senator was bent on destroying the RFC. He expected Fulbright to continue to attack Truman's appointments to the board of directors. He knew that the committee had developed charges against Truman's appointees, the most serious being that Rowe had obtained an RFC loan under favorable conditions just four months prior to appointment to the board, apparently because of friendship with Willett. Dawson argued against another Fulbright proposal—replacement of the board of directors with a single administrator. Fulbright had been frustrated in his attempts to fix responsibility for the corporation's questionable loans (and consequently the director's reluctance to accept responsibility) and believed that one person should bear responsibility. Dawson responded that the job was too much, that the staff would be making all key decisions.

When Fulbright met with the president on 12 December, he was accompanied by Senator Tobey, the committee's leading Republican, and Sen. Paul H. Douglas, an Illinois Democrat. The delegation urged the president to accept the committee's proposals for reorganization, emphasizing that reform could be implemented without embarrassment to the administration. Fulbright later described the president's mood as congenial; the group left feeling that the mission had been a success. Fulbright waited to see what the White House response would be, but Truman's reaction was inconclusive. On 28 December, the president resubmitted the names he had endorsed. Nine days later, he informed Fulbright he was still considering the single administrator plan.[23]

By the end of January 1951, Fulbright's patience ran out. He had been urging presidential attention to committee observations on the RFC for more than four months and had been rebuffed. The most powerful weapon in the committee's arsenal was the long-awaited report, and Fulbright prepared to use it. George Meader, who had written the report, urged caution, suggesting release of executive session testimony first. He argued that Truman ought to be informed when charges were leveled at members of his official family. Fulbright and Douglas, however, judged that they had extended sufficient courtesy to the president and decided to release the report.[24]

The interim report, entitled "Favoritism and Influence," appeared on 2 February 1951 and was a devastating attack that accused the leadership of being responsive to outside persons. At the center of the allegations was Dawson, whom the committee claimed to have "apparently exercised considerable influence over certain of the Directors of the R.F.C." The report blasted the Dawson-Willett-Dunham connection, charging that there were "close personal relationships" between Dawson, Merl Young, Rex Jacobs, James Windham, and RFC directors Dunham and Willett. "These friends with others constitute a group who appear to have exercised influence over the R.F.C. Former Chairman Hise and Director Dunham of the R.F.C. have stated that Dawson tried to dominate the R.F.C. Hise said that he resisted domination by Dawson, but Dunham acknowledged that he did not. Hise, Dunham and former Director Gunderson, all three, have asserted that Willett does what Dawson requires of him as an R.F.C. Director."[25]

The report included accusations of other improprieties and suspicious relationships. It claimed approval of loans in spite of evidence that they should have been rejected. It said that attorney Joseph H. Rosenbaum claimed to have Willett and Dunham "in his hip pocket." Young, the former RFC examiner and a close friend of Dawson, was said to be "the individual named most frequently in the reports of alleged influence." He had risen from an annual salary of $1,080 in 1940 to over $60,000 in 1950. Both Young and Dawson were from Missouri. The report drew the committee's perspective in broad brush strokes, presenting accusations based on testimony to date. It was an interim report, scarcely a brief. Charges were set forth with slight substantiation, particularly in the section that identified alleged wielders of influence.

If "Favoritism and Influence" was a tossing of the gauntlet, the battle quickly was joined. At a press conference on 8

February, Truman scornfully dismissed the report as "asinine" and accused Fulbright of leaving town when he heard the president wanted to see him. Fulbright flatly denied the charge.[26] Truman then moved to seize the initiative. Almost certainly in response to a suggestion from Dawson, he asked the RFC to screen its files for letters from congressmen on behalf of prospective borrowers. Shortly after the 8 February press conference, batches of letters were delivered to Dawson at the White House. On 15 February, in a hand-delivered letter, Truman advised Willett, "I sincerely hope that you will get all the facts together and show exactly where undue influence rests with regard to the R.F.C. Board. There are an immense number of pressure letters from nearly every member of Congress, particularly members of the Banking and Currency Committee, with which I think you ought to fortify yourself and be able to quote from when they hold hearings on your confirmation."[27]

Truman became even more direct. He placed a call to the Capitol and had Senator Tobey summoned from an executive session of the Fulbright committee. Senator Douglas later recalled Tobey's return. With a "solemn and pale face," Tobey informed the committee of the president's words: "The real crooks and influence peddlers were members of this committee, as we might soon find out."[28] Truman further charged that "a great many" members of Congress had accepted fees for their influence in getting RFC loans for constituents.[29]

The president had struck a nerve. Douglas reviewed his own correspondence with the RFC, and in an attempt to head off criticism read into the *Congressional Record* three letters he had written to the RFC. He admitted that perhaps he had gone too far in advocacy. He claimed he had written no letters after March or April 1949, although the nine hundred letters Truman reviewed included six from Douglas written after that date. Although it was not revealed at the time, Fulbright himself was in a sensitive position, since he had given two letters in support of a loan application, which was approved, to a resort hotel in Hot Springs. (During the hearings, Fulbright criticized RFC loans to hotels as having little or no public interest.)[30]

Truman soon ended his criticism of congressional pressure on the RFC. On 23 February, 1951, Joseph Short, who had replaced Ross as press secretary, issued a prepared statement in which he gave the cover story that the letters had been solicited in conjunction with reorganization plans. Since there was "no evidence of illegal influence on the R.F.C. by any member of the executive branch or the legislative branch," the letters would not be made public, though they would be available to the committee on request.[31] But the president had succeeded in planting doubts concerning the integrity of some members of Congress.

Meanwhile, Truman submitted a reorganization plan that seemed almost conciliatory. Its principal feature was the reform for which Fulbright had been asking for months: replacement of the board of directors by a single administrator. It proposed a five-member Loan Policy Board composed of the administrator, deputy administrator, the secretaries of the Departments of Treasury and Commerce, and a member selected by the president. The board would establish loan policies to be executed by the administrator. Fulbright and Douglas quickly expressed approval, although another member of the committee, Republican Sen. Homer Capehart of Indiana, opposed on the ground that a "dictator" might be no less subject to influence than the current directors.[32] Had a similar reorganization plan been offered a few months earlier, it might have ended criticism of both the RFC and the administration. By late February 1951, however, matters had gone too far. Truman's approach— using letters to attack the committee while he was putting the finishing touches on a conciliatory reorganization bill— had caused too much trouble.

Other actions by the administration and the committee demonstrated the animosity on both sides. Stories had circulated that Fulbright's dispute with the president had cost him patronage. Senator Douglas was summoned for a tax audit shortly after the dispute over the letters. At the request of administrative assistant David K. Niles, Sen. Kenneth S. Wherry relayed a message to Senator Tobey to "go easy" on Dawson, and Tobey indignantly made the appeal public, calling it "improper and unethical."[33]

Dawson continued to be Truman's primary source for information on behind-the-scenes activities of the committee, and Truman saw a continuing campaign of harassment. Dawson told him that the committee had an investigator in the RFC building waiting for mistakes in daily operations, that other investigators were attempting to develop critical material on the private lives of the directors, that the RFC believed phone lines were tapped. Senator Douglas allegedly had told Democratic National Committee Chairman William Boyle, when asked what he had against Willett, that although he did not have anything against him, he would get something. Truman was informed that the committee had taken Dunham's personal diary and refused to allow the president to see even a copy.[34]

Dawson himself had remained a shadowy figure through the unfolding of the RFC intrigue. The focal point of the committee's "Favoritism and Influence," the man who had the greatest role in shaping Truman's understanding of the RFC, he had avoided publicity. The catharsis that the committee needed to complete its business was testimony of this key individual.

Dawson's testimony was needed to still the public clamor for a resolution of the affair. Criticism had been stirred by "Favoritism and Influence" and not quelled by discussion of the congressional letters or submission of the reorganization plan. After the tumultuous release of "Favoritism and Influence," it was revealed that E. Merl Young had given his wife, a White House stenographer, a $9,540 "natural royal pastel mink coat" charged to the account of attorney Rosenbaum, who represented a firm that shortly obtained approval of its application for an RFC loan. As with the deep freezers during the five-percenter inquiry, the mink coat became a symbol of high-level corruption. Young became the current version of the crooked operator that Maragon had been in the five-percenter case, and Dawson became the Truman crony who abused the president's authority in the mold of Vaughan. Even in demeanor Young recalled Maragon; with his cavalier attitude as he flashed his White House pass to meet his wife, he grated the Truman staff as Maragon had earlier.[35]

Two old themes emerged in the RFC problem. The first was an attack on the administration for what the *Philadelphia*

Enquirer called Truman's misplaced loyalty to cronies.[36] Comparison with the scandals of the Harding administration abounded, although most of it did not consider Truman as culpable as the earlier chief executive. John O'Donnell of the *New York Daily News* wrote, "No scandal of the Truman Administration has yet flamed so high as that of Harding's Teapot Dome disaster." Still, he added that it will come: "It's in the books, no doubt of that."[37] Truman responded to the charge of cronyism at a 15 March 1951 press conference, insisting that all his people were honorable.[38] But in a rare unguarded moment, his private resolve on behalf of his associates seemed less certain. When Senators Fulbright and Douglas visited him in the Oval Office to urge that he allow Dawson to testify, Douglas remarked that the president had been loyal to friends who had not returned his loyalty. Truman gazed out the window for a moment and murmured, "I guess you are right."[39]

The other theme of the RFC confrontation was the tendency of critics to attack the agency itself. The *Philadelphia Enquirer* registered an opinion that was being heard regularly—"There is a simple solution to the problem raised by the R.F.C. investigation: abolish the R.F.C."[40]

Nevertheless, just as General Vaughan had been the centerpiece of the five-percenter investigation, the RFC inquiry increasingly focused on Dawson. But there were fundamental differences about the allegations against these two men. While Vaughan was closer to the president, the attack on Dawson represented an attack on the White House staff. Truman commented that one of his most difficult responsibilities was to persuade good men to take jobs in government, and Dawson was Truman's talent scout, a position he handled in a fashion that had won admiration and the respect of virtually everyone. Charles S. Murphy, White House special counsel, observed that nobody who had been screened by Dawson became entangled in the scandals that plagued the administration.[41]

Dawson opened his testimony on 10 May by reading a statement apparently prepared by Murphy.[42] He denied influence over any of the RFC directors. Quoting statements from "Favoritism and Influence," he offered contrary evidence, often from testimony by other RFC principals. He claimed he had not had any business dealings with Young. He admitted accepting free lodging at the Saxony Hotel in Florida but disavowed any role in the RFC loan subsequently obtained by that hostelry. As Dawson's testimony developed over the next two days, the committee failed to demonstrate that he had influenced any loan. He had arranged a routine appointment for a prospective borrower; beyond that, any connection with loans was incidental or inferred by circumstantial evidence. Dawson had luncheon dates with corporation director Dunham but insisted that loans were never discussed. He did not deny interest in RFC affairs—he had spent several years as an employee. He denied having control over appointments; indeed, he once had supported an unsuccessful candidate for secretary of the RFC while Fulbright was supporting the successful candidate.[43]

Even Douglas had to concede that "Dawson made a good showing, and only minor peccadilloes were proved against him."[44] Fulbright's closing statement was a convoluted presentation that was in part an apology to Dawson for any embarrassment, in part an attempt to reiterate the point of the committee's investigation. The senator remarked a difference between the way Dawson viewed his relation with the RFC and the way in which the committee viewed it. Fulbright read from the committee's report: "In presenting this report, the subcommittee wishes to distinguish between improper influence as such and the improper use of the Corporation's authority in response to influences which in themselves may be perfectly proper. This report deals primarily with the latter. The subcommittee believes that the Corporation's authority has been seriously abused by the Directors, and that this constitutes an important impropriety." He then addressed Dawson directly, saying, "For your benefit, the objective of this study and of the hearings was not an attempt to embarrass you in any respect. You were sort of a necessary background. The study was directed toward the R.F.C., and I think that may throw some light upon what our objective was."[45]

The remarks demonstrate a problem throughout the investigation. Fulbright was trying to focus on improprieties as opposed to illegalities and was faced with the problem of marking the fine line between what he called "improper influence as such" as opposed to "improper use of the Corporation's authority in response to influences which in themselves may be perfectly proper." (Dawson later remarked sardonically that he never did understand what Fulbright meant.) Fulbright was headed off by administration spokesmen who denied illegalities, and at one point he commented in frustration, "I think it is setting a low level if our only goal for official conduct is that it be legal instead of illegal."[46] In a speech entitled "The Moral Deterioration of American Democracy," delivered on the Senate floor, 27 March 1951, he complained, "Scandals in our Government are not new phenomena in our history. What seems to be new about these scandals is the blindness or callousness which allows those in responsible positions to accept the practices which the facts reveal."[47]

Dawson was embittered by his appearance before the committee. He characterized the investigation as "intellectual McCarthyism," accusing Fullbright of "not seeking information, but vindication." He claimed that Fulbright and the committee were hypocritical and deceptive, creating faulty inferences regarding his actions.[48]

Several circumstances conspired to rob the Fulbright committee of a chance to make a lasting contribution. First, Stuart Symington, who had been sworn in as RFC administrator on 1 May 1951, had taken command in a fashion that took the sting out of the committee's allegations. Symington approached his job not only as an administrative position but as a public relations job—which it was. (Dawson considered him too publicity conscious, and another critic commented that "one could be sure that if Symington did not reform the R.F.C., he would talk about it as though he had."[49]) In a press conference a month after assuming his post, Symington announced that the RFC would announce weekly all loans that had been approved. He declared that the RFC ought to "bristle with integrity" and backed that assertion with the firing of several people tainted by the Fulbright investigation—including Dawson's wife, a file clerk whose reputation was damaged solely by circumstantial allegations. Admitting that there had been problems in the RFC, Symington disclosed improper behavior overlooked by the Fulbright committee and took actions on the committee's recommendations. His efforts to stay on top of operations led subordinates to call him "Doctor Facts." By the time of the committee's report, the crusading impulse that had governed the most visible moments of the committee had been adopted by Symington.[50] Indeed, when the final report was released in August 1951, it was an anticlimactic gesture that had none of the effect of "Favoritism and Influence." The nature of the final report itself also diminished its effect. Reflecting the temperament of its author, it was a measured document and failed to address how independent agencies ought to be regulated. Two conservative Republicans, Sen. Homer E. Capehart of Indiana and Sen. John Bricker of Ohio, shattered previous committee unanimity when they published a minority report that was laden with invective and innuendo; Fulbright dismissed it as a "political diatribe."[51]

Finally, the burden of the investigation had been lifted from the Fulbright committee. Days after the report was issued, Senator Hoey announced that his subcommittee of the Senate Expenditures Committee would investigate charges that Democratic National Committee Chairman Boyle had used his influence to gain a $565,000 RFC loan for a former legal client, the American Lithofold Corporation. Assured by Charles Murphy that Boyle had done nothing improper, Truman stood behind him. Nevertheless, Boyle resigned as national chairman in October 1951, citing ill health. The Hoey committee concluded that Boyle had done nothing illegal but that he had not conducted himself in such a manner as to avoid the appearance of impropriety.[52]

The Fulbright committee, torn by dissension, had been outmaneuvered by Truman, out-crusaded by Symington, and upstaged by Hoey. It expired quietly. After months of testimony and headlines, the committee had not resolved even the fundamental question of whether the corporation would be abolished. The fate of the agency was held in the balance until the Eisenhower years, when it was succeeded by the Small Business Administration.

6. THE BUREAU OF INTERNAL ■
REVENUE SCANDAL ▬▬▬▬▬▬▬

The five-percenter investigation and the Reconstruction Finance Corporation hearings demonstrated that there was need for tighter accountability of public funds disbursed through negotiated contracts and business loans. By the time Donald Dawson completed his testimony before the Fulbright committee in the spring of 1951, it was clear that the other side of the federal ledger, collection of public monies, was also in need of careful scrutiny.

The Bureau of Internal Revenue (BIR) of the late 1940s paralleled in many respects the institutional weaknesses of the RFC. Both had expanded rapidly, well beyond their initial charters and without significant structural adjustments. Both dealt in increasingly large sums with controls that were slight. And both had been manipulated for political purposes, particularly in appointments. As with the RFC, the seeds of scandal had been planted in the BIR before Truman became president. Many problems centered in offices of collectors of internal revenue, the sixty-four men who headed each of the revenue districts across the nation. There is no doubt, considering their responsibilities, that the collectors were underpaid, which discouraged talented, qualified individuals. Several men who held these offices took outside jobs that impinged on the time they could devote to revenue duties and occasionally created conflicts of interest. More serious was the fact that the office of collector had become a place for patronage, since it was subject to presidential appointment and Senate confirmation. Indeed, several collectorships had slipped into virtual control of Democratic political machines within their districts. The political nature of appointments often led to a perspective that created conflict between collectors and civil service bureaucrats with whom they dealt in Washington.[1]

Other factors that created the potential for corruption developed out of the sheer growth of the BIR. From the time the Sixteenth Amendment was ratified in 1913, instituting the modern income tax and vastly expanding responsibilities of the bureau, there had been only one reorganization, in 1917. Collections had increased fiftyfold, and there were nearly twelve times as many employees.[2] The existing structure had become unwieldy. As Rep. Cecil R. King's subcommittee would observe, the bureau "was exposed not only to the hazards of duplication of authority and effort but also to underdiffusion of responsibility."[3]

In spite of the potential for problems, not until well into Truman's second term was it apparent that the potential had been translated into sordid reality. As late as November 1950, the president was effusive in praise of the BIR. Before an informal gathering of collectors in his office, Truman remarked, "From what I hear from [commissioner] George Schoeneman, he says he has the most effective organization that has ever been in existence in the history of the Bureau of Internal Revenue. I am proud of that and I hope you will keep that reputation."[4] By that time, however, the reputation had been undermined. Within months, revelations began that led to the most damaging scandal of the Truman years, climaxed by yet another congressional investigation. When the lengthy hearings were completed, charges would touch both the Treasury and Justice departments and lead to wholesale dismissals and indictments. For the first time, the president's official family entered the revelations, with a cabinet officer dismissed and a high-level staff member imprisoned.

The first indication of the corruption passed almost without notice. Freshman Sen. John J. Williams, a conservative Republican from Delaware, revealed in a speech on 19 December 1947 that a cashier in the Wilmington collector's office had embezzled over thirty thousand dollars during the preceding seven years by manipulating taxpayer accounts. The cashier, Maurice A. Flynn, pleaded guilty the following month and was sentenced to four years in prison. What troubled Williams more than Flynn's transgression, however, was that bureau officials, including Wilmington collector Norman Collison, had to be prodded to action by a speech on the Senate floor. The senator intimated that Flynn's political connections—he had been Democratic floor leader in the Delaware House—may have discouraged prosecution.

Disclosures regarding the Wilmington collector's office, while minor in comparison to later revelations, opened the question of the integrity of the bureau and brought Senator Williams to national attention. He had also gained the confidence of BIR employees and others who later gave him information that helped to expose corruption in other collectors' offices. Wilmington's collector, Collison, had been negligent, but he had not been involved in any corrupt activities. Soon, however, a series of disclosures pointed to collectors in St. Louis, Boston, New York, and San Francisco. Early in his administration, Truman had told a group of collectors that they could be "either a tremendous asset to the administration or . . . cause the administration all sorts of embarrassment."[5] Those words now took on the tone of prophecy.

The revelations about the office of the St. Louis collector, James P. Finnegan, were the most damaging to the administration, not only because they focused on the president's home state but also because of Finnegan's indirect connections to Truman. Finnegan was appointed to the post in April 1944 largely because of the backing of Robert E. Hannegan, chairman of the Democratic National Committee. In the 1940 senatorial primary campaign, which Truman described as the "crucial battle of my political career," he considered his "biggest break" to have been Hannegan's decision to switch support from Gov. Lloyd C. Stark, enabling Truman to carry St. Louis.[6] Truman had paid his political debt by teaming with his Missouri Senate colleague, Bennett Clark, in backing Hannegan for St. Louis collector in 1942. President Roosevelt assented, in spite of opposition from both St. Louis newspapers. Hannegan made an indisputedly fine record as collector and was elevated to commissioner of internal revenue in October 1943.

Hannegan's tenure as commissioner was brief—less than six months—but several observers have attributed to his leadership a change in approach that led to the later scandals. Hannegan's predecessor had been conservative and exacting, and the new commissioner set out to change what he saw as a stodgy bureau. He relied on patronage for appointment of collectors. The four collectors who received the most notoriety in 1951 (Finnegan in St. Louis, Denis W. Delaney in Boston, Joseph P. Marcelle in Brooklyn, and James G. Smyth in San Francisco) received their appointments within two years of Hannegan's appointment as commissioner. Joseph Nunan, who succeeded Hannegan and was later convicted of tax fraud, fully subscribed to Hannegan's policy. All four discredited collectors were products of urban political machines.

One of Truman's defenses against the charges stemming from the BIR scandal was that the four disgraced collectors had been appointed before he assumed the presidency. This defense, however, overlooks two aspects of these appointments. First, it was Truman's backing that initiated Hannegan's rapid political rise and gave him the responsibilities that allowed him to change appointment policy. Second, Truman implicitly endorsed the policy himself. Frank Pace, the budget director, once asked Truman why he continued to allow machine politicians to influence the administration: Truman chuckled and gently admonished Pace, "Frank, you make a splendid Director of the Budget, but a lousy politician."[7]

The dismissal of Finnegan, Hannegan's hand-picked St. Louis protégé, was illustrative of problems created by Hannegan's patronage policy. Finnegan, freely acknowledging that he was not a tax expert, had taken the job only with assurance that he could continue his private law practice. Hannegan told him, "This is a position [in which] you possibly could assist me in our program," which Finnegan took to mean he could get jobs for people. He saw his responsibilities as those of an administrator and public relations man.[8] Often working only three or four hours a day as collector, occasionally only calling in, Finnegan had ample time for other pursuits, and, inevitably, a conflict of interest developed. Finnegan, using influential contacts to enhance his private legal practice, took fees from corporations seeking loans from the RFC, and was thus in violation of criminal statutes. In the most celebrated case of this nature, Finnegan and Democratic National Chairman William Boyle received retainers from the American Lithofold Corporation after allegedly assisting the company in procuring the $565,000 RFC loan that precipitated Boyle's resignation. But Finnegan's transgressions went far beyond mere conflicts of interest. Reports circulated that St. Louis tax attorneys fixed tax cases through his office. He collaborated with John Martin Brodsky, an insurance agent, in a scheme to sell policies to St. Louis firms with tax delinquencies. In a final ironic twist, it was found that Finnegan himself was in arrears in his taxes by $2,444 for the period from 1947 to 1949.

As if Finnegan's misconduct was not enough, the handling of his dismissal brought further embarrassment. Because of his indirect ties to the president (some critics inaccurately described Finnegan as Truman's friend) and his more direct ties to Democratic power brokers Hannegan and Boyle, Finnegan had more visibility than the other collectors who got into trouble. Truman defended the administration's handling of Finnegan, reiterating that the latter "was dispensed with long before anything was looked into by any committee."[9] This contention obscured the delays that preceded Finnegan's resignation on 4 April 1951. Publicly, little of the Finnegan record was known until after he resigned. Senator Williams added to it in the following weeks, and Finnegan's appearance before the King committee and his indictment by a St. Louis grand jury came that October. But before the resignation the Treasury Department had information on Finnegan's misconduct. Four revenue agents conducted an internal investigation of the St. Louis collector's office early in 1950; their reports in July of that year revealed Finnegan's personal tax delinquencies, as well as weaknesses in administration. Secretary of the Treasury John W. Snyder claimed that he had asked for Finnegan's resignation in August 1950, yet despite initial consent the resignation did not come in. Finnegan testified that he had offered to resign several times, including once in October 1950 when he spoke to the bureau's commissioner, Schoeneman, to the president's appointments secretary, Matthew Connelly, and to the president himself. All urged him to stay, he asserted. Truman hedged when presented with Finnegan's testimony. He first said that his memory was hazy but later stated unequivocally that he had backed Snyder's first request for a resignation. Either way, there were mixed feelings in the White House at the time of Finnegan's resignation. While Truman's letter responding to the collector's resignation was a terse one-sentence acceptance, an earlier draft was a four-paragraph letter expressing regret, understanding, and appreciation for services rendered. Truman never overcame his ambivalence regarding Finnegan. Even after leaving office, the president suspected that the collector might have been persecuted by Judge George Moore, who had called the St. Louis grand jury.[10] Considered individually, the cases of the other collectors dismissed in 1951 should have been less damaging politically to the Truman administration. But they came after the resignation of Finnegan and followed closely in the wake of the RFC disclosures, thus fostering the impression that not only the Bureau of Internal Revenue but also the entire executive branch was full of scandal.

Denis W. Delaney of the Boston office was the next collector dismissed. Like Finnegan, he was the product of a big-city Democratic machine. He had been engaged as commissioner during Hannegan's tenure, despite a questionable background that included bankruptcy and court-imposed probation for larceny.[11] Delaney's office was first investigated in late 1947 by the House Appropriations Committee in conjunction with BIR budget cuts; operations were found to be lax and inefficient. The committee alleged that Delaney and some of his subordinates engaged in political activity in possible violation of the Hatch Act.[12] Prodded by the Appropriations Committee, the BIR initiated its own investigation, and the bureau found irregularities in Delaney's personal returns. A subsequent internal investigation in May 1951 was conducted by Brig. Gen. John B. Dunlap, later named commissioner of internal revenue. His report, along with accumulated evidence, precipitated Delaney's discharge on 17 July 1951. Later hearings before the King subcommittee revealed even more disturbing details. He had been involved in an insurance scheme with Finnegan's brother Hugh that was patterned after the St. Louis operation. Delaney, moreover, had accepted bribes in return for writing off tax delinquencies. Eventually, he pleaded guilty to tax evasion and bribery and was sentenced to a year in prison.[13]

Politics also provided the rationale for appointments to the New York City collector's office. When Nunan was promoted to replace Hannegan as commissioner in the spring of 1944, a replacement was needed for the New York City first collection district, centered in Brooklyn. Nunan backed his old assistant, James B. E. Olson, but Hannegan bowed to the wishes of Frank V. Kelly, head of the Democratic organization in Brooklyn, and named Joseph P. Marcelle as collector. Olson received a consolation prize when he became district supervisor of the alcohol tax unit in the neighboring third district (Manhattan). In the tumultuous closing months of 1951, both men had to resign. Each had been involved in outside activities while working for the bureau. During his seven years as collector, Marcelle's law practice had garnered $235,000 to complement his $10,750 salary as a collector, much of which he preserved with unsubstantiated deductions on his own tax returns. His close association with gamblers in New York led to the investigation that exposed him. The third collection district had a reputation worse than Marcelle's first district. Collector James W. Johnson of the third district became another casualty in the epidemic of collector dismissals in August 1951, not because of any misconduct on his part but because he had allowed corruption within his office. Asked to resign late in 1950, Johnson refused. It was only after Senator Williams introduced a resolution calling for his dismissal that he was finally forced out. The administration failed to screen Johnson's successor, Monroe Dowling, who was asked to resign because of irregularities on his personal tax return in March 1952, just seven months after assuming his position as collector. He thus bore the inglorious distinction of being the first collector appointed by Truman to be fired.[14]

The San Francisco collector's office had a reputation as a notoriously independent outfit, a reputation that Washington had done little to curb. The charges that ended this independence and unseated collector James G. Smyth were initiated in an internal report filed in April 1950 by Treasury special agent William F. Buckett. The California Crime Commission treated the allegations lightly, but the Kefauver committee drew attention to them. Renewed investigations revealed irregularities ranging from tax fixing to embezzlement. The most serious involved an extortion scheme by Ernest M. "Mike" Schino, chief field deputy of the office, who had conspired to sell worthless stock in a nonoperating mine to taxpayers in difficulty. Schino was indicted in March 1951. On 27 September 1951, the ax fell on Smyth and eight of his assistants involved in a variety of transgressions, such as backdating receipts, embezzling, and conspiring to impede due process of law. When the King committee wrapped up its probe into the San Francisco irregularities, Chairman Cecil King summarized the findings in a statement that was as appropriate for the other wayward collectors' offices as for the case at hand.

> Control of the office . . . had fallen into the hands of a top echelon of political appointees whose chief failing was their gross incompetence. Their second, and also serious failing, was a devotion to political interests which transcended their loyalty to the Revenue Service and caused them to engage in petty and sometimes criminal manipulations. In these they were encouraged and protected by the complacency and indifference of an inept top administration in Washington. Political and personal favoritism in the treatment of taxpayers and in the handling of personnel problems has been the result. . . . The former Commissioners of Internal Revenue and the Treasury Department in Washington cannot escape their share of ultimate responsibility.[15]

King's criticism of former commissioners pinpointed one of the root causes of the bureau's problems. It was Robert Hannegan who instituted the practice of relying on patronage for appointment of collectors, but his choice of a successor had an equally devastating effect on the bureau. Nunan served as commissioner from March 1944 to June 1947, was a product of the patronage system, and carried out Hannegan's ideas, appointing most of the collectors who embarrassed the bureau in 1951. Nunan admitted he was not a tax expert, but Hannegan, as he had done with Finnegan, assured him that the job was political. Nunan continued his New York law practice, receiving annual legal fees of $27,000 and $57,000 during his two years as commissioner. Nunan's full legacy appeared after the Truman administration left office, when he was convicted for evading $91,086 in personal income taxes for the years from 1946 to 1950.[16]

In spite of a laudatory letter to Nunan upon his resignation, Truman professed to have no confidence in him. Appointing a successor, the president seemingly sought to overcome the weaknesses that political operatives had brought to the office. Truman selected from his own staff the administrative assistant for personnel, George Schoeneman, who had earned a reputation as a good administrator during a twenty-two-year career with the BIR. But Schoeneman was not an innovator, and the bureau was sorely in need of reform. Newspaperman Blair Bolles, assessing Schoeneman's service, commented, "The careerist of long standing learns to be discreet, to do his tasks well, but not to press for change and reform. . . . The whole environment of his employment has taught him to be persistent but not aggressive, a servant but not a creator."[17] Schoeneman was not an aggressive commissioner. Secretary Snyder observed that he "did not know how to be firm with his chief associates."[18] When the 1951 scandals broke, Schoeneman could not deal with them. As corruption in the Boston collector's office reached a climax, Schoeneman submitted his resignation, citing ill health. Accepting it, Truman graciously praised his former staff member for a long career of "loyal and devoted service."[19]

Second-line leadership in the bureau was also suspect. Daniel A. Bolich, the assistant commissioner of internal revenue, resigned three months after Schoeneman, also citing ill health. He was later revealed to be under investigation by the King committee. Protracted litigation finally cleared Bolich in 1959, but the circumstances of his resignation in 1951 cast a pall on the bureau.[20]

By the autumn of 1951, the BIR was an institution rotting from within, with weak leadership in Washington and corruption in collectors' offices from coast to coast. It was ironic, then, that the man who came to symbolize the tax scandals to many was a member of neither the bureau nor even the Treasury Department. Assistant Attorney General T. Lamar Caudle nonetheless had an important position in the nation's tax system; as head of the tax division of the Department of Justice, he was responsible for prosecution of tax cases referred to the department.

The Caudle case was as tragic as any coming out of the tax scandals. The congressional committee that investigated the Justice Department considered him a weak and naive man who made errors of judgment. The man closest to President Truman's decision to fire Caudle, special counsel

Charles S. Murphy, described him as stupid. Neither the Chelf-Keating committee, responsible for the House investigations, nor Murphy considered his actions venal. The committee, with only one dissenting voice, concluded, "Every member of the subcommittee and its staff who observed Caudle and listened to his testimony over a long period shares the opinion that he is an honorably motivated man."[21]

Caudle was brought to Washington in September 1945 by Attorney General Tom Clark, who had been drawn to Caudle and impressed by the job he was doing as U.S. attorney in Clark's home state of North Carolina. Caudle worked closely with Clark in the early stages of the Kansas City vote fraud investigation in 1946. Though he had nothing to do with the case after it gained national attention, he earlier had written a memo recommending that it be closed. In April 1947, he assumed leadership of the tax division, where his naïveté caught up with him.[22] Unable to resist favors that created clear-cut conflicts of interest, he drifted into a position that made his resignation inevitable.

In one celebrated case, Caudle delayed (and attempted to prevent) the tax-evasion trial of Samuel Aaron and Jacob Freidus. While the trial was pending, Caudle received a $5,000 commission for sale of a $30,000 Lockheed Lodestar; the purchaser was an investigator for Aaron and Freidus.[23] On another occasion, Caudle along with his close friend Charles Oliphant, chief counsel in the BIR, accepted a paid vacation in Florida from Troy Whitehead, a North Carolina manufacturer being investigated on a tax case. When a lien was placed on his property, Whitehead called Caudle, who with Oliphant's help had the lien lifted. In another instance, Caudle and his wife contributed to the declining status value of the mink coat, solidifying its image as a symbol of corruption. Mrs. Caudle's $2,400 coat had been purchased through Jacob Landau, a tax attorney who had often dealt with the tax division. She had paid $1,500 as a downpayment for the coat, and although she claimed to have paid the balance, she had no receipt. In fact, Landau had written off the balance as a business expense; he called Mrs. Caudle to demand the balance just prior to Caudle's testimony before the King subcommittee, however.[24]

In a highly publicized Alabama case, wholesale jewelry salesmen Joseph Mitchell and Samuel Ripps and their wives were indicted in early 1950 for understating their income by nearly $750,000. Prior to the indictment, Alabama Rep. Frank Boykin had taken an unusual interest in the case, discouraging prosecution. The investigator, John H. Mitchell, testified that he was led to believe that Caudle also did not want the case prosecuted. Furthermore, when John Mitchell asked Caudle about rumors that Ripps and Joseph Mitchell had made large contributions to the Democratic National Committee, Caudle replied, "I told them not to do it, but Frank [Boykin] went ahead and took the money." Shortly thereafter, Deputy Attorney General Peyton Ford, who was no friend of Caudle, instructed John Mitchell to report directly to him. Caudle froze the investigator out of further work in the tax division.[25]

Caudle tried to establish a relationship with President Truman and had reason to believe he was succeeding. His letters to the president were laden with praise. In October 1951, despite charges against him, Caudle accompanied the president's party to the attorney's alma mater, Wake Forest College. Replying to Caudle's letter of thanks less than a month before dismissing Caudle, the president wrote, "Men like you and Jess Larson make it possible to carry on in this job."[26] Caudle later told the King subcommittee, "I really thought I was making some time. I sure did. I thought I was making some progress with the Chief."[27]

In mid-November, as the president's party was preparing to depart for Key West, Murphy received a call from the King subcommittee's counsel, Adrian De Wind, urging him to take a look at transcripts of closed testimony regarding Caudle. Murphy sent his assistant, David Stowe, who phoned Murphy in Key West after perusing the transcript, relating in detail some of Caudle's indiscretions and errors of judgment. Murphy advised Truman to allow Caudle to resign voluntarily, and the president agreed. Caudle, already under fire, suffered further embarrassment by what happened next. Murphy could not reach Attorney General J. Howard McGrath; his deputy, Peyton Ford, "hemmed and hawed." When McGrath finally was contacted, he called Key West to argue Caudle's case. Truman did not relent. A shell-shocked Caudle was summoned to McGrath's office and informed. Thus, by the time he got his letter of resignation in the mail, a few days had elapsed since the president made his decision. Truman's patience ran out; before receiving the letter, the president announced that Caudle had been fired.[28]

Even as Caudle was making his unceremonious exit, the guillotine was being readied for his opposite number in the BIR, Charles Oliphant. The son of distinguished law professor and Treasury general counsel Herman Oliphant, he had brought charges against several figures prominent in organized crime, including the brother of Al Capone. But Oliphant's penchant for accepting gifts was even greater than that of his friend Caudle. He traveled to the World Series baseball games and other sporting events in the private plane of Poncet Davis, a friend under investigation for tax fraud. To his credit, Oliphant disqualified himself from Davis's case, but the subcommittee chairman, Cecil King, criticized him for lack of discretion.

Indeed, it was testimony before the King committee that proved most damaging to Oliphant. It was revealed that he had accepted loans and gifts from a high-powered Washington investigator, lobbyist, and influence peddler, Henry "the Dutchman" Grunewald, and had given BIR jobs to Gunewald-backed applicants. The testimony that precipitated Oliphant's downfall was given by former Capone lawyer Abraham Teitelbaum in a dramatic session on 4 December 1951. Teitelbaum claimed that he had been the victim of a half-million dollar shakedown perpetrated by two unsavory characters who told him of their connection with a Washington clique that involved Oliphant, Nunan, and Jess Larson, former head of the War Assets Administration. From another source, Teitelbaum claimed that the two shakedown artists claimed to have "Mr. O. . . . and Mr. Caudle in their vest pocket."[29] Oliphant resigned the next day, in a letter in which he denied culpability and whined that "attacks, vilification, rumor and innuendo are beyond the point of human endurance." Oliphant argued, in a defense likely to engender a sympathetic response in the White House, "Without inquiry of me, without a shred of credence to link my name to the alleged plot, the forum of a responsible Congressional

Committee was made available for hurtling sensational and irresponsible charges throughout the country."[30]

Although the president promptly accepted Oliphant's resignation, the reference to congressional committees was timely, for Truman was as perturbed by the King subcommittee as he had been earlier by the Hoey and Fulbright committees. His relationship with Cecil King remained on a higher plane than with Senator Fulbright during their skirmishes over the RFC, but differences between King and the president emerged. (Later, when Williams of Delaware increased the pace of his investigations, it proved prudent for Truman to cooperate with King, using King's moderate approach as a foil for what the administration saw as the excessive and self-serving zeal of Williams.)

Earlier in 1951, Truman had pledged cooperation with committees investigating the BIR. In the waning months of the year, a contention arose as to how free committee access should be to files within the purview of the executive. While the president and his party were in Key West in November 1951, the committee requested broad access to Department of Justice files. The department argued against such disclosure. Murphy, the president's wise special counsel, urged cooperation between adversaries and individual review when agreement was not reached. Truman, reacting both to Murphy's advice and to his own indignation at the increasing impertinence of the committee, scrawled a note at the bottom of a letter from the committee's counsel regarding the request. "Mr. Murphy: this guy believes in asking for the sun, moon + stars and wants a comet thrown in. We'll give him what he wants for specific cases—no more."[31] Given the decision to proceed on a case-by-case basis, the question of access—to executive department files and to tax returns—would be raised with regularity over the next year. Truman's irritation never diminished. He became intransigent.

The autumn of 1951 witnessed another change in the administration's approach to BIR corruption. The president's staff was concerned that the White House had dealt only with accusations and had not investigated possible malfeasance. The administration had been on the defensive, reacting, seldom initiating change. An exception had been the appointment of John B. Dunlap as commissioner of internal revenue on 1 August 1951, for Dunlap proved a dynamic take-charge leader. But even that had been a reaction, a result of the resignation of a week leader—Schoeneman— who had seen his organization crumbling. The challenge was to take the offense, to initiate, to show that the president was correcting weaknesses. A memo expressed the goal, emphasizing style over substance: "It seems to me that the President should take publicly impressive action in connection with the Internal Revenue Bureau. . . . Politically, it seems to me imperative that the President put himself on the side of the angels in a way that will be unmistakenly plain."[32]

As the president and his staff pondered action, recommendations fell into two categories: reforms and rule changes that would inhibit malfeasance; investigations that would uncover violations. Some reforms and rule changes were adopted as part of a reorganization of the bureau, and the bureau instituted others. Many proposals concerned selecting collectors. Suggestions included the system used by congressmen to make appointments to the military academies and a method of appointment by the commissioner of internal revenue without Senate approval. Placing collectors under Civil Service received endorsement from the staff, former Secretary of Labor Frances Perkins, and the new chairman of the Democratic National Committee, Frank E. McKinney. The president initially opposed the idea, believing that Civil Service would make removal of wayward collectors difficult, but Truman relented and included it in the BIR reorganization plan. Another staff recommendation, prohibiting collectors from engaging in outside work, was not specifically implemented, though Dunlap issued instructions requiring all employees to give "a full measure of devotion" to their jobs.[33] Dunlap's office took several other actions to prevent abuses revealed in the King subcommittee hearings, including establishment of the Internal Revenue Inspection Service and elimination of the health of the taxpayer as a reason for refraining from prosecution.[34]

Investigations of abuses received more staff attention than the less dramatic rule changes. One such proposal envisioned transfer of the investigation of criminal acts from the Treasury Department to the FBI as a means of counteracting adverse BIR publicity. David E. Bell, one of Murphy's assistants, stopped short of suggesting involvement of the FBI, but he did recommend that FBI Director J. Edgar Hoover might head an independent investigation. Bell believed that the selection of Hoover would "make it perfectly plain that the president wants the Bureau investigated fast, expertly, and thoroughly." He suggested a special assistant to the attorney general who would insure vigorous prosecution.[35] Former Attorney General Francis Biddle, acting as national chairman of the Americans for Democratic Action, recommended that the president appoint a Democrat and a Republican as prosecutors. Biddle appealed to Truman's political sense, cautioning, "It is inconceivable that the matter will blow over as some optimistic Democrats occasionally suggest. The enemies of your administration will keep it stirred up, and the public is outraged, uncertain, and almost ready to believe anything. In view of these circumstances, leaving action in the ordinary administrative channels will not stem the tide of rising indignation."[36]

Truman took the recommendations under advisement. While finishing touches were being put on the BIR reorganization plan, it was nevertheless becoming clear that the plan would not assuage increasing public indignation. During a 13 December 1951 press conference, the president abandoned his usual reticence to offer more than terse, monosyllabic responses to questions touching on the scandals. In a number of expansive answers, he not only defended his administration's record in dealing with the charges but also revealed bitterness toward some of the miscreants. Asked if he felt he had been "sold down the river," Truman shot back, "Well, who wouldn't feel that way?" When pressed, he granted that the feeling applied to all those fired. Defending his actions, he cited "drastic action," moving on cases involving the collectors and even Caudle before pressure forced his hand. He claimed no increase in numbers of people fired, despite headline treatment. Questioned about a possible investigation, he hinted that one might be forthcoming: "If there is one . . ."[37]

Truman's defense of his "drastic action" was unconvincing. With the Caudle dismissal fresh in everyone's memory, the administration's resolve was open to question. Although the administration had conducted its own half-hearted investigation, it was publicity by the King subcommittee that determined the dismissals of both Caudle and Oliphant. The president's statement on the numbers of firings was also misleading. Dismissals had reached unprecedented levels; a staff study after the press conference revealed that the rate of BIR dismissals for 1951 had more than doubled after the King subcommittee began open hearings.[38] Public perception of the BIR problems more closely approximated correspondent William V. Shannon's conclusion in a *New Republic* article that appeared shortly before the press conference. "Had President Truman and Secretary Snyder insisted long ago on really wiping away the slime before public and Congressional indignation forced them to act," he wrote, "the shortcomings in the tax offices would have seemed no more sinister than embezzlement in a bank. But as a result of the Administration's letting the shortcomings fester out of sight, they have attained their present eminence as a symbol of political scandal."[39]

The day following the volatile 13 December press conference, the move for an independent investigation gained momentum. King visited Truman to discuss his investigation. He urged the president to initiate action on behalf of the executive branch, including special grant juries and "appointment of an investigative chief or Commission, reporting directly to the President, with jurisdiction over both Treasury and Justice Department tax functions, and complete access to files and personnel of both Departments."[40] King's advice made clear that an independent investigation would not affect congressional prerogatives. The administration was pondering such an investigation. The idea of a three-member committee had the most support. Mentioned for such a committee was Judge Thomas F. Murphy of New York, who had earned his reputation by reorganizing the New York City police department and for prosecuting Alger Hiss. Murphy accepted the appointment, as did the Reverend Daniel Polling, a prominent Baptist cleric from Philadelphia. A third member—a prominent Chicago attorney—had been named. The commission disintegrated before it received sanction, however. Murphy and Polling disagreed on the chairmanship, and Murphy withdrew, citing a ruling that he would not be allowed to serve on such a commission while acting as a federal judge.[41]

By mid-January, Truman had decided to let Attorney General McGrath handle the problem, a curious decision, because McGrath had been under fire since the Caudle dismissal. Questions regarding McGarth's status had become features at press conferences, and the president's staff had begun to question the Justice Department's handling of the BIR scandal. Having decided to stick with McGrath, Truman seized the opportunity to demonstrate confidence in his attorney general and quell rumor of McGrath's resignation. Because the commission had never been announced, the decision represented no demonstrable change of policy.[42]

A former governor of Rhode Island, the personable, driving attorney general had moved up rapidly in politics and was labeled "one of the fastest comers in the Democratic party" when he left his Senate seat in 1947 to become national chairman of the party.[43] His loyalty to the administration—he had a 99 percent pro-administration voting record in the Senate and had been a key campaign strategist in 1948—helped influence the president to name him as successor to Tom Clark, appointed to the Supreme Court in 1949.[44] McGrath appreciated the opportunity the president had given him, and he expressed gratitude at a cabinet meeting in early January 1952. He soon let it be known that he intended to appoint a special assistant to search out corruption. He remembered an earlier conversation with Judge Learned Hand when searching for someone to take Caudle's place: Hand had recommended his son-in-law, Newbold Morris. That recommendation and Morris's reputation satisfied McGrath, who shortly appointed the New York attorney.[45] Morris seemed to be an ideal appointment. Descendant of a patrican New York family, he was a Republican with a reputation as a liberal and a good-government reformer. He had been associated with Mayor Fiorello La Guardia and had run unsuccessfully for mayor twice on a reform ticket.[46]

Morris had another attribute that made him especially attractive to the attorney general. Morris "really had no experience in investigating, and he was the kind of person that it might have been assumed could be reasonably directed or led, or the wool pulled over his eyes,"[47] which suited Mc-Grath, who wanted to limit any investigation. At a White House meeting even before Morris was appointed, McGrath explained he was looking for someone to serve for ninety days; it was to be a "short-run operation." As McGrath's people explained, few federal officials had been guilty of misconduct, and it made no sense to "equip ourselves with a large sledge hammer to drive a few tacks."[48] McGrath's intentions became even clearer. At a luncheon meeting, the attorney general assured Morris that his job would not be taxing. "You can clean the whole thing up in several months," he explained.[49] The attorney general provided his new special assistant with space in the Justice Department and promised cooperation.

Harold Seidman was lent to Morris from the Bureau of the Budget to serve as a contact with the White House. Seidman had known Morris slightly in New York. Their first meeting in Washington was over dinner in Morris's Carlton Hotel room, a ritual repeated during the next two months. Conversing for a while, Seidman began to understand Morris's dilemma. He had received an office and could request any document he wished, but without a staff he would not know where to begin. "You've been had," Seidman warned him. "It's perfectly obvious what McGrath will do. He'll have you sit in your office for six months or a year then announce that Newbold Morris was unable to find any corruption in Washington, which will be perfectly true, because you never really had an opportunity to look. He is playing you for a patsy."[50]

Seidman recommended that Morris meet McGrath, Hoover, and Murphy, and he outlined subjects to discuss with each man to determine his authority, budget, and manpower. At the White House, Seidman and Louis Yavner, another Morris associate, met with David Lloyd and Donald Hansen (on loan to the White House from the Treasury Department) to warn that the way Morris was being treated could be embarrassing to the president. Hansen told Murphy, "The great point at issue will be how much authority, help, and independence Morris will have. It appears from what Yavner and Seidman have told me that Justice doesn't intend for Morris to make much of a splash."[51]

Morris met the president at Blair House on 11 February 1952, and Truman promised space, clerical help, and ample funds. Morris left convinced he had the president's support. Three days later, Truman issued a statement directing federal departments and agencies to give total cooperation to Morris.[52] Nevertheless, the shell that had been constructed quickly began to crumble, a casualty of structural weakness, imprudent and confused leadership, and lack of cooperation. "This was really an impossible thing," Hansen observed. Morris "just couldn't do a job like this because a job like that couldn't be done. You can't set up a new separate agency and recruit some people for it and all of a sudden get on to the job of rooting out corruption in Government which is a job that the F.B.I. and some of the other investigative agencies of the Government and the Criminal Division of the Department of Justice had been working on for years."[53]

Weaknesses in the investigation were compounded. On 14 February, the joint resolution intended to grant Morris subpoena power was introduced. A provision would have granted Morris the right to grant immunity, a power not requested. Some congressmen even opposed granting subpoena power, and inclusion of the additional request ended any chance for passage. "Someone in the Justice Department had slipped that request for power to grant immunity into the draft of the President's message, without my sponsorship," Morris asserted, convinced he had been betrayed. "In retrospect it looks as though this extreme request had been deliberately sneaked in to irritate the Congress needlessly and to drive it into turning down the granting of *any* powers. And that is exactly what happened. I feel that I was tripped up from behind even before I reached the scrimmage line."[54] Truman blamed the House Judiciary Committee, which had rejected the appeal, for preventing the investigator from doing "a bangup job." The president, however, took personal responsibility for adding the power to grant immunity to the bill.[55]

Morris and the New Yorkers on his staff turned to a device that had been used with some success by the New York City Department of Investigation. They devised an intricate and detailed questionnaire, including a complete personal financial statement, designed on the premise that while a respondent might be able to conceal income it would be difficult to conceal expenditure. The intent was to show that U.S. attorneys devoted time and effort to outside pursuits, which, while well known at the time and not illegal, was certainly undesirable.[56] Yet before any of the questionnaires circulated, it became evident that Morris simply was not suited for the job. Hansen considered him "a very able fellow" and "a perfect gentlemen," but he also asserted that Morris "had more enthusiasm than judgment when he started off on this operation."[57] Seidman was less generous in his assessment, claiming Morris "lacked the interest, talent and ability to conduct an investigation. Morris was concerned only with enhancing his own public reputation."[58] Seidman found Morris unable to withstand pressure. Evening sessions at the Carlton became strained. Seidman later recalled that "it was very difficult because I found in talking to Mr. Morris, at some point he'd always put his head down and put his arms over his head. He didn't want to face up to the tough decisions, or, in fact, make any decisions at all."[59]

Moreover, charges circulated that Morris's law firm had arranged an illegal sale of oil tankers to Chinese Nationalists. According to his law partner, Morris had shared in the profits. Given a chance to explain before a Senate panel, Morris damaged his position by asserting that the senators had "diseased minds" and were seeking "character destruction."[60] Indeed, it seemed that Morris was bent on self-destruction. New York reporters said he had been "born with a silver foot in his mouth."[61] Appearing on "Meet the Press" on 2 March 1952, he blundered into embarrassing statements that eroded his credibility. Queried about General Vaughan, he responded, "I don't think I'd have had General Vaughan there to start with." A reporter retorted, "But he wasn't dismissed, was he, after all those things were revealed?" "Not yet," declared Morris, leaving the implication that he was going after Vaughan.[62] Later, several of his advisers cornered Morris in his office one evening and only half in jest told him to raise his right hand and swear, "I will not appear on any more television programs.[63]

The following Thursday, 6 March, Morris again met with

Truman and apologized for any misunderstanding. Truman brushed it off. Morris then raised the issue of the questionnaire. The president endorsed the idea and told an astonished Morris he did not want to see one until he received a copy to fill out. Morris was buoyed by the response.[64] The questionnaire soon became the focal point of the investigation. The fault lay with Morris, who Seidman claimed failed to grasp the purpose for which his advisers had intended to document. "I think the only thing that Mr. Morris ever understood, of anything we ever told him," said Seidman, "was that we had a questionnaire."[65] Morris foolishly hand delivered copies to the Justice Department on 18 April while McGrath was out of town. The forms were not distributed, even after the attorney general returned. McGrath unreservedly opposed it. At a cabinet meeting on 28 March, he blasted the questionnaire as a violation of personal rights. Testifying before Rep. Frank Chelf's subcommittee investigating the Department of Justice, he was asked if he planned to fill out his copy of the document. "I have not yet decided," he replied, "whether I will permit anybody in the department or advise anybody in the government to do it."[66] McGrath was technically Morris's boss, in spite of the independence promised the special assistant. McGrath also was head of the department that Morris had targeted for initial emphasis. It was a challenge both to McGrath's leadership and to his political acumen. He did not handle it well.

By late March, McGrath had reason to believe he could move against Morris, made vulnerable by his gaffes and by his unpopular questionnaire, against which McGrath heard rumblings within the administration. He recalled Secretary of Defense Robert Lovett remarking, "Every man I have working for me will go home if he has to fill that out."[67] And after reading the questionnaire even Truman decided not to use it.[68] But McGrath was not operating from strength. Discontent with Morris did nothing to enhance McGrath's position, for he had brought Morris to Washington. Members of the president's staff, led by Murphy and press secretary Joseph Short, believed McGrath an ineffective attorney general who should be held responsible for the problems in the Department of Justice. By the end of March, they had come to the conclusion that McGrath would have to go. Short argued that McGrath was not doing his job, that his handling

of the Caudle and questionnaire issues were prime examples. Murphy advised the president that the "relationship
between the Attorney General and Newbold Morris has become so bad that it will be extremely difficult and probably
impossible to continue the present situation."[69] He argued
that McGrath's uncertainty over the questionnaire was a
questioning of a presidential executive order, because the 20
February order that delineated Morris's powers gave him
the right to request such information.

McGrath forced the issue. He went to see Truman on 2
April to express his opposition to the questionnaires, and he
left with the impression that the president both disapproved
of the questionnaire and wanted him to fire Morris. As
McGrath remembered the incident, Murphy called a few
hours later saying that Truman had told *him* (Murphy) to
fire Morris. Further conversation between the two men
could not clarify the confusion, so Murphy said he would
check with the president. That afternoon, McGrath and
other members of the cabinet gathered at the airport to help
the president greet Queen Juliana of the Netherlands.
Catching Truman alone, McGrath pressed for a resolution.
Halfway through his recapitulation of the morning conversation, McGrath saw Short nearby and called him over to
join the discussion. "He came over," McGrath recalled,

> and my God, no sooner were the words out of my mouth than
> the son of a bitch exploded, "What has the President got to do
> with this? You brought Morris down here." Well, I was dumb-
> founded. I said, "I brought him here with the President's ap-
> proval and consent, and you took him over. You gave him his
> independence. Are you mad?" With this the President is smart;
> he walks away. The press gets the story that a disagreement is
> going on in a public place, and I said, "Look, Joe, let's not argue
> it here. I'll meet you at the White House." So back we went. . . .
> it was about six o'clock. Murphy and Joe are there. They are
> violent . . . blaming me for Morris. The whole thing was bitched
> up. They said the President was being made the victim. "You
> brought him down," Short is saying. . . . I said, "Well you sons
> of bitches, I'll get rid of him. Don't think you can pull this crap
> on me. I know what you're up to. I can handle this myself." And
> I left.[70]

The next morning, 3 April, McGrath told the story to J.
Edgar Hoover, concluding that he had decided to dismiss

Morris. Hoover prevailed upon McGrath to inform Truman of his decision. As McGrath remembered, Truman responded by saying, "Howard, you always come up with the right answer." That sealed Morris's fate. By one o'clock that afternoon, McGrath had ordered him out. Truman, at his scheduled press conference later in the day, denied that McGrath talked to him before firing Morris. He claimed that he had been involved in discussions regarding the dismissal but that he was not aware it was "to take place right away" and had learned of the firing from the press service ticker.[71]

The final act of McGrath's tenure as attorney general played out. Just before Truman's 4:00P.M. press conference, the president met with his staff. Short took the lead in urging McGrath's dismissal, but he was not alone. Assistant press secretary Roger Tubby, echoing the sentiments of his boss, argued that many of Truman's supporters felt that McGrath had "betrayed" the president. The closest anyone came to backing McGrath was a snort from John Steelman when Tubby used the word *betrayed*. Truman, deep in thought, sat drumming his fingers on his desk, mulling the arguments. In a low voice, he said he thought he would have to let McGrath go. Short urged that Truman make the announcement that afternoon or risk being charged with succumbing to public pressure. The president needed no prompting. He phoned McGrath and told the shocked attorney general, "I have a press conference in a little while and I think I ought to announce your resignation." McGrath, stunned, could do little more than acquiesce.[72]

The president, wanting to announce a new attorney general at a press conference that was only minutes away, turned to Matt Connelly for a recommendation. Connelly, without hesitation, nominated James P. McGranery, a federal district judge from Philadelphia whom Truman had known since his days in the Senate and who had been an assistant attorney general under Clark. The president concurred, saying McGranery was the man he had in mind. Announcement was made at the press conference.[73]

The decision to replace McGrath was not taken lightly, nor was it the hasty move that the flurry of staff phone calls made it appear. Truman had been considering the move. He had offered the job to Judge Samuel I. Rosenman of New York, who turned it down on the basis of friendship with the president, saying the public would be skeptical of his willingness to expose corruption in the administration. Taking Rosenman's suggestion, Truman called Sen. Wayne Morse of Oregon who also declined. Short and Tubby's protests of betrayal actually had not moved the president. Nor was there the slightest bit of rancor in the dismissal. "I don't think there was the slightest thing wrong with Howard personally at all," he later reflected. The basis for the decision was McGrath's "inability to get on top of the situation."[74] Two weeks after the events of 3 April, Truman wrote McGrath to reassure him: "I want you to know that my fondness for you has not changed one bit. Political situations sometimes cause one much pain. I am ready, if at any time in the future, you become interested in any other place in public service, to do anything I can do for you. I'll go all out!"[75]

Truman's behavior during the RFC and BIR scandals revealed his attitude toward those who served him. His statement during the Fulbright revelations that all his people were honorable has been cited as evidence of blind loyalty to subordinates. Yet this statement must be tempered with a defense of his administration during the BIR firings, when he boasted that the discredited collectors were brought in before his presidency. These were not "his" people.

The contrast is evident in Truman's attitude regarding two collectors, Finnegan and Delaney. Finnegan's ties to the president through Hannegan made him one of the president's men. As Finnegan's indiscretions appeared, the president urged him to stay on. When Truman did fire him, it was with reluctance and with a cursory note accepting his "resignation," only after he considered a flattering note that praised Finnegan's service. Afterward, Truman suspected that Finnegan had been "persecuted." In sharp contrast was the president's attitude toward Delaney, who was brought in during the Roosevelt administration. When Treasury Under Secretary Edward J. Foley took the recommendation for Delaney's dismissal to the president, Truman's only comment was "Where do I sign?"[76]

McGrath's firing hence was a painful decision, for McGrath was honorable and loyal and unmistakably one of

Truman's men. Indeed, after the president had begun to consider replacement, McGrath was given one more chance. Even then, after the Morris affair backfired, the decision was made only with regret. On the other hand, the departure of McGrath and appointment of McGranery brought about a change in attitude in the Justice Department. The siege mentality engendered by McGrath's defensiveness was replaced by a constructive attitude. The Chelf committee was gratified by the new cooperation.[77]

Truman's personnel problems resulted not so much from "blind" loyalty, then, as from a dualistic view of people, a facile tendency to divide people into categories: Goats or Rabbits, Democrats or Republicans, friends or foes, his people or others'. It was a limited, and limiting, perspective.

7. THE SEARCH FOR A ▇▇▇▇▇
POSITIVE RESPONSE ▇▇▇▇▇

During the closing weeks of 1951, there was a shift in the Truman administration's response to allegations of corruption and cronyism. Outward signs of change were few; they seemed imperceptible to observers. In the president's 13 December press conference he dealt with the BIR scandal in frank terms and promised to continue "drastic action."[1] To the amazement of observers he meant it. Initially, the administration had denied any problem. During the attacks on Pauley and Vaughan, Truman viewed corruption as a creation of newspapers. Through the five-percenter inquiry and well into the RFC hearings, he maintained that disclosures were political. Aside from the individuals involved, there was little staff work on the subject. In Truman's view, such involvement was not necessary because serious corruption did not exist.

In 1951 events dictated administrative response. As the BIR disclosures followed the RFC debacle, critics charged that corruption was everywhere. Truman and staff became testy and indignant. But toward the latter part of the year, the staff began to feel that corruption was indeed an issue. There was a discomfiture, a concern that the administration was being tarnished by the issue, a frustration over the inability to counter it.

Beginning in mid-December 1951 and continuing through the first half of 1952, the administration attempted to take the initiative, both in countering charges and in developing programs to prevent future corruption. This active response was characterized both by intense staff involvement and by more willingness on the part of the president to comment publicly, defending the record of his administration and advocating solutions.

It was early in 1951 that the unraveling of the RFC investigation forced reevaluation. Corruption seemed likely to provide Republicans with an easy issue during the approaching campaign year. On 7 February, Kenneth Hechler, special assistant to the president, returned to the White House from a visit with his parents, active Republicans, and warned of Republican strategy, which included an attack on the competence of Truman's staff. "It seems to me," he suggested, "that some serious work should be done to build up the fact that the president's staff does not consist of 'incompetent political cronies.'"[2]

Translating concern into action was another matter. The next several months saw only one development, the reactivation of the Research Division of the Democratic National Committee, which had served the party during the 1948 campaign. The research division had operated with relative independence from the national committee in 1948 and lapsed because of a jurisdictional dispute as well as a lack of money. In belief that the Democrats had suffered in the 1950 off-year elections partly as a consequence, several members of the staff (including George Elsey, Richard Neustadt, David Lloyd, and James Lanigan) raised the issue: "Analyze opposition attacks on the Democratic Party, nailing lies as soon as they are spread, and prepare materials for counter-battery against opposition charges."[3] When Murphy made a pitch to Truman on behalf of reactivation, he built his case around this need. "It seems to me," he argued, "that this is a matter of the utmost importance. I believe that our efforts to take the offensive against the smear campaign of the Republicans are severely limited in their effectiveness because we lack the machinery to put our side of the case down in good, concrete, usable form, day after day, and week after week."[4] Nevertheless, a director for the group was not even named until the end of December 1951.[5]

There were other instances in which the administration revealed its frustration by lashing out against initiators of charges. Nowhere was this better illustrated than in Truman's response to two articles that appeared early in 1951, both of which he considered irresponsible. The first was an editorial in the *Chicago Daily Tribune* of 13 February, which called for Truman's impeachment. Blaming Truman for waging illegal war in Korea and for instituting "Pendergast spoils in the White House," the editorial made the familiar recitation of corruption charges, from Vaughan and the five percenters to the RFC. The editorial concluded, "Truman is crooked as well as incompetent. That is sufficient ground for the impeachment of any official."[6] Truman was enraged. He considered the statement libelous, and asked the attorney general to "proceed with whatever action is necessary to get the right result" and to "go after these people with hammer and tongs."[7]

By the time the Department of Justice reached the question of whether to sue the *Tribune* two months had elapsed, and Truman's fury had lessened. When both the Department of Justice and attorneys for the Democratic National Committee recommended against suit, the president decided to drop the idea. He was not quite ready to let it go, however, and in a letter to his former special counsel, Clark Clifford, revealed both the depth of his feeling about the press attack and an effort to place the matter in historical context. "I am wondering if all the libelous statements, particularly this one and several others that we are familiar with, could not be kept until sometime in the future when we could make use of them not for gain but for historical purposes," he wrote. "There have been only two or three Presidents who have been as roundly abused and misrepresented in certain sections of the press as I have. . . . I have just finished going through McElroy's life of Cleveland and I don't think there ever was a President as thoroughly misrepresented by the press as he was, and I don't think there ever was a more honorable man in the Presidency, although he followed the program of going straight ahead with his policies when they were as unpopular as they could be."[8]

Truman barely had put the *Tribune* editorial behind him when a more insidious attack came from another quarter. William Bradford Huie, editor of *The American Mercury*, was the perpetrator of this assault, a vicious article in the April 1951 issue of *Cosmopolitan*. Rufus Burrus, an attorney in Independence and friend of the president, wrote to Huie objecting to his total lack of objectivity and failure to check his story. But the *Cosmopolitan* article paled in comparison to what came next, for as Truman told Burrus, Huie "wrote a worse article."[9] The editorial—appearing in *The American Mercury* under the heading "Is President Truman an Honorable Man?"—was a denigrating personal attack on the president that argued that Truman "is devoid of personal integrity. We believe that he is a fixer among fixers, that his influence in this country is debilitating and evil."[10] Huie set out two incidents from Truman's days in Independence. First, he claimed Truman had settled the debts from the haberdashery unscrupulously, using political pressure to strong-arm creditors into accepting miniscule amounts. Second, Huie asserted that in 1938 Truman had borrowed $35,000 from the Jackson County school fund illegally, using his mother's farm as security; that in subsequent years Truman allegedly refused to pay interest on the loan; and that he allowed the mortgage to be foreclosed and his mother forced out of the house.

Huie's charges were not original. Jonathan Daniels, familiar with Truman's early career as a result of research for his 1950 biography of the president, *The Man of Independence*, commented, "There is absolutely nothing new in the whole piece except the effort of this fellow William Bradford Huie to make new violence out of warmed over venom. . . . All that he says in both cases has been said before and showed up before. Furthermore, this Huie knows that the charges he now makes have been examined and demolished before. He does not misunderstand; he deliberately disregards the facts which are bound to be known to him for the purposes of his slander."[11]

Tempered by legal advice after the *Chicago Tribune* editorial, Truman did not contemplate suit against Huie. Nevertheless, there was feeling that something ought to be done. After a discussion with Hechler, Elsey suggested to press secretary Short that the facts on Huie's charges might be researched and "held in reserve for future use, in a effort to protect the president from this kind of writing."[12] Elsey further suggested that Short's former assistant press secretary, Eben Ayers, might be a likely choice to undertake such an investigation. Ayers had been assembling information for the president concerning Truman's personal papers and records. The idea appealed to the president, who suggested a few people Ayers might talk to in Kansas City to begin his research and promised to ask them to cooperate. There was still no notion of what would be done once Ayers gathered the data. The investigation was still little more than a vague effort to strike back in some way. As Ayers remembered,

Truman "seemed to feel that if the truth were obtained it would disprove the malicious charges."[13] Ayers spent the next few weeks preparing for his trip, gathering papers and conferring with Daniels and the president. The precise purpose of the trip was ill defined because both Daniels and Ayers were unsure that anything new could turn up. Daniels suggested what should not be done. "Of one thing I am sure," he told Ayers, "and that is that it would do no good for any friend of the President to notice this Huie. He would like nothing better than to be a magnified son-of-a-bitch."[14]

Ayers drove to Kansas City late in June. He spent four days there, gathering information and talking to former business associates of the president. Assisted principally by Eddie Jacobson, Truman's partner in the haberdashery from 1919 to 1922, and the president's brother, Vivian, Ayers conducted interviews, assembled records, and made contacts.[15]

Ayers's objectivity in assembling his report might be questioned. He was, after all, a special assistant to Truman and had traveled to Kansas City to disprove Huie's allegations. A comparison of Ayers's documentation, however, with the unsubstantiated evidence provided in Huie's article overwhelmingly favors Ayers. Huie quoted by name only Roger Sermon, former mayor of Independence, who had died the preceding year, and the quotation dealt solely with the nature of the school fund, not with Truman's involvement. Huie had quoted "the lawyer who represented the President's brother in the mortgage foreclosure on the President's mother's farm." Among statements attributed to this lawyer, the following were the most serious: "Harry Truman is a deadbeat and has been all his life. Vivian is a splendid citizen, honest and responsible; Harry is the bad apple in that barrel. . . . As a person Harry Truman is a liar and a deadbeat; and as a willing tool of Tom Pendergast he was the enemy of every decent citizen in this community."[16] The lawyer was Omar Robinson, who admitted to Ayers that he had talked to Huie, but categorically denied the statements attributed to him and referred to Huie as a "G— d—— lying son-of-a-bitch."[17] In addition to interviews, Ayers solicited letters from people who had business or legal contacts with

Truman, as well as documents and bank records still available that had bearing on either the Truman-Jacobson partnership or the loan from the school fund. Some records had been destroyed, but Ayers felt confident enough in his work to conclude, "While I know there are some gaps in [the material], I think it makes a pretty good case."[18]

In regard to the Truman-Jacobson partnership, controversy revolved around a loan from the Security State Bank, assets of which were taken over by the Continental Bank. Ayers concluded that "from the negotiation of the loan until final liquidation of the banks involved, Truman and Jacobson sought in every way possible to carry out all of their financial, legal and moral obligations under this loan. In addition to cash payments which they made at various times and the eventual purchase of the note at a price above that paid for many similar bank assets, Mr. Truman forfeited all title to ownership in a 160-acre farm and an equity in that property which he had valued at more than the face value of the original loan."[19]

The school-fund loan issue left even less room for criticism. Truman was not directly involved in the loan; Vivian had negotiated it and handled its repayment. Further, when the foreclosed farm was repurchased by the Trumans, the price netted the county $10,900. Daniels turned Huie's allegations around, saying the loan provided "the best possible evidence for any fair-minded person of Truman's honesty in politics," since Truman had been involved in politics for eighteen years and had been spending millions on county roads, and still he had to stand by while his mother's farm was sold.[20]

Ayers took his information to the president, who expressed satisfaction. Ayers indicated that he still needed a few items, so final disposition of the information was left unresolved.[21] A short time later, the August issue of *The American Mercury* appeared, with another Huie article attacking Truman in a similar vein. Ayers noted that "the boys around the White House were a little excited about it," and he took the opportunity to discuss it with the president. Ayers told Truman that the new article, which the president had not seen, contained a few points not covered during his investigation, but the two men agreed they were of little consequence. Discussion turned to the question of a response. Ayers echoed Daniels's earlier advice that such a public controversy should be avoided. Truman concurred and closed the issue with a quotation he attributed to Calvin Coolidge: "never enter into a p—— contest with a skunk."[22] Despite the restraint shown in not using the information from Ayers, the entire project showed a curious lapse in presidential discretion. Dispatching an official drawing a government salary to document the president's record of personal integrity might have left Truman susceptible to a new set of charges had he chosen to use Ayers's data.

Handling of the Huie charges reflected the administration's lowkey attitude toward the corruption issue in the summer of 1951: information should be gathered, but results kept in reserve. In July, the president asked that cabinet members submit to him a list of investigations conducted by outside agencies that related to their departments. Advisers including Murphy and Steelman agreed that the results of the compilation should not be published.[23] It was a typically rearguard action that revealed the lack of any plan either to counter attacks or to prevent attacks from being made. The subdued attitude of the summer soon gave way to apprehension, and discussions began concerning the offensive. In a memorandum that foreshadowed the attitude that Truman and his staff would take over the next months, Lloyd saw corruption charges as political and mentioned the need to counter them: "It is fatal to allow these matters to become political footballs to be used against the administration. It is furthermore important that the administration take the offensive and be ahead of the game so that it is not constantly in a defensive position."[24] Lloyd, with Murphy and Lanigan, suggested what Murphy lightly referred to as "the dirty tricks department." The three men proposed coordinating the government's foreign and domestic investigative and law-enforcement functions.

December 1951 was a month of torment. With the twin issues of Korea and corruption, Truman's popularity plunged to a new low, 23 percent on the Gallup poll. With the BIR revelations reaching flood tide and Democratic party leaders and supporters ruminating that corruption could become the issue of 1952, Truman could no longer ignore it. The president became uncharacteristically moody. Having placed a premium on loyalty, he felt betrayed. Angry over the BIR developments and frustrated over inability to address the problem, a dispirited president faced reporters for the revealing and expansive 13 December press conference. An aide confessed that he had never seen the president so despondent. The feeling that events were getting out of hand pervaded the administration. "There is no memo or file of the facts on corruption yet," Elsey lamented to Clifford. "Things are moving too fast for the staff to prepare any such memorandum."[25]

The sense of urgency that permeated the administration and party began to generate suggestions. It remained an article of faith that the scandals were not nearly as bad as outsiders portrayed them. Recommendations for action, especially from those outside the president's immediate staff, were usually couched in such terms. Carl V. Rice, national committeeman for Kansas, claimed Republicans were blowing the scandals out of proportion. Federal Trade Commissioner John Carson asserted that previous scandals "were cancerous as compared with the scrofula of these days."[26] Washington attorney Nathaniel Ely commented confidently, "The president now has full grasp of the situation."[27] Even among the president's advisers there was a tendency to minimize the problem. Dawson referred to the scandals as "a relatively few cases of petty wrongdoing."[28] As if trying to convince themselves, Democrats talking to Democrats continued to insist that little was wrong. Responsibility fell to Murphy, who was becoming more and more what another member of the White House staff, Neustadt, later referred to as "the cleaner-upper of nasty operational crises."[29] Murphy had performed one of the more successful efforts of countering scandal-related charges in helping to defuse the RFC issue a few months earlier. His closest associates were those whom Neustadt described as "the 'idea' boys, the bright young men of Truman's White House, responsible, indefatigable [men who had] . . . a real network of close, informal relationships [with] . . . bright, able, imaginative staff men all over Washington."[30]

Bearing responsibility in the corruption countermeasures campaign, Murphy's group consisted of Lloyd, Donald Hansen, and Hechler. Lloyd had been primarily a speech writer, promoted to administrative assistant on 22 December 1951, and countermeasures were one of his early assignments.[31] Hansen, Murphy's assistant, worked with Lloyd and coordinated particularly the Bureau of the Budget. Hechler was Lloyd's assistant and had a reputation as "a lightning-fast researcher, fact-finder, and compiler of background information, particularly in the field of 'political' research."[32] The activities of the group after mid-December represented in no way a radical program, for Murphy had been involved in similar activities for months. It was, rather, more of a responsibility inherited by default, a continuation of previous tasks. New, however, were the heightened concern and the consequent increase in time devoted to countering charges. The Murphy group operated behind the scenes, not only developing ideas but also coordinating proposals.

The administration first had to address the BIR. Truman's 13 December press conference already had set in motion what would become Newbold Morris's investigation. Another proposal was a formal reorganization plan. It had circulated within the bureau, so planning had not been tied to the current controversy. After Hansen conferred with Treasury officials, it was decided to link the reorganization plan to corruption charges. Treasury worried that the bill might be controversial, but the department could gain leverage in rallying support since an opponent would be cast in the uncomfortable role of voting *for* corruption. At the same time, the White House could demonstrate that it was developing a positive anticorruption program. Yet the approach was not free of risk because it might allow opponents to charge that the plan was a slap-dash proposal.[33]

Truman's handling of the BIR reorganization plan demonstrated that he regarded the corruption issue with a sense of urgency. He customarily kept reorganization plans secret until ready to present them, when they would be "more or less just sprung on the Congress," according to Harold Seidman, who knew reorganization procedures well from the perspective of the Bureau of the Budget.[34] In the case of the BIR plan, Truman announced in advance the salient details. In a 2 January 1952 statement, the president called the plan "part of a program to prevent improper conduct in the public service" and declared, "We must rid the Government of any employees who misuse their official positions for personal gain."[35] The plan would replace the sixty-four collectors' offices with twenty-five district offices, each headed by a civil service appointee. He also proposed inspection service, independent of the BIR.

The immediate reaction pleased the administration. Snyder told a cabinet meeting two days after the president's statement that the plan had been well received. Dawson, encouraged by the "very fine public reception" for the plan, suggested similar measures for the Department of Justice and the Bureau of Customs.[36]

The plan went to Congress on 14 January 1952 with a forceful statement by Truman linking it to the cleanup campaign. "The thorough reorganization of the Bureau of Internal Revenue which I propose is an integral part of a program to prevent improper conduct in public service, to protect the Government from insidious influence peddlers and favor seekers, to expose and punish wrongdoers, and to improve the management and efficiency of the executive branch."[37] There was an air of urgency that reflected the new approach. Meanwhile, Hansen and Lloyd had developed proposals for the anticorruption campaign. The two men outlined suggestions to clarify ethical responsibilities of federal employees and citizens doing business with the government. Hansen advised that a cleanup committee was "necessary from a public relations standpoint."[38] In an ironic foreshadowing of Morris's questionnaire fiasco, Hansen suggested that government employees file financial statements. In preparation for a 24 January White House meeting on corruption, Murphy reviewed the Hansen-Lloyd suggestions and incorporated them into his own recommendations.

The 24 January White House meeting signaled a subtle shift in the administration's campaign. Emphasis shifted to two actions—the Morris investigation and government reorganization. Murphy had expected the meeting to discuss approaches, but Truman used it to give McGrath the vote of confidence that preceded the appointment of Morris. Regarding other tactics, William Finan, who represented the Bureau of the Budget at the meeting, recalled that the president said he planned "a series of actions over a long period of time."[39] The consequence was to place McGrath (and subsequently Morris) at the center. Murphy and men—overburdened in other areas—monitored the McGrath-Morris melodrama and served as White House liaison.

The administration continued to be pleased with public response to the BIR plan. A Gallup poll released on 23 January revealed that 84 percent of those who had heard of the proposal to place BIR collectors under the Civil Service approved. Murphy informed Truman that the proposal had been "very favorably received by the public."[40] The plan was bolstered by the Citizens Committee for the Hoover Report, a Republican-dominated group often at odds with the administration. Although the director of research of the citizens committee, Robert L. L. McCormick, believed Truman had submitted the plan to get himself "off the hook," he saw it as consistent with Hoover Commission proposals and testified forcefully in support.[41] The plan passed the House without significant opposition on 30 January 1952.

The positive response to the BIR plan generated administration interest in others. Truman suggested placing U.S. attorneys under civil service at the 24 January meeting, and discussions ensued about doing the same for collectors of customs, postmasters, and U.S. marshals. In the Bureau of the Budget, Finan urged Director Frederick J. Lawton to get Truman's permission to plan along these lines.[42] Weary of being portrayed by Congress as condoning opportunities for corruption, Truman was delighted. His feisty attitude reappeared: "There is going to be a howl from the patronage boys all the way down the street. But I will fight for this vital and urgent change."[43]

Opposition developed in the Senate, where Walter George, a Georgia Democrat and a power on the Finance Committee, and his Republican colleague, Eugene Millikin of Colorado, bristled at Truman's charge that opponents were interested in patronage. George attacked the proposal for failing to conform with the Reorganization Act of 1949, for failing either to specify the future form of the BIR or to create a statutory structure to replace that which would be eliminated by the plan, and for failing to guarantee the right of taxpayers to sue collectors.[44]

Ensuing Senate proposals to counter or complement the BIR plan complicated the administration defense. John McClellan, Democrat from Arkansas, threatened legislation to replace the BIR plan. Four Democrats more charitably disposed toward the administration (Mike Monroney of Oklahoma, Blair Moody of Michigan, John Sparkman of Alabama, and George Smathers of Florida) introduced a bill that they called the "Clean Government Act of 1952," claiming that their proposal would "go much farther than, but not conflict with, the Internal Revenue Bureau reorganization plan."[45] The bill proposed to make the commissioner of internal revenue a civil service appointee, to create a position within the Civil Service Commission for constant BIR review, to prohibit outside interference in tax cases, to extend the definition of bribery, to require public disclosure of RFC transactions, and to prohibit pensions to government employees convicted of felonies in connection with their jobs. This measure was an irritant to the administration if for no other reason than it diverted attention from the BIR plan and required careful handling, particularly because Monroney was one of the leading supporters of the administration's plan. Reports from agencies (Treasury, Bureau of the Budget, Civil Service Commission, RFC) recommended against provisions of the bill and offered faint praise for others. When Monroney queried the president about the bill, Truman praised the positive approach and found the provision regarding noninterference in tax cases laudatory, but he stressed that, as far as the BIR was concerned, "The most important thing to do right now is to gain Senate acceptance of my Reorganization Plan."[46]

The fight became bitter. With forty-nine Senate votes needed to kill the measure, opponents reportedly garnered forty-five by late February and forty-seven as the final vote neared two weeks later. The administration was committed and, in the words of Budget Director Lawton, "put muscle" into the fight.[47] The BIR assembled research materials. Democratic Sen. Hubert Humphrey of Minnesota carried the fight on the Hill. On 7 March, Truman, in an open letter to Vice-President Alben Barkley, urged favorable action, labeling the measure a key solution to corruption: "This reorganization plan is an essential part of a program to assure honesty, integrity and efficiency in government. Unfortunately, those who find it to their advantage to preserve the present system, or to play politics with the integrity of the public service, have raised specious arguments against the plan that obscure the real issue." Added the president, "Disapproval of the plan would be a defeat for civil service reform—and a victory for the proponents of a political patronage system."[48] This theme was echoed by three of the plan's chief supporters in the Senate; Humphrey, Monroney, and Moody, in a Government Operations Committee minority report, termed the plan the cornerstone of the anticorruption drive.[49]

On 13 March 1952, the Senate voted on a resolution offered by Senators George and Millikin, without which the plan would automatically become law the next day. The resolution was defeated by a surprisingly wide margin, fifty-three to thirty-seven, as ten opponents apparently switched at the last minute. Hansen said, "The only reason that reorganization went through was because of the issue of corruption in Government and a lot of senators didn't want to vote . . . *for* sin, so we got some Republican votes on that that probably wouldn't have come along otherwise."[50]

The success of the BIR plan gave momentum to the notion of reorganization as an anticorruption device, momentum that was carried over to similar proposals that had been under consideration for some time. Removing presidential responsibility for appointment of postmasters, U.S. marshals, and customs collectors (as well as internal revenue collectors) had been proposed as early as 1937 by the President's Committee on Administrative Management (Brownlow committee). The Hoover Commission had proposed placing postmasters under civil service. The president had mentioned the same proposal for U.S marshals and attorneys. The Treasury and Post Office departments developed plans, although Secretary of the Treasury Snyder resisted new plans before BIR reorganization won approval. The Justice Department, embroiled in the Morris affair and its consequences, complained of legal problems.[51]

Truman introduced three new plans on 10 April. Reorganization Plan No. 2 of 1952 proposed to eliminate presidential appointment and Senate confirmation of postmasters at first-, second-, and third-class post offices. Plan No. 3 eliminated from presidential appointment the collector of customs, comptroller of customs, surveyor of customs, and appraiser of merchandise; continuation of these services would fall under the jurisdiction of new civil service offices subject to appointment by the secretary of the treasury. The final proposal called for U.S. marshals to be considered for civil service appointment by the attorney general. In a special message to Congress introducing the new plans, the president alluded to charges of corruption in a statement intended to link the new plans to the cleanup campaign but to minimize the significance of the scandals: "I know, from personal experience in both the Congress and the Presidency, how much time and effort is lost and how we have been distracted from the consideration of issues of paramount national importance by the present method of appointing the officials covered by these reorganization plans. We must relieve ourselves of this burden of minor personnel actions in order to devote our efforts to the greater issues confronting our Government today."[52]

The administration based its case on patronage. Senator George, again an ardent opponent, seized this issue for opposition. He complained that the plans would "concentrate more power" in the executive departments and urged that "Congress should be more responsible, rather than less, for appointments."[53] Administration opponents, who had come within a few votes of defeating the BIR plan, had better prospects in the renewed battle. Truman's continual attacks on the Congress as a den of patronage-hungry wolves had alienated some potential supporters, and the absence of scandals in the target agencies robbed the current proposals of the urgency that had punctuated the debate over BIR reorganization.

When the measures came before the Senate in June, they were all turned back by substantial margins,[54] effectively ending what remained of the administration's effort. The anticorruption program had produced meager results and had done little to defuse the corruption issue in the election, less than five months away.

8. THE CORRUPTION ISSUE IN THE 1952 CAMPAIGN

During the early months of 1952, while President Truman's political lieutenants attempted to defuse the corruption issue, Republicans began to use it as one of their campaign themes. It was not a difficult case for the GOP. The Democrats unwittingly had prepared the way in a manner that would have brought credit to the most imaginative Republican press agent. Indeed, the Republicans received an issue packaged with all the elements for an advertising promotion. Images of mink coats and deep freezers were in the public mind. Readily identifiable "villains," including Vaughan and Dawson, were still in the administration. There was constant attention as RFC and BIR disclosures came out in a way that kept them before the public. The opposition was divided by internecine political warfare, as Democratic committee chairmen sparred with the president over the investigation of executive agencies. A vocabulary of catchwords could raise public indignation—five percenter, crony, influence. Finally, McGrath and Morris provided melodramatic tension within the administration.

Nor did Republicans underestimate the corruption issue. In a November 1951 Gallup poll of Republican county chairmen, corruption was the most frequently mentioned issue for the approaching campaign. One of the respondents proclaimed: "Oust the thieves, robbers, Commies, the ten percenters, the mink coats and all forms of dishonesty and corruption in our national government."[1] The early front-runner for the Republican presidential nomination, Sen. Robert A. Taft of Ohio, exploited the issue, declaring in New Hampshire, "The entire nation has been shocked over and over again by the low state of morality in the administration."[2]

Analyzing a single issue is risky, however, and interpretation appears skewed as if the election hinges on that issue. The 1952 campaign did not turn on corruption, an issue that actually diminished toward the end. But that does not deny its importance. Using Sen. Karl Mundt's formula of K_1C_2, Republicans included Korea and Communism with corruption. Nor was corruption solely a Republican lament. Adlai Stevenson, in what John Bartlow Martin, the Democratic standard-bearer's biographer, considered perhaps his worst error, accepted the Republican issue agenda, forcing himself to respond constantly from the defensive.[3]

Truman campaigned vigorously, insisting that the Democratic party would have to stand or fall on the record of his administration. Scandals were part of that record, and the president, so recently hesitant to offer more than staccato, single-sentence responses on corruption, was now loquacious in defense. Like Stevenson, he accepted Republican ground rules that established corruption as a key issue. Unlike Stevenson, Truman's posture was an unavoidable result of his imcumbency. He was campaigning, perhaps, for the position of his administration in history.

Most observers expected Truman to seek reelection, in spite of the steady erosion of his popularity. The Korean War and the BIR continued to sap his presidency, however, and in March 1952 Sen. Estes Kefauver of Tennessee outpolled Truman in New Hampshire. Truman announced his decision not to run on 29 March, almost sixteen years to the day before another Democratic president embroiled in another Asian war would make a similar announcement under remarkably similar circumstances, although there were significant differences. Truman had decided long before not to seek reelection, while Lyndon Johnson was pressed into his withdrawal by political realities.[4] Johnson's decision also reflected his intention to remove himself from active participation in the campaign, while Truman's declaration was a political speech that indicated his expectation to participate.

Indeed, Truman's speech anticipated his next seven months of campaigning. He defended his administration. He enumerated three corruption-related themes that he would reiterate. He underscored his personal integrity and abhorrence of dishonesty in government: "I stand for honest government. I have worked for it. I have probably done more for it than any other President. . . . I hate corruption everywhere, but I hate it most of all in a Democratic officeholder."[5] The president also stressed efforts to counter corruption. This part of his speech was brief, reflecting the loss of momentum in the White House anticorruption offensive. He alluded to reorganization and expansion of civil service, complaining that allegations of scandal hurt the honest majority of federal employees. Truman likewise attacked the hypocrisy of Republicans who alleged that the administration was corrupt. Harkening back to a suggestion from Donald Dawson that Truman initiate a series of speeches on what Dawson called "The Big Steal," the president criticized Republican devotion to "private selfish interests" that were "robbing the public."[6] He asserted that Republicans "can't have it both ways—they can't be for morality on Tuesday and Thursday, and then be for special privileges for their clients on Monday, Wednesday and Friday."[7]

With Truman out, attention turned to others. Truman's support was expected to boost any of them. Corruption-related issues helped him make his selection, particularly when it came to choosing between Kefauver and Stevenson. Before the group narrowed, Truman first contemplated backing Supreme Court Chief Justice Fred M. Vinson, who removed his name from consideration. Other contenders had liabilities. New York's Averell Harriman was too inexperienced in politics. Sen. Robert S. Kerr of Oklahoma was too closely associated with oil. Truman believed that anyone from the Deep South would have a difficult task, so he denied Richard Russell, Senator from Georgia, his endorsement. He considered Vice-President Alben Barkley too old at seventy-four, though Barkley did gain presidential backing when Truman's preferred candidate, Stevenson, wavered.

Of all potential Democratic nominees, the president had the least difficulty eliminating Kefauver. Contention between the two had arisen out of the corruption issue when Kefauver came to national attention as chairman of the Special Senate Crime Investigating Committee in 1950 and 1951. It gained Kefauver a reputation as a crusader, but it cost him the support of influential Democrats whose organizations were touched by the investigation. He had supported most of Truman's programs but was compelled to criticize the administration to maintain himself as a corruption fighter. Truman had little use for "Mr. Cow Fever," whom he considered a "peculiar person. He is ignorant of history, an amateur in politics and intellectually dishonest."[9] Kefauver's crime investigation seemed to delight in embarrassing the administration. After beginning in Kansas City and finding nothing, he took his investigation to St. Louis. There, Truman observed, "He found something in *East* St. Louis, Illinois. But *St. Louis, Mo.* was used for the *headlines.* So the President of the United States had all the credit for Illinois crime. . . . When the time came for a report to the United States Senate the 'great crime investigator' took his report, copyrighted it and sold it as a book over his own name! Talk about ethics—well he has none."[10]

The corruption issue was a factor in Truman's decision to endorse Stevenson. In spite of certain reservations, Truman considered Stevenson the best available man by virtue of background, experience, and capacity. "I like Stevenson's political and administrative background," the president wrote in his memoirs.[11] The political training of the two had remarkable parallels. Eric Sevareid once described the Illinois governor as "that rare creature, a reformer who was elected with the support of the hard-bitten political machine,"[12] words that could have been pulled from descriptions of the president during his work with the Truman committee. Indeed, both men had shown integrity while working with political machines. Stevenson had not turned from the patronage system; he accepted it as part of politics in much the same fashion as Truman had done in Jackson County. Stevenson saw patronage as a necessary evil that he justified in a political quick-step that may have been expressed in more erudite terms than those used by the president but was Truman-like in conclusion: "The patronage method of job dispensation is a substantial part of the price we have paid for the organized party activity which is vital in a democracy. . . . The party managers have been discerningly practical sociologists. They have made, in the main, an accurate appraisal of what is required to make political parties tick and thereby serve the larger purposes of democratic government. Perhaps the net result has been that a greater amount of good has come from a lesser amount of evil."[13] Carl McGowan, an associate of Stevenson, remarked that the governor's "relations with the Democratic politicians were pretty good. He didn't give the Chicago organization much trouble about appointments."[14] It was a position that Truman would have found comfortable. Stevenson's biographer has suggested that Stevenson insisted that he was a citizen rather than a politician, an attitude that partly explains Truman's later disillusionment with him.

Stevenson was summoned to Blair House early in January and during the hour-long discussion learned of Truman's decision not to seek reelection—and that the governor was his choice. Stevenson appeared flabergasted and turned down the offer. Throughout the spring, he continued to insist that he was a candidate only for governor and that he could not run for two offices.[15] Protests to the contrary, Stevenson was hounded about his presidential aspirations by the administration as well as the press. The president sent Charles Murphy to see him in mid-March. It was a tense session, with a perturbed Stevenson asking why he should feel compelled to run because Truman disliked Kefauver. The governor enumerated his differences with Truman on a broad range of issues, including corruption. Federal employees found guilty of wrongdoing should not simply be fired; they ought to be prosecuted, he insisted.

As fortune had it, Stevenson was slated for an appearance on "Meet the Press" the day after Truman announced his intention not to run. Stevenson again insisted that he had no intention other than to seek reelection as governor. His comments on corruption looked to the question of public morality rather than specific allegations. His remarks were not far from what Truman had said. "The level of morals in public life," Stevenson asserted, "can never be much different from the level of morals in civilian life." The closest he came to criticizing the administration was to say that government "must take the lead" and be "like Caesar's wife."[16]

With Stevenson refusing, Kefauver was the front-runner. The senator had called on Truman in January and informed the president that he was considering a run at the nomination but would do so only if the president was not going to seek reelection. Truman claimed he had not yet made up his mind. Still, he was friendly, even fatherly, though pehaps it was only a tactic to delay the senator's entry. Frustrated by the inability to get clear direction, Kefauver decided to enter regardless of Truman's intentions. Knowing that his handling of the corruption issue might be the key to nomination, he downplayed it in his 23 January 1952 announcement to run. He could not ignore what was indisputably the basis of his national reputation, but to press hard could alienate party regulars and make him appear willing to sacrifice the party. When a reporter's question broached the issue, Kefauver stepped over "a fine line between pointing out that more needed to be done and asking why the Administration was not taking the proper steps."[17] Asked if he thought the administration had done all it could to stamp out corruption, Kefauver replied, "No, I don't think so. I do think some good things have been done, but I think much more must be done. More stress must be put on morality and clean government in the Federal Government, and we must take the leadership in showing the way and giving the inspiration to local people to help them clean up their criminal conditions."[18] Kefauver straddled the line separating loyalist from reformer. He acknowledged the viability of corruption as a campaign issue and tried to stay away from Truman. Later he regretted the strategy: "It would have been better to have made a definite break with President Truman. As it was, I criticized the shortcomings of his administration . . . but still tried to avoid a final and conclusive break with him. My campaign would have been stronger and I would have lost nothing."[19]

By the spring of 1952, it was clear that corruption was going to be a major campaign issue. Kefauver's success in New Hampshire, volleys of Republican attacks, and opinion polls all demonstrated public sensitivity to corruption, and the erosion of the White House effort to form a positive response made it apparent that the administration would not head off the issue. The Democratic National Committee, particularly its research division, shared the burden of presenting the White House point of view. Bert Gross, who had been effective as executive secretary of the Council of Economic Advisers, was named to head the research division. He had demonstrated loyalty to the party, and his appointment was supported by administrative political workers such as David Lloyd, Kenneth Hechler, and George Elsey—all of whom had expressed concern about corruption.[20]

The research division and the national committee were in

Truman's corner. Kefauver's lieutenants were frustrated in efforts to get cooperation from national chairman Frank McKinney and even had to resort to subterfuge to secure a copy of a mailing list. Gross maintained regular contact with the White House staff through Donald Hansen. When his staff developed a position paper on corruption, it reflected the president's point of view, even incorporating portions of Truman's Jefferson-Jackson Day dinner speech in which the president defended the record of his administration. The paper argued that Democrats had "constantly ferreted out favoritism and corruption without fear or favor" and that Democrats had "steadily raised the level of public morality." A political document, the report would deserve little attention save that it reflected Truman's approach to the campaign. It gave Truman credit for reforms implemented under political duress, such as the reorganization of the RFC. Other reorganization plans, some from the Hoover Commission's report or earlier sources, were again gathered under the administration's anticorruption effort. Divisions and disagreements were ignored; Democrats who were giving little assistance to Kefauver took credit for his accomplishments. Most remarkable in a document full of exaggeration were sentences underscored, as if emphasis would overcome evidence. Disputes with Representative Hoey and Senator Fulbright were brushed aside: "*The administration has cooperated closely with Congressional committees in developing information on corruption and misfeasance.*" Patronage was forgotten: "[Government employees] *were selected on the basis of their ability—not political 'pull.'*" The paper concluded with a section echoing the theme launched earlier by the president, that of attacking Republicans as the party of privilege.[21] Democrats would complain—often with justification—of Republican exaggeration of the corruption issue. With the research division's paper establishing a counterpoint, campaign talk on corruption degenerated into hyperbole and self-congratulation. Ironically, this style was perhaps more effective than the countermeasures campaign. As the campaign went on and Republicans were caught in trouble of their own, talk on both sides robbed the corruption issue of its effect, rendering it less effective for the Republicans than it might have been.

The Republicans, of course, had a searing primary contest

between Sen. Robert A. Taft and Gen. Dwight D. Eisenhower. Taft had used the corruption issue while Eisenhower concluded his tour of duty with NATO in Europe. When the general returned only a month before the Republican convention, he made his first appearance in Abilene. Speaking to local citizens and a national television audience on a rainy 4 June afternoon, Eisenhower referred only obliquely to corruption, celebrating Midwestern moral values: "In spite of the difficulties of the problems we have, I ask you this one question: If each of us in his own mind would dwell more upon those simple virtues—integrity, courage, self-confidence, an unshakable belief in the Bible—would not some of these problems tend to simplify themselves?"[22]

When the Republicans assembled in Chicago on 6 July, both Taft and Eisenhower helped to make the party's platform. On corruption neither side risked political capital. Mentioned in the preamble, corruption received detailed treatment as one of the topical sections on issues of the campaign. Here the GOP let go:

> The present Administration's sordid record of corruption has shocked and sickened the American people. Its leaders have forfeited any right to public faith by the way they transact the Federal Government's business.
>
> Fraud, bribery, graft, favoritism and influence peddling have come to light. Immorality and unethical behavior have been found to exist among some who were entrusted with high policymaking positions. . . .
>
> Under public pressure, the Administration took reluctant steps to clean house. But it was so eager to cover up and block more revelations that its clean-up drive launched with much fanfare ended in a farce.
>
> The Republican party pledges to put an end to corruption, to oust the crooks and grafters, to administer tax laws fairly and impartially, and to restore honest government to the people.[23]

Eisenhower became the Republican nominee when a flurry of delegate switches after the first ballot carried him to victory over the Taft forces. In his acceptance speech, the general declared that he intended to "sweep from office an Administration which has fastened on every one of us the wastefulness, the arrogance and corruption in high places, the heavy burden and anxieties of a party too long in power."[24]

The party in power followed the Republicans to Chicago on 20 July, and corruption was a less popular topic. Stevenson neither avoided it nor criticized Truman. He made the most of a sensitive matter, transforming a liability into a rallying point: "Where we have erred, let there be no denial: where we have wronged the public trust, let there be no excuses. Self-criticism is the secret weapon of democracy, and candor and confession are good for the political soul. But we will never appease, we will never apologize for our leadership of the great events of this critical century all the way from Woodrow Wilson to Harry Truman!"[25]

Awkwardness between the Democratic standard-bearer and the president emerged soon after the convention, in their interpretations of what had happened in Chicago. Truman believed that he had not only passed the mantle to Stevenson but also was responsible for his nomination. "Had I not come to Chicago when I did," Truman wrote, "the squirrel headed coonskin cap man . . . who has no sense of honor [Kefauver] would have been the nominee."[26] The president believed Stevenson both owed loyalty and was beholden to him for the nomination. When Stevenson failed to defer, the president considered him politically naive and an ingrate. Stevenson saw things differently and explained to a friend, "I am *not* Truman's candidate. He asked me and I turned it down. He then turned to Harriman, then to Barkley, but the convention turned to me after I had repeatedly said I was not a candidate and didn't want it."[27] Although Stevenson desired distance between himself and the White House, his actions in the first month after the convention—both purposeful and inadvertent—so separated him from the president that the two men could barely deal with each other. Truman saw each of Stevenson's moves toward independence as insults to his administration and violations of party loyalty; the president thus resisted Stevenson's inclination toward an independent campaign. "I am the key of the campaign," Truman insisted, emphasizing that "the Democratic Party has to run on the record of the Roosevelt-Truman administration."[28]

A controversial move by Stevenson was replacement of

McKinney as national chairman. Jack Arvey, a powerful
Cook County Democrat, opposed it, but another Stevenson
adviser, Carl McGowan, recalled that "to rid himself of Truman" Stevenson could not keep McKinney.[29] In his *Memoirs*
Truman claimed, "The first mistake he made was to fire the
chairman of the Democratic National Committee and to
move his campaign headquarters to Springfield, Illinois, giving the impression that he was seeking to disassociate himself from the administration in Washington, and perhaps
from me." Truman said that this did not give Stevenson free-
dom of action but instead "needlessly sacrificed basic political backing and perhaps millions in votes."[30]

Stevenson's next affront strengthened the Republicans'
ability to exploit the corruption issue. Queried by the *Oregon
Journal* as to whether he could "clean up the mess in Washington," Stevenson foolishly restated the question: "As to
whether I can clean up the mess in Washington, I would
bespeak the careful scrutiny of what I inherited in Illinois
and what has been accomplished in three years."[31] Republicans pointed out that even the Democratic nominee acknowledged a mess in the nation's capital. McGowan took
the blame, saying he had dictated the letter without putting
the phrase in quotation marks. Others blamed the typist.
Stevenson apologized to the president, but the damage was
done.

Publicly, Truman refused to give the "mess in Washington" letter any more attention than it had received. Asked
to comment on it at a press conference, he replied simply, "I
have no comment, because I know nothing about any
'mess.'"[32] Although he graciously accepted Stevenson's apology, he was infuriated. The result was a letter that, fortu-
nately, he did not send:

> My dear Governor:
> Your letter to Oregon is a surprising document. It makes the
> campaign rather ridiculous. It seems to me that the Presidential
> Nominee and his running mate are trying to beat the Demo-
> cratic President instead of the Republicans and the General of
> the Army who heads their ticket.
> There is no mess in Washington except the sabotage
> press. . . .

I've come to the conclusion that if you want to run against your friends, they should retire from the scene and let you do it. When you say that you are indebted to no one for your nomination, that makes nice reading in the sabotage press, but it gets you no votes because it isn't true. . . .

You fired and balled up the Democratic Committee Organization that I've been creating over the last four years. . . . Cowfever could not have treated me any more shabbily than have you. . . .

Best of luck to you from a bystander who has become disinterested.[33]

Four months later, Truman was still bitter:

The Governor found it very difficult to believe that a life-long politician can be a honest man. He did not and does not yet understand the necessity of organization from the precinct to the National Committee.

He and Franklin Roosevelt experienced contact with two rotten, money grabbing machines—Kelly-Nash and Tammany Hall. It did not occur to the Governor or to the President that even these terrible machines usually present honest men for public office. . . .

There are more honest men who are professional politicians than there are honest bankers and businessmen. The word of a successful man in politics is worth more than the bond of a banker, of [a] big businessman.

So the Governor distrusted the President, the Chairman of the National Committee and the Democratic Party. He had read Bertie McCormick's awful *Tribune* and Hearst's Chicago sewer sheet until he more than half believed what they had to say about Roosevelt's New Deal and the President's Fair Deal. A half-hearted approach never won in a political campaign.[34]

On their side, the Republicans were far from half-hearted: campaign material was exhaustive and detailed on the issue of corruption. The most complete examination of the corruption issue was compiled by the staff of the Senate Minority Policy Committee. In a twenty-one-page section of a report on issues, each incident bordering on a scandal during the Truman years was reviewed.[35] A resource book for Republican speakers, "Democrats Run on Truman Record," included a section of quotes and quips such as these: "The only thing the Democrats have to fear is—fur itself";

"Probably the reason the Truman people like to go to Key West is because so many of them have been suffering from exposure."[36] A handbill proclaimed that "A Vote for Ike and Dick is a vote *against corruption.* A vote for Ike and Dick is a vote *for morality*."[37] A pamphlet entitled "Want Another Truman?" portrayed the Stevenson administration in Illinois as founded on corruption, comparing the records of Stevenson and Truman.[38]

Eisenhower mentioned corruption at nearly every campaign stop. He seldom dealt in specifics, relying instead on catch phrases, promising to "cast away the incompetent, the unfit, the cronies, and the chiselers."[39] He indicted Stevenson as well as Truman: "Their nominee for President has lately been quoted as admitting that there is a mess in Washington. The head of the Administration himself has announced that their Presidential nominee must run on one issue—the record of the Administration. On both of these points I am in hearty agreement with the opposition."[40] Eisenhower was evasive in his solution to the problem, however. He spoke only of getting rid of the perpetrators, proposing to "root out of government those who would betray our system or abuse our confidence."[41] He beheld a new breed of honest politicians, "men and women to whom low public morals are unthinkable."[42]

Shortly after the convention, Truman had planned an extensive whistle-stop tour for the last month of the campaign, but the tension between Stevenson and Truman in August left Stevenson's advisers unsure that Truman's participation would be an asset. Stevenson wrote to the president: "I know how sincere you are about helping us and of your almost limitless energy, but we shall try not to impose on you unreasonably."[43] Truman, moreover, had second thoughts as his support of Stevenson waned. He scrawled one of his caustic unsent letters, complaining of "snub after snub" by Stevenson and his campaign manager, Wilson Wyatt. Truman closed with a reference to his campaign trip, saying, "I shall go to the dedication of the Hungry Horse Dam in Montana [scheduled for 1 October], make a public power speech, get in a plane and come back to Washington and stay there. You and Wilson can now run your campaign without interference or advice."[44] Nevertheless, party loyalty and disdain for the opposition overcame his reservations. So did Stevenson's campaign, which had not repeated the affronts of August. But Truman's involvement during the last month of the campaign had little to do with Stevenson and much to do with Truman himself. Columnist Doris Fleeson commented that there was an essential difference between the 1948 tour, when Truman was "fighting recklessly for office," and the 1952 trip: "He is fighting now for his place in history and that is a much more careful and deeply felt effort."[45]

Yet Truman's style was reminiscent of 1948. He no longer defended the administration's record on corruption; he was now constantly on the attack. He accused the Republicans of running what he variously labeled "a smear campaign," a "gutter campaign," or a "'back street' campaign."[46] He claimed, as he had in 1948, that the letters GOP properly stood for "Gluttons of Privilege."[47] He intimated that former generals make poor presidents who often preside over corrupt administrations.[48]

Republican rhetoric in October 1952 was an even match for Truman's vitriolic accusations as the campaign degenerated to mudslinging vilification on both sides. The Republicans launched a "scandal-a-day" project in October, a series of twelve whistlestop speeches.[49] Reborn to righteousness after the Checkers speech in which he answered charges that he had benefitted from a "slush fund" financed by wealthy Californians, vice-presidential candidate Richard Nixon referred to Truman and several members of his administration as "crooks and incompetents." He charged that under Truman, "We find embezzlement, thievery, knavery and criminal carelessness rife in the American Government."[50] On another occasion, Nixon called Truman "the champion lemon picker of all time."[51] Eisenhower, in spite of his protestations of being nonpolitical and above the fray, scrapped with the others. He exhumed the Kansas City machine and its boss: "Tom Pendergast is dead. But his political influence, his political morals, his political offspring, they all go marching on."[52] The campaign did have its high moments—notably in the magnetic personality of one candidate and the literary style of the other—but the corruption issue did nothing to elevate either the candidates or the campaign.

How much influence did the corruption issue have on the

results of the election? Scholars who have examined the outcome have decided that the issue did not aid the Republicans
as much as had been anticipated. Truman's staff concluded
that Korea was the most important factor in the campaign,
followed by communism and the desire for a change, of
which corruption was an aspect. That these issues remained
prominent to the end is a tribute to Republican strategy, a
criticism of Stevenson's acquiescence, and a validation of
Truman's instinct that the governor ought not to take the
defense.[53] In fact, the corruption issue hurt the Democrats
more in provoking the division between Stevenson and Truman. Stevenson felt compelled to disassociate himself from
Truman, though he sought to prevent a breach that would
jeopardize party support. Seeking balance, he lost on both
sides. "Had the election of 1952 been close," Truman wrote
in retrospect, "the discharge of the National Committee
Chairman, the lack of faith in the administration of Roosevelt and Truman would have lost that election even to Robert
Taft."[54]

The magnitude of Eisenhower's triumph might have been
a repudiation of the incumbent president. Truman never
saw it as such but viewed the election in terms of political
strategy, and while he admired Stevenson's eloquence and
intellectual courage, he was critical of many of Stevenson's
strategic decisions. He viewed the outcome as a vindication
of his own political philosophy, which placed a premium on
party unity, trust within party circles, and fidelity to party
tradition. Stevenson, on the other hand, restructured party
organization, failed to trust Truman's operatives, lacked
faith in the Roosevelt-Truman tradition—and lost the election. In Truman's opinion, moreover, the governor had been
too defensive and had called on the president too late in the
campaign. It was not the assessment of a man who bore any
remorse for having bogged down a losing ticket but that of
a consummate politician who felt secure that he had been
faithful to his personal political code in the face of condi-
tional loyalty by others.

9. POSTPRESIDENTIAL YEARS

As President Truman took the train back to Independence and private life in January 1953, he left behind the responsibilities of the presidency, but the conclusion of his term of office did not signal the end of Truman's relationship with his official family. He kept in touch with men who had suffered through charges of scandal. He relaxed with them, reminisced, and often came to their defense. The reduced pace of his life also gave time not only for social and political activities but for reflection as well.

Some former members of the administration privately expressed concern about what they considered Truman's undue loyalty to subordinates. Charles Sawyer believed he was "too loyal to third-rate friends, perhaps second-rate . . . but it was an appealing weakness."[1] A Kansas City businessman, Tom Evans, a friend of the president since the 1920s, said that unconditional support for friends was Truman's "greatest weakness, if you can call it a weakness."[2] Martin Friedman's observations typified those of staff members, that Truman possessed "a quality that endeared him to his staff because he sort of adopted them, and if you were a member of his staff you were one of his people and he had tremendous loyalty to his people."[3] Frank Pace noted, "If you were in difficulty, your job was to keep Mr. Truman from rushing out and taking up the cudgels on your behalf, and to remind him that you were there to take the blows."[4] Truman was reluctant to censure. George Elsey speculated that a president might have to be "cruel . . . and cold-blooded and cast friends aside," but Truman "couldn't quite cast aside some people."[5]

In retirement, Truman demonstrated a commendable consistency toward associates and the charges against them. In preparation for his memoirs, he ruminated about corruption. He discussed ethics of officials and his own code of ethics during his career. "In all this long career I had certain rules which I followed win, lose or draw," he insisted, noting that he never handled political money, that he refused gifts and favors, and that he made no speeches for money or expenses while holding national office. "There were opportunities by the wholesale for making immense amounts of money at the county level and also in the Senate. I lived on the salary I was entitled to and considered that I was employed by the taxpayers, and the people of my county, state and nation." Truman concluded, "I would much rather be an honorable public servant and known as such than to be the richest man in the world."[6] In a short memo on political ethics, Truman claimed that a public official is "a servant of all the people in his constituency. He cannot honestly serve the people if he is in the employment of outside interests." After examining regulations for reporting receipts and monitoring contributions, he stated, "The objective of all these rules and regulations is to have public officials without obligation to special interests."[7]

In the spring of 1953, weeks after leaving the White House, the Trumans joined Edwin Pauley and his family at the Pauley's Hawaiian retreat, Coconut Island. It was the first real vacation Truman enjoyed in many years. Although Pauley's nomination as under secretary of the navy had caused embarrassment to the administration in its early days, the relationship between the two men had continued to be warm. When Pauley's civic activities in Los Angeles led to Vice-President Richard M. Nixon's attendance at a reception at his house, Pauley assured Truman that he had nothing to do with inviting Nixon. Truman reassured Pauley by saying, "You know me well enough to know that whenever I have reason to disagree with one of my friends, he hears about it before anyone else does."[8] Later, in 1969, when Truman was so infirm that he could hardly leave his home in Independence, Pauley and his wife came for a visit, to pay their respects to their friend, to stand by him.

In retirement, Truman suffered the humiliation of having his former appointments secretary, Matthew J. Connelly, and a former assistant attorney general, T. Lamar Caudle, indicted by a federal grand jury on a charge of conspiracy to defraud the government. The indictments came out of the 1951 conviction of a St. Louis shoe broker, Irving Sachs, president of Shu-Stiles, who had pleaded guilty to income-tax evasion and had been fined $40,000 but avoided a prison term because of ill health. According to the indictment, Sachs's attorney, Harry J. Schwimmer (himself indicted two weeks before Caudle and Connelly) had offered money, negotiable instruments, and gifts to Connelly and Caudle to prevent Sachs's indictment, prosecution, and imprisonment. Connelly's association with the former president went back to the Truman committee, when he had become acquainted with Truman's friend Tom Evans and Evans's attorney, Schwimmer. Connelly provided Washington introductions and assistance to Evans and Schwimmer on a range of matters, none of which he considered improper. On Schwimmer's recommendation, Evans in 1949 lent Connelly $750 to inspect oil stocks. Unknown to Connelly, Schwimmer repaid Evans and added $2,850 to the investment, purchasing a $3,600 royalty. Schwimmer sent Connelly monthly dividends and later arranged sale of the royalties for $1,650. Schwimmer made gifts of clothing to Connelly. These transactions, coupled with evidence that Connelly had spoken to Internal Revenue Commissioner George Schoeneman, to the chief counsel for BIR, Charles Oliphant, and to Caudle about the Sachs case, provided the substance of the government's charges against Connelly.[9] The former presidential aide claimed that his involvement in the case resulted from the manipulations of Schwimmer, that he had made phone calls as a favor to Evans. When he explained the situation to Truman, he recalled that the president told him, "Well, you know, and I know, they're not after you, they're after me." Connelly responded, "In other words, I'm the fall guy." "You could say that," Truman replied.[10]

The trial took several bizarre twists that formed the basis for subsequent appeals. The Schwimmer case was severed from that of Connelly and Caudle when Schwimmer suffered a heart attack on 23 May 1956. Schwimmer's absence prevented testimony on ambiguous evidence in the case against Connelly.[11] When the jury returned a guilty verdict on 14 June, Connelly and Caudle filed motions for acquittal or mistrial based on disputed evidence, and they contested rulings of the court on evidence, constitution of the jury (jurors were admitted only from rural areas surrounding St. Louis), and venue. Judge Rubey M. Hulen, who had been under medication for severe depression during the course of the trial, reserved judgment. He expressed ambivalence about Connelly's guilt, describing him as "a glad hander and a greeter" who had "done nothing more than I might have done."[12] On the day the judge was to enter a hospital for electroshock therapy, and shortly before he was to rule on the pending motions, he committed suicide. Hulen's successor, Judge Gunnar H. Nordbye, refused to grant the Connelly and Caudle petitions because, he ruled, actions of the two defendants had furthered the scheme perpetrated by Schwimmer and Sachs. "The crucial question is did they do so with an evil and corrupt intent, as charged in the indictment? The jury concluded that they did." Nordbye let that decision stand.[13] The case was appealed, but the Supreme Court refused to review.

Truman considered the verdict "a travesty which I am sure will be straightened out eventually."[14] Convinced of Connelly's innocence, he had only the highest praise for him. "Matthew Connelly is in a class by himself," the president wrote. "There never was a better man in his position!"[15] Members of Truman's presidential staff were similarly incredulous at the verdict. George E. Allen, formerly director of the RFC, Rep. Morgan M. Moulder, and former Republican House Majority Leader Charles Halleck were character witnesses at the trial. Others were convinced of a political vendetta by the Eisenhower administration. Donald Dawson called Connelly a "victim of politics."[16] Brig. Gen. C. J. Mara considered the case "completely political," that Attorney General Herbert Brownell was behind it.[17] Charles Murphy saw "one of the worst cases of political persecution that I've ever heard of. It appears to me that the Eisenhower administration, at least the Attorney General, came into office with the purpose of doing everything he possibly could do to discover and make some kind of case of wrongdoing against the Truman administration."[18] Moulder suggested that the jury may have been "carefully selected to return a verdict of guilty."[19] Evans considered the case a personal tragedy; he realized too late that Schwimmer was using their friendship to curry favor with an innocent Connelly, who "never did anything crooked in his life."[20]

While the case was under appeal, Truman agreed to speak

at a hundred-dollar-a-plate dinner organized to defray Connelly's legal expenses on 19 September, 1959 in Boston. House Majority Leader John W. McCormack served as chairman of the dinner, and Richard Cardinal Cushing was on the dais. Connelly's attorney, Jacob Lashly, feared that the publicity might jeopardize Connelly's appeal, but Truman assured him it was a "testimonial dinner."[21] Dewey Stone, a Boston businessman, warned that the idea of a dinner was "not in good taste."[22] Nevertheless, Truman gave a fiery speech that delighted Democratic partisans, blasting the Eisenhower administration for its "unprecedented *persecution* and not prosecution of members of my staff" (emphasis added). He alleged that "individual rights of the people haven't been protected since 1952."[23] The Boston press reported $150,000 raised for Connelly. Actually, receipts had been less than $56,000, of which Connelly received $28,467.95.[24]

Connelly's appeal then ran its course. He and Caudle began their prison terms on 4 May 1960. Truman described the sentence as one of the worst miscarriages of justice in his time: "I think Mr. Connelly was railroaded."[25] The cartoonist Herblock portrayed Connelly and Caudle entering prison together, heads bowed over the caption, "They were imprudent in the wrong administration."[26]

Connelly spent only six months in prison, but Truman was not ready to let the matter drop. In 1961 he sought a full pardon for his former appointments secretary, and he wrote Attorney General Robert Kennedy, claiming Connelly and Caudle had been "victims of injustice growing out of a calculated campaign by the Republican Administration to cast a shadow on my Administration." He said that Judge George Moore, who had called the grand jury, had gone to "more than usual lengths" to have Connelly and Caudle indicted. He described Judge Nordbye, who took the case after the death of Hulen, as a "violent partisan."[27] Kennedy responded on 24 April to inform Truman that he was studying the matter carefully and that he would let him know when he had decided on the proper disposition of the case.[28]

Truman wrote again to thank Kennedy, providing a more detailed account of his perspective on the Connelly case. "There was a condition in Missouri at the time they were persecuted [*sic*] that was most deplorable," Truman wrote. He explained that both Judge Moore, "who was very prejudiced against the Administration of which I was the head," and Judge Hulen had been appointed while Truman was in the Senate because of the recommendation of his colleague, Sen. Bennett Clark. Truman continued:

> Judge Moore called a Grand Jury and instructed them to indict anyone possible who had served with me or under me. That Grand Jury indicted Matthew Connelly on the strength of the fact that some $750.00 had not been reported on his income tax return. It was a ridiculous procedure. Rubey Hulen tried the cases and as soon as they were over he went out in the back yard of his home and shot himself because he knew he had not handled the cases in the interest of justice. Then the Court of Appeals sent an old Republican Judge from Minnesota to review them and he did not even read the record but he refused another trial. That is the situation as it is today. It was a fixed Grand Jury, an unjust trial and an unjust review—not for justice but for a political attempt to discredit a former President of the United States.[29]

Truman was convinced of an injustice, but he was unfamiliar with the most basic details of the case. Connelly had not been charged with failing to report $750. Though the $750 in question had been entered into evidence, it was not the subject of the indictment. Truman impugned the motives of all three judges in the case, condemning their actions on the basis of misleading or incomplete information. The assertion that Hulen had committed suicide because he had mishandled the case ignored Hulen's treatment for depression. The inference that Nordbye had not read the record of the trial was likewise erroneous; Nordbye rendered a considered decision that reflected intimate knowledge of the evidence that had been presented.[30] There were procedural decisions made during the course of the trial on which an appeal or a pardon might well have been based; Truman touched on none of them in his petition to Kennedy. His defense of Connelly was not based on the substance of the case.

Kennedy answered Truman with a handwritten note, saying, "I know how much your heart is set on the Caudle Connelly matter," and guaranteeing his personal attention.[31]

Truman thanked him on 12 June. The matter rested
through the year, however, and by the beginning of 1962,
Truman's patience had run out. There had been trouble
between Truman and Robert Kennedy earlier; their relationship never would be cordial. Truman had given Kennedy a lecture when they met during the 1960 campaign.
He remarked privately that "they say young Bobby has
changed for the better. . . . I can never understand and
never will if I live to be a hundred . . . why it takes so long
these days for somebody to learn the difference between
right and wrong."[32] Angered by the delay, he wrote Kennedy again, this time without the trim of courtesy. "I've
never spoken to your brother about this and I don't intend
to. But if you think that I enjoy mistreatment and injustice
to one of my best employees, you are mistaken, so don't
smile at me any more unless you want to do justice to Matt
Connelly, which is the right thing—a full pardon."[33]

A few months later, Truman sent Connelly an encouraging note, although his opinion of Kennedy had not moder-
ated. "Matt: It looks as if that damned Irish Atty. Gen. may
come across. He had a letter from me not long ago he'll
never forget. I don't like him!"[34] Connelly still had several
months to wait. Finally, on 22 November, 1962, President
Kennedy issued the pardon. Truman thanked the president
for erasing the "unjust conviction."[35]

Truman always had confidence in Connelly; not so in Caudle. Shortly after the latter's dismissal late in 1951, Truman
wrote, "Caudle was discharged because he did not handle
his office efficiently."[36] In September 1954, Drew Pearson
wrote Truman on Caudle's behalf, having learned of a com-
forting letter Truman had written to Attorney General J.
Howard McGrath after his dismissal in April 1952. Pearson
urged a similar letter to Caudle, suggesting that Caudle had
remained loyal to Truman and had demonstrated no bitterness about the firing. Truman replied curtly, "I am not in
any position to write the letter which you suggest. I regret it
very much."[37] Adversaries in the past, Truman and Pearson
again were opposed diametrically on the Connelly-Caudle
case. Pearson later wrote in his diary, "I have always thought
that Connelly was guilty as hell but that Caudle, while dumb,
was innocent."[38] But Truman was unmoved by a pleading

letter in which Caudle proclaimed his innocence in the Sachs
case. Although the president mentioned Caudle along with
Connelly in his first letters appealing to Robert Kennedy for
a pardon, he did so only because their cases had been joined.
Subsequent exchanges referred only to Connelly; when only
Connelly was pardoned, Truman thanked the president
profusely without mention of Caudle.[39] Caudle was eventually pardoned in 1965 by President Lyndon B. Johnson.
What distinguished Connelly from Caudle was Truman's
personal relationship with his former appointments secretary. Truman trusted his own political instincts and his ability
to judge men. When someone close to him was criticized,
Truman consistently interpreted the attack as against the
president rather than the individual. Defending his associates, Truman was defending himself, his record, his personal integrity. Caudle had neither a personal relationship
nor an official position close enough to the president that
Truman himself would feel threatened by charges against
the former assistant attorney general. Further, Truman considered Caudle to have been inefficient. Distance both per-
mitted and promoted greater objectivity than would likely
have existed in the assessment of the performance of close
associates.

Perhaps the closest of those associates, Harry Vaughan,
kept in close touch with Truman during retirement, and
their correspondence touched the five-percenter inquiry
of 1949 and other charges of improprieties. Truman always was sympathetic—consoling, encouraging, reassuring.
Vaughan provided his boss with nostalgic reminiscence, kept
him posted on associates, and monitored the press for comment on Truman's presidency.

The first years of retirement were personally difficult for
Vaughan. It was not simply the slower pace. Vaughan and
Colonel Mara, his friend and former assistant military aide,
sought to form an import-export business, but after a year,
Vaughan informed Truman, "Neal Mara and I have concluded that we might as well face the facts. Drew [Pearson]
and his friends of the press have discredited me to such an
extent that I am unable to get a client. There is no use being
indignant about it and saying that it is an injustice. It's a fact
and there is nothing to do about it. A friend of mine might

not believe a word of all that has been said but he fears that any potential customers might believe it."[40] Truman encouraged his friend. "I have always understood these people better than they think they understand themselves, and I think you are a shining example of the political situation when conditions change radically." He assured Vaughan he should not get discouraged, that things could not always be dismal.[41] Vaughan continued to be perturbed and complained to Truman. "I have decided that anyone connected with the newspaper racket should be greeted by a poke in the nose. In payment for what he is sure to do."[42] Truman counseled that there was no "reason for your 'closing' up entirely. Of course, these fellows always like to make out you and I are something we are not but they have never proved it."[43]

An article in the *Saturday Evening Post* finally prompted Vaughan to sue. He had been upset by previous articles in the magazine; he had written a letter denying the charges in one and considered suing over another early in 1955. The basis for Vaughan's suit was the caption of a picture of him accompanying an article by Pearson in the issue of 3 November 1956: "Many Pearson charges against Harry Vaughan were later confirmed by testimony before Senate committee."[44] In his lawsuit, Vaughan maintained that the caption made it appear that he had committed an offense while in office and that he had been officially "charged" with such an offense.[45] The case went to trial early in 1959 and Vaughan claimed that the judge, whom he characterized as "the biggest dope I ever saw on the bench," tried it in a prejudicial manner, doing "everything he could do to block us."[46] Mara agreed that the judge ruled constantly for the defense,[47] but a judgement was rendered in Vaughan's favor, for $10,000.

Vaughan then turned to writing a book in defense of his White House employment. Within a year, he and his wife completed a manuscript of seventy thousand words, "Whipping Boy First Class," that gave his point of view. The Vaughans showed the manuscript to several publishers but received a cool reception. Louis Zara of Crown Publishers expressed interest and suggested a foreword by President Truman.[48] Margaret Vaughan appealed to Truman. "We have had to slowly face the fact, and acknowledge it over the past two years, that Harry is a scorned and discredited man.

I—and I am sure you—do not want that to be what he must live with for the remaining years of his life. If, as Louis Zara believes, we can change this through an effort of our own, that I want to do."[49]

When Truman sent the foreword, it was everything the Vaughans had hoped for. The first six pages of the nine-page, handwritten document recounted a long relationship, concluding that Vaughan was "an efficient, able and energetic public official."[50] The balance was a bitter attack on the press for its treatment of Vaughan and other members of the administration, written with such vitriol that Vaughan suggested it should be made less argumentive. In the final pages of the foreword, Truman claimed that soon after he took office,

> Such slick purveyors of untruth as *Time*, *Newsweek*, and the *United States News & World Report* along with Billy Hearst's sewer press and Bertie McCormick's sabotage sheets [*Chicago Tribune*] began a campaign of misrepresentation and vilification hardly ever equalled in this country's history. . . . *Time* put a special reporter on the job to follow Harry Vaughan with instructions to distort and misquote every action and statement of my military aide. . . . But it is to the everlasting credit of [Secretary of State Dean] Acheson, [Secretary of the Treasury John W.] Snyder, [Secretary of State George C.] Marshall and Harry Vaughan that they faced the lies and misrepresentations with fortitude and did their jobs as duty called for with honor and credit to this great "free press" Republic of the United States of America.[51]

Crown Publishers backed out, however, and the manuscript never was published.

*   *   *

Truman assuredly had his troubles as president. Although he never was charged with personal involvement in corruption, the issue hounded him. The Pendergast association was hard to shake and was revived during the Kefauver crime investigation. Opportunities for private gain abounded in an uncertain postwar economy, and expanding layers of bureaucracy shielded wrongdoers while problems festered. But these were conditions, not causes. It was Truman's remarkable inability to separate himself from inconvenient people, coupled with his proclivity to judge issues in terms of personalities, that produced tempests from teapots. Truman found it hard to censure friends and harder still to break with them. His conviction that attacks on associates were aimed at the president was a rationale that aggravated these tendencies because it made all such criticism seem political rather than substantial, causing Truman to rely more on his judgment of people than on evidence that might have implicated them.

Harsh criticism resulting from these probably minor flaws in Truman's makeup dominated contemporary assessments of the administration. Uncompromising defense of subordinates made the president seem intransigent and hardened adversary relationships with congressional committees and columnists. Issues were magnified as resistance intensified and led to impasse. Joined with Korea and Communism, these issues contributed to the plunge in Truman's public rating in the early 1950s.

The postpresidential tribulations of Connelly, Caudle, and Vaughan were echoes of corruption that gradually disappeared during Truman's retirement; the administration is remembered less for scandal than for the integrity of its president. As his successors encountered troubles of their own, the corruption under Truman paled. After campaigning on corruption in 1952, both Eisenhower and Nixon experienced more serious problems during their presidencies. One student of the Eisenhower years beheld more conflicts of interest there than in the administration whose "mess" the general had promised to clean up and suggested that the Eisenhower incidents were more serious.[52] President Nixon's entrapment in Watergate coincided with a revival of interest in Truman. The feisty, forthright, "buck-stops-here" assertiveness of Truman offered an attractive contrast to the leaf-by-leaf revelations of the Watergate coverup. Even as Nixon insisted that he was not a crook, biographies informed readers that Truman had affixed three-cent stamps to personal letters while in the White House, refusing to misuse his franking privilege.[53] Truman's shortcomings, moreover, now seem less onerous, intense loyalty to subordinates seeming preferable to Nixon's acceptance of a subordinate's proposal to leave a director of the FBI "twisting slowly, slowly in the wind."

Truman's reputation in the 1980s is strong. The seeming impotence of the presidency in later years enhanced his image as an executive who simplified the complexities of the postwar world. If some writers have continued to criticize Truman as an architect of the Cold War, the American people now look back with pride on an era of national strength, world leadership, and presidential decisiveness.

NOTES

Notes to Chapter 1
A Political Philosophy

1. Frank McNaughton and Walter Hehmeyer, *This Man Truman*, p. 122. The figure of $15 billion saved by the committee is from Alfred Steinberg, *The Man from Missouri: The Life and Times of Harry S. Truman*, p. 187.

2. Frank Mason, *Truman and the Pendergasts*, p. 156.

3. Truman, personal notes, 3 December 1930–14 May 1934, transcribed by Eben A. Ayers, Harry S. Truman Personal Handwritten Notes folder, Ayers Papers, Truman Library. It is in these notes that Truman discussed at length his relationship with Pendergast. The original of these autobiographical notes, in Truman's handwriting on Pickwick Hotel stationery, is in the Harry S. Truman, County Judge folder, PSF Longhand Notes File, Truman Library (hereinafter Pickwick Hotel Notes). Excerpts from these notes have been published in Robert H. Ferrell, ed., *The Autobiography of Harry S. Truman*.

4. Truman, autobiographical statement, 1945, p. 12, Truman Autobiography—Autobiographical Sketch folder, PSF Biographical File, Truman Papers, Truman Library (hereinafter Truman, autobiographical statement, 1945). This document was written during the brief months of Truman's vice-presidency. It has been published in Charles Robbins, *Last of His Kind: An Informal Portrait of Harry S. Truman*, pp. 29–31, 36–38 passim. It also has been used as the principle source for Ferrell, ed., *The Autobiography of Harry S. Truman*, pp. 17–20 passim. Other information on Truman's relationship with his mother in this paragraph is from Jonathan Daniels, *The Man of Independence*, pp. 49–50.

5. Henry A. Bundschu, Truman Biography, 15 December 1948, p. 8, Truman Biography—Henry A. Bundschu folder, PSF Biographical File, Truman Papers, Truman Library.

6. Truman, autobiographical statement, 1945, p. 13. The preceding information on Truman's biblical training is from Truman, Pickwick Hotel Notes, 14 May 1934; Truman, autobiographical statement, 1945, p. 12.

7. Truman, Masonic history, Longhand Personal Names Memos folder, PSF Longhand Notes File, Truman Papers, Truman Library.

8. Truman, personal note, 15 August 1950, Longhand Notes, undated folder, PSF Longhand Notes File, Truman Papers, Truman Library. Truman recorded the prayer on White House stationery with an introductory note, "A prayer said over and over all my life from eighteen years old and younger." He also wrote it on another occasion on an undated slip of paper, explaining that he had said the prayer since his high school days; the note recounted positions he had held during that period, from working in an Independence drugstore to the presidency. The reminiscing, nostalgic tone of the note underscores the significance the prayer held for Truman. In its entirety, the prayer read: "Oh! Almighty and Everlasting God, Creator of Heaven, Earth and the Universe: Help me to be, to think, to act what is right, because it is right; make me truthful, honest and hon-

orable in all things; make me intellectually honest for the sake of right and honor and without thought of reward of me. Give me the ability to be charitable, forgiving and patient with my fellowmen—help me to understand their motives and their shortcomings even as Thou understandest mine! Amen, Amen, Amen."

9. Harold F. Gosnell, *Truman's Crisis: A Political Biography of Harry S. Truman*, p. 10.

10. Truman, autobiographical statement, 1945, p. 15.

11. Truman, Pickwick Hotel Notes, 15 May 1934.

12. Truman, autobiographical statement, 1945, p. 15.

13. Ferrell, ed., *The Autobiography of Harry S. Truman*, p. 55. The preceding information in this paragraph is from Steinberg, *The Man from Missouri*, pp. 54–56; Daniels, *The Man of Independence*, pp. 105–7; Truman, autobiographical statement, 1945, pp. 24–25.

14. Steinberg, *The Man from Missouri*, pp. 56–58; Daniels, *The Man of Independence*, pp. 107–9; Truman to Boxley, 2 March 1935, Fred A. Boxley folder, PSF Historical Files—Pre-Presidential Files, Truman Papers, Truman Library.

15. Truman, Interview, p. 4, Merchandising Venture, 1919–1921 folder, PPF Memoirs File, Truman Papers, Truman Library.

16. Truman, Pickwick Hotel Hotes, 15 May 1934. The rest of the paragraph is based on Cyril Clemens, *The Man from Missouri: A Biography of Harry S. Truman*, p. 44; Gosnell, *Truman's Crisis*, p. 47; "Is President Truman an Honorable Man?" *The American Mercury* 72: 546–50; Boxley to Truman, 8 January 1935, 17 January 1935, 26 February 1935, and Truman to Boxley, 11 January 1935, 2 March 1935, Fred A. Boxley folder, PSF Historical Files—Pre-Presidential Files, Truman Papers, Truman Library; Daniels, *The Man of Independence*, p. 108.

17. Gosnell, *Truman's Crisis*, pp. 66–68; Truman, memo, 10 January 1952, Longhand Personal Memos, 1952 folder, PSF Longhand Notes File, Truman Papers, Truman Library.

18. Daniels, *The Man of Independence*, p. 113.

19. Harry S. Truman, *Year of Decisions*, vol. 1 of *Memoirs by Harry S. Truman*, pp. 136–37; Daniels, *The Man of Independence*, p. 113; Truman, autobiographical statement, 1945, pp. 26–27; Missouri Politics folder, PPF Memoirs File, Truman Papers, Truman Library; Lyle W. Dorsett, *The Pendergast Machine*, p. 71.

20. Dorsett, *The Pendergast Machine*, p. 71.

21. Truman, "Jackson County," Longhand Personal Memos, 1952 folder, PSF Longhand Notes File, Truman Papers, Truman Library.

22. Mason, *Truman and the Pendergasts*, p. 112.

23. Maurice M. Milligan, *Missouri Waltz: The Inside Story of the Pendergast Machine by the Man Who Smashed It*, p. 218.

24. Truman, memo, 10 January 1952, Longhand Personal Memos, 1952 folder, PSF Longhand Notes File, Truman Papers, Truman Library.

25. Milligan, *Missouri Waltz*, pp. 218–19.

26. Ibid., p. 20.

27. Lyle W. Dorsett, "Truman and the Pendergast Machine," pp. 5–6; Eugene Francis Schmidtlein, "Truman the Senator," p. 51.

28. Truman, Pickwick Hotel Notes.

29. Truman, memo, 10 January 1952, Longhand Personal Memos, 1952 folder, PSF Longhand Notes Files, Truman Papers, Truman Library.

Comment on Truman's acceptance of patronage as political spoils is in Dorestt, "Truman and the Pendergast Machine," p. 6.

30. Truman to A. V. Burrowes, 8 January 1944, Truman—Personal 1944 folder, Lou E. Holland Papers, Truman Library; Truman, autobiographical statement, 1945, pp. 28–35; Truman, memo, 10 January 1952, Longhand Personal Memos, 1952 folder, PSF Longhand Notes File, Truman Papers, Truman Library; William Hillman, *Mr. President*, pp. 185–89. (Hillman's account is based on the 10 January 1952 memo); Walter Hehmeyer, Oral History Interview by James R. Fuchs, p. 48 (Hehmeyer referred to a five- or six-page, single-spaced statement Truman dictated on the Pendergast days that Hehmeyer and Frank McNaughton used in preparation of their book, *This Man Truman*; the account of the Truman-Pendergast relationship in that book conforms to the others described here; McNaughton and Hehmeyer, *This Man Truman*, pp. 64–70); Truman, *Year of Decisions*, pp. 139–41; Robbins, *Last of His Kind*, pp. 62–63 (Robbins recounts an interview with Col. Rufus Burrus, a friend of Truman; Burrus asserted that Truman had claimed that he made no commitment to Pendergast when Truman first ran for Eastern District judge and that Pendergast "never at any time asked me to do anything about appointing anybody," though Truman admitted to consulting with Pendergast on some appointments); Robert Irvin, Oral History Interview, pp. 59–60.

31. Truman, Pickwick Hotel Notes, 3 December 1930–11 May 1934. Margaret Truman used this account in the preparation of her biography of her father and published excerpts of it therein. Margaret Truman, *Harry S. Truman*, pp. 71–75.

32. Truman, memo, 10 January 1952, Longhand Personal Memos, 1952 folder, PSF Longhand Notes File, Truman Papers, Truman Library.

33. Truman, Pickwick Hotel Notes.

34. Truman, memo, 10 January 1952, Longhand Personal Memos, 1952 folder, PSF Longhand Notes File, Truman Papers, Truman Library; Truman, *Year of Decisions*, pp. 140–41; Hillman, *Mr. President*, p. 187; McNaughton and Hehmeyer, *This Man Truman*, p. 68; Daniels, *The Man of Independence*, pp. 146–47; Steinberg, *The Man from Missouri*, p. 89; Mason, *Truman and the Pendergasts*, pp. 83–84; Robbins, *The Last of His Kind*, p. 72.

35. Truman, Pickwick Hotel Notes. Harold Gosnell, in his political biography of Truman, noted another exception to Truman's supposed independence from Tom Pendergast that is related to the incident concerning the contractors. When Truman sought to place a bond issue on the ballot to finance roads and other civic improvements, he felt compelled to get Pendergast's approval to go forward with the proposal. Gosnell correctly commented that Truman's action was "an interesting recognition of Pendergast's power," since the Boss had no official government position to sanction bond issues. Gosnell, *Truman's Crises*, p. 85.

36. Truman, Pickwick Hotel Notes.

37. Schmidtlein, "Truman the Senator," pp. 46–48.

38. Truman, Pickwick Hotel Notes.

39. Margaret Truman, *Harry S. Truman*, p. 73. An account of the incident is in Steinberg, *The Man from Missouri*, p. 97.

40. Truman, memo, 10 January 1952, Longhand Personal Memos, 1952 folder, PSF Longhand Notes File, Truman Papers, Truman Library.

41. Truman, Pickwick Hotel Notes.

42. Truman, memo, 10 January 1952, Longhand Personal Memos, 1952 folder, PSF Longhand Notes File, Truman Library; Truman to A. V. Burrowes, 8 January 1944, Truman—Personal 1944 folder, Holland Papers, Truman Library.

43. Truman, speech, untitled and undated, p. 4, and Truman, speech, untitled and undated on County Court stationery, p. 7, Addresses of Harry S. Truman, 1929–1933 folder, PSF Historical Files—Pre-Presidential File, Truman Papers, Truman Library.

44. Truman, speech, untitled and undated, p. 4, and Truman, speech, apparently URICH homecoming, undated, Addresses of Harry S. Truman, 1929–1933 folder, PSF Historical Files—Pre-Presidential File, Truman Papers, Truman Library.

45. Truman, speech, apparently URICH homecoming, undated, Addresses of Harry S. Truman, 1929–1933 folder, PSF Historical Files—Pre-Presidential File, Truman Papers, Truman Library.

46. Truman, speech, untitled and undated but after 7 October 1929, Addresses of Harry S. Truman, 1929–1933 folder, PSF Historical Files—Pre-Presidential File, Truman Papers, Truman Library. Information on the Kansas City Law School speech is in Daniels, *The Man of Independence*, p. 128.

47. Truman, speech, Raytown High School Commencement, 14 May 1931, Addresses of Harry S. Truman, 1929–1933 folder, PSF Historical File—Pre-Presidential File, Truman Papers, Truman Library.

48. Truman, Pickwick Hotel Notes.

49. Truman, memo, 10 January 1952, Longhand Personal Memos, 1952 folder, PSF Longhand Notes File, Truman Papers, Truman Library.

50. Truman, Pickwick Hotel Notes.

51. Gosnell, *Truman's Crises*, p. 102; Daniels, *The Man of Independence*, pp. 162, 170.

52. Daniels, *The Man of Independence*, p. 170. Information on charges of fraudulent election procedures is from Gosnell, *Truman's Crises*, pp. 104–6.

53. Schmidtlein, "Truman the Senator," pp. 102–03; Dorestt, "Truman and the Pendergrast Machine," p. 6; Dorsett; *The Pendergast Machine*, pp. 110–11; Gosnell, *Truman's Crises*, p. 117; Truman, memo, 10 January 1952, Longhand Personal Memos, 1952 folder, PSF Longhand Notes File, Truman Papers, Truman Library. Peter Brandt, a reporter for the *St. Louis Post-Dispatch*, told of an instance in which railroad officials attempted to pressure Truman, through Pendergast, to call off an investigation of their company. Truman refused. Raymond P. Brandt, Oral History Interview by Jerry N. Hess, p. 7.

54. Margaret Truman, *Harry S. Truman*, pp. 114–17; Dorsett, *The Pendergast Machine*, pp. 133–36. Although Jim Pendergast was a personal friend, Truman quickly lost respect for his political acumen. In 1948, Truman wrote in his sporadically maintained diary: "Jim Pendergast has turned out to be a dud. What a chance he had—in spite of old Tom's weaknesses. Jim can't keep his word. Tom never failed to keep his." Truman, diary, 2 August 1948, Memoirs—Diaries folder, PPF Memoirs File, Truman Papers, Truman Library.

55. Cited in Steinberg, *The Man from Missouri*, pp. 159–61.

56. Margaret Truman, *Harry S. Truman*, p. 117.

57. Daniels, *The Man of Independence*, pp. 197–99; Brandt, Oral History

Interview, p. 91; Dorsett, *The Pendergast Machine*, p. 136; Gosnell, *Truman's Crises*, p. 148.
   58. Ferrell, ed., *The Autobiography of Harry S. Truman*, pp. 55, 130; Daniels, *The Man of Independence*, pp. 213–14; Robbins, *Last of His Kind*, p. 85; Margaret Truman, *Harry S. Truman*, p. 135.
   59. Daniels, *The Man of Independence*, pp. 213–14; Gosnell, *Truman's Crises*, pp. 150–51; Truman, *Year of Decisions*, pp. 162–63; Margaret Truman, *Harry S. Truman*, p. 136.
   60. Ferrell, ed., *The Autobiography of Harry S. Truman*, pp. 68–70, 131.
   61. Truman, untitled and undated notes on Senate career, p. 4, Longhand Personal Memos, PSF Longhand Notes File, Truman Papers, Truman Library.
   62. Steinberg, *The Man from Missouri*, pp. 180–81; Gosnell, *Truman's Crises*, pp. 154–57. The membership of the committee, which initially numbered seven, was soon expanded to ten. Six of these were Democrats: Truman, Tom Connally of Texas, Carl Hatch of New Mexico, James Mead of New York, Mon Wallgren of Washington, and Harley Kilgore of West Virginia. The four committee Republicans were Joseph Ball of Minnesota, Owen Brewster of Maine, Harold Burton of Ohio, and Homer Ferguson of Michigan. Committee membership is discussed in Truman, *Year of Decisions*, pp. 164–65, 186.
   63. Truman, *Year of Decisions*, p. 167. The evaluation of the committee's strengths in this paragraph is based on Gosnell, *Truman Crises*, p. 157.
   64. Wilbur Sparks, Oral History Interview by Jerry N. Hess, pp. 29–30. Other sources for this discussion of the committee staff are Sister M. Patrick Ellen Maher, "The Role of the Chairman of a Congressional Investigating Committee of the Senate to Investigate the National Defense Programs, 1941–1948," p. 251; Daniels, *The Man of Independence*, p. 225; Truman, *Year of Decisions*, pp. 166–67; Sparks, Oral History Interview, pp. 28, 55, 56, 59–61; George Meader, Oral History Interview by Charles T. Morrissey, p. 13; Hehmeyer, Oral History Interview, pp. 2, 3, 123.
   65. Truman to Vaughan, 1 September 1942, Harry H. Vaughan—Personal File folder, Senatorial File, Truman Papers, Truman Library. Sources for information on Truman's leadership of the committee are Truman, untitled biographical statement, undated, Longhand Personal Memos, undated folder, PSF Longhand Notes File, Truman Papers, Truman Library; Maher, "The Role of the Chairman," pp. 250–51; Schmidtlein, "Truman the Senator," pp. 240–41; Meader, Oral History Interview, p. 13; Sparks, Oral History Interview, p. 186.
   66. Truman, memo, Truman Committee folder, PPF Memoirs File, Truman Papers, Truman Library.
   67. "Senator Truman," *Kansas City Star*, 8 March 1943, Harry S. Truman—Personal, January 1943 folder, Senatorial and Vice-Presidential Files, Truman Papers, Truman Library.

Notes to Chapter 2
Early Allegations

   1. Margaret Truman, *Harry S. Truman*, p. 284.
   2. Ibid.; Robert J. Donovan, *Conflict and Crisis: The Presidency of Harry S. Truman, 1945–1948*, pp. 177–78; Eleanor W. Schoenebaum, ed., *Political Profiles: The Truman Years*, p. 577.

3. Harold L. Ickes, "Man to Man!" undated (approximately May 1946), OF 210B (1952–1953) folder, Truman Papers, Truman Library.

4. Information on the Allen nomination and critical comment are found in Donovan, *Conflict and Crisis*, p. 177; Matthew J. Connelly, Oral History Interview by Jerry N. Hess, pp. 244–45; Schoenebaum, ed., *Political Profiles: The Truman Years*, p. 8; Frank McNaughton to David Hulburd, 19 January 1946, Allen-Symington-Pauley appointments folder, Mc-Naughton Papers, Truman Library. Allen's response is explained in George E. Allen, Oral History Interview by Jerry N. Hess, pp. 42–43; Allen to Truman, 25 March 1946, George E. Allen folder, PSF Chronological Name File, Truman Papers, Truman Library.

5. Schoenebaum, ed., *Political Profiles: The Truman Years*, p. 435; Truman, Personal Memo, 2 June 1954, Longhead Personal Memos, 1954 folder, PSF Longhand Notes File, Truman Papers, Truman Library.

6. Margaret Truman, *Harry S. Truman*, p. 291. Information on early support for Pauley by Roosevelt, Forrestal, and Truman in this and the following paragraph is found in Forrestal, memorandum to Roosevelt, 15 March 1945, Cabinet, Secretary of the Navy folder, PSF Subject File, Truman Papers, Truman Library; Forrestal, memorandum to Truman, 29 October 1945, Edwin Pauley folder, PSF, Truman Papers, Truman Library; Truman, memo, undated (13 or 14 February 1946), Longhand Personal Memos, 1946 folder, PSF Longhand Note File, Truman Papers, Truman Library; Truman, interview by Harris, p. 5, Cabinet folder, PPF Memoirs File—Interviews with Truman, Truman Papers, Truman Library; Harry S. Truman, *Year of Decisions*, vol. 1 of *Memoirs by Harry S. Truman*, p. 553.

7. Eben A. Ayers, diary, 18 January 1946, Ayers Papers, Truman Library.

8. Truman to Jonathan Daniels (unsent), 26 February 1950, Jonathan Daniels folder, PSF Personal File, Truman Papers, Truman Library. Other Truman assessments of Ickes are in Truman, *Year of the Decisions*, pp. 554–55; Truman, memo evaluating cabinet members, undated, p. 10, Longhand Personal Memos folder, PSF Longhand Notes File, Truman Papers, Truman Library; Truman, memo, 14 January 1952, Longhand Personal Memos, 1952 folder, PSF Longhand Notes File, Truman Papers, Truman Library.

9. Margaret Truman, *Harry S. Truman*, p. 291; Matthew J. Connelly, Oral History Interview by Jerry N. Hess, p. 366.

10. Ernest R. Bartley, *The Tidelands Oil Controversy: A Legal and Historical Analysis*, pp. 3–6, 131–38; Michael W. Straus, memo to Ickes, 31 May 1945, Edwin Pauley Correspondence folder, Secretary of the Interior File, Box 223, Ickes Papers, Library of Congress.

11. Robert Engler, *The Politics of Oil: A Study of Private Power and Democratic Directions*, pp. 341–45; Ed Hidalgo, memo to Forrestal, 17 February 1946, General Correspondence 1944–1947 folder, Box 126, Records of the Secretary of the Navy James Forrestal, Record Group 80, General Records of the Department of the Navy, National Archives, Washington, D.C.; Bartley, *The Tidelands Oil Controversy*, pp. 144–58.

12. Harold L. Ickes, *The Lowering Clouds, 1939–41*, vol. 3 of *The Secret Diary of Harold L. Ickes*, pp. 58, 486, 624; Engler, *The Politics of Oil*, p. 341.

13. Cited in Donovan, *Conflict and Crisis*, p. 179; Ickes's diary entries of

29 April 1945 and 20 October 1945 referred to Pauley's efforts on behalf of the oil industry. Ibid., pp. 179–80.

14. Truman, memo, undated (13 or 14 February 1946), Longhand Personal Memos, 1946 folder, PSF Longhand Notes File, Truman Papers, Truman Library.

15. Donovan, *Conflict and Crisis*, p. 180.

16. McNaughton to David Hulburd, 19 January 1946, Allen-Symington-Pauley Appointments folder, McNaughton Papers, Truman Library; Truman memo, undated (13 or 14 February 1946), Longhand Personal Memos, 1946 folder, PSF Longhand Notes File, Truman Papers, Truman Library.

17. Tristam Coffin, *Missouri Compromise*, pp. 47–48. Other comments on the senators of the committee are in Engler, *The Politics of Oil*, p. 342; Donovan, *Conflict and Crisis*, p. 180.

18. Cited in Donovan, *Conflict and Crisis*, p. 180.

19. Truman, memo, undated (13 or 14 February 1946), Longhand Personal Memos, 1946 folder, PSF Longhand Notes File, Truman Papers, Truman Library. The next sentence in Truman's longhand memo was crossed out: "I said this because I knew his propensity for sensational statements making himself the hero." Truman recalled in his memoirs that he said to Ickes, "'Tell 'em the truth and be kind to Ed." Truman, *Year of Decisions*, p. 554.

20. Pauley statement, 4 February 1946, Edwin W. Pauley Correspondence folder, Box 223, Secretary of the Interior File, Ickes Papers, Library of Congress.

21. Warner W. Gardner, memo to Ickes, 13 February 1946, Edwin W. Pauley, 1946–1948 folder, Box 402, Ickes Papers, Library of Congress; Engler, *The Politics of Oil*, pp. 343–44.

22. Pauley statement, 4 February 1946, Edwin W. Pauley Correspondence folder, Box 223, Secretary of the Interior File, Ickes Papers, Library of Congress.

23. McNaughton to David Hulburd, 6 February 1946, p. 2, Ed Pauley folder, McNaughton Papers, Truman Library.

24. Ibid., pp. 2–6; Gardner, memo to Ickes, 13 February 1946, Edwin W. Pauley, 1946–1948 folder, Box 402, Ickes Papers, Library of Congress; "Edwin W. Pauley," Edwin W. Pauley Correspondence folder, Box 223, Secretary of the Interior File, Ickes Papers, Library of Congress.

25. "Edwin W. Pauley: September 6, 1944," Edwin W. Pauley Correspondence folder, Box 223, Secretary of the Interior File, Ickes Papers, Library of Congress. The ensuing discussion of this meeting is based on this memo and "Edwin W. Pauley," Edwin W. Pauley Correspondence folder, Box 223, Secretary of the Interior File, Ickes Papers, Library of Congress; McNaughton to Hulburd, 6 February 1946, Ed Pauley folder, McNaughton Papers, Truman Library; Memo on Abe Fortas testimony, Edwin W. Pauley, 1946–1948 folder, Box 402, Ickes Papers, Library of Congress; Helen E. Cunningham, memo to Ickes, 4 February 1946, Edwin W. Pauley Correspondence folder, Box 223, Secretary of the Interior File, Ickes Papers, Library of Congress.

26. Ickes, "Ed Pauley vs. Ed Pauley," Edwin W. Pauley Correspondence folder, Box 223, Secretary of the Interior File, Ickes Papers, Library of Congress.

27. Gardner, memo to Ickes, 13 February 1946, Edwin W. Pauley, 1946–1948 folder, Box 402, Ickes Papers, Library of Congress.

28. McNaughton to Hulburd, 6 February 1946, Ed Pauley folder, McNaughton Papers, Truman Library; Ayers, diary, 6 February 1946, Ayers Papers, Truman Library.

29. *Public Papers of the Presidents of the United States, Harry S. Truman, 1946*, p. 111.

30. Ickes to Truman, 12 February 1946, cited in *Baltimore Sun*, 14 February 1946, Truman Appointments folder, Democratic National Committee Clipping File, Truman Library.

31. *Baltimore Sun*, 14 February 1946, Truman Appointments folder, Democratic National Committee Clipping File, Truman Library.

32. Ayers, diary, 13 February 1946, Ayers Papers, Truman Library. The rest of this paragraph is based on this source. The following paragraph is based on Ayers's diary, 14 February 1946.

33. Truman, memo undated (13 or 14 February 1946), Longhand Personal Memos, 1946 folder, PSF Longhand Notes File, Truman Papers, Truman Library.

34. Donovan, *Conflict and Crisis*, p. 181.

35. *Public Papers of the Presidents, Truman, 1946*, pp. 119–21, 128.

36. Ibid., pp. 134, 146; Walter Lippmann, "Pauley Muddle as of Now," Assistant Secretary folder, OF 18A, Truman Papers, Truman Library.

37. "Evaluation Memorandum (M–55)," 71–1–7 folder, Box 126, Records of the Secretary of the Navy James Forrestal, 1940–1947, Record Group 80, General Records of the Department of the Navy, National Archives.

38. *Public Papers of the Presidents, Truman, 1946*, pp. 153–54.

39. Harold F. Gosnell, *Truman's Crises: A Political Biography of Harry S. Truman*, p. 286.

40. *Chicago Daily Tribune*, 14 March 1946, Truman Appointments folder, Democratic National Committee Clipping File, Truman Library.

41. Davis to Truman, 15 February 1946, and Truman to Davis, 21 February 1946, 931 Ickes folder, OF Name File, Truman Papers, Truman Library.

42. *Chicago Daily Tribune*, 14 March 1946, Truman Appointments folder, Democratic National Committee Clipping File, Truman Library.

43. Truman, memo, 14 January 1952, Longhand Personal Memos, 1952 folder, PSF Longhand Notes File, Truman Papers, Truman Library.

44. *Washington Daily News*, 15 February 1946, Truman Appointments folder, Democratic National Committee Clipping File, Truman Library. One analysis of the Ickes-Pauley dispute concluded, "The President responded with tactics that soon became familiar in his administration: he supported the man while taking action against his policy" (James Boylan, "Harry S. Truman, 1945–53," in C. Vann Woodward, ed., *Responses of the Presidents to Charges of Misconduct*, p. 326). While this conclusion is somewhat misleading in its general application, it is certainly valid in this case. In 1953, just before leaving office, Truman declared off-shore oil deposits a naval petroleum reserve. This was seen as political because of General Eisenhower's campaign promise to transfer tidelands oil from federal to state control. *Chicago Sun Times*, 18 January 1953, Post-Election 1953—Appraisals of the Truman Administration folder, Democratic National Committee Clipping File, Truman Library.

45. The account of the Kansas City vote fraud case is drawn from U.S. Congress, Senate, Subcommittee of the Committee on the Judiciary, *Kansas City Vote Fraud: Hearings on S. Res. 116*, 80th Cong., 1st sess., 28 May, 5, 6 June 1947 (hereinafter *Kansas City Vote Fraud: Hearings*); "Report of the Activities of the Department of Justice in Connection with the Kansas City Primary Elections of 1946;" Kansas City Elections of 1946 folder, Clark M. Clifford Papers, Truman Library; Boylan, "Harry S. Truman, 1945–53," pp. 326–27; U.S. Congress, House, Committee on the Judiciary, *Investigation of the Department of Justice: Report pursuant to H. Res. 50*, 83d Cong., 1st sess., 1953, pp. 92–95 (hereinafter *Investigation of the Department of Justice*).

46. *Kansas City Vote Fraud: Hearings*, pp. 224–25.

47. *Investigation of the Department of Justice*, p. 94.

48. *Kansas City Vote Fraud: Hearings*, p. 227.

49. *Investigation of the Department of Justice*, pp. 94–95.

50. *Public Papers of the Presidents of the United States, Harry S. Truman, 1947*, p. 265.

51. Ibid., p. 456.

52. Ayers, diary, 17 October 1947, Ayers Papers, Truman Library.

53. *Public Papers of the Presidents, Truman, 1947*, p. 467.

54. Frank McNaughton to Don Bermingham, 9 January 1948, Speculation folder, McNaughton Papers, Truman Library; Donovan, *Conflict and Crisis*, p. 349; Boylan, "Harry S. Truman, 1945–53," p. 328.

55. Ayers, diary, 29–31 December 1947, Ayers Papers, Truman Library; *New York Times*, 1 January 1948, p. 1; *Public Papers of the Presidents, Truman, 1947*, p. 536; Donovan, *Conflict and Crisis*, p. 349.

56. Assistant Attorney General John F. Sonnett, memo to Director, FBI, 2 January 1948, Wallace H. Graham folder, PSF Personal File, Truman Papers, Truman Library; Blair Bolles, *How to Get Rich in Washington: Rich Man's Division of the Welfare State*, p. 41.

57. Ayers, diary, 19 January 1948, Ayers Papers, Truman Library.

Notes to Chapter 3
The Case of General Vaughan

1. Harry H. Vaughan, "Whipping Boy First Class," p. 6, Vaughan Papers, Truman Library; Jonathan Daniels, *The Man of Independence*, pp. 93–94.

2. Vaughan, "Whipping Boy First Class," pp. 7–13; Eleanora W. Schoenebaum, ed., *Political Profiles: The Truman Years*, p. 578. In 1925, Vaughan and Truman were joined at Fort Riley by John Snyder, who was later to be labeled, along with Vaughan, as part of the "Missouri Gang." In the 1920s, each of the three was a colonel in charge of one of the artillery components of the 102d Reserve Division; they were referred to as the "Three Cannoneers" by their men.

3. Vaughan, "Whipping Boy First Class," p. 6.

4. Cornelius J. Mara, Oral History Interview by Jerry N. Hess, p. 61.

5. Roger Tubby, Oral History Interview by Jerry N. Hess, p. 139.

6. Stephen J. Spingarn, Oral History Interview by Jerry N. Hess, p. 150. Other information in this paragraph is drawn from Spingarn and from Roger Tubby, Oral History Interview by Jerry N. Hess, pp. 14, 64, 138–39.

7. Merriman Smith quoted in Vaughan, "Whipping Boy First Class," p. 25.

8. Mara, Oral History Interview, p. 61.

9. Harry S. Truman, Interview, p. 9, Politics: Cronyism folder, PPF Memoirs File, Truman Papers, Truman Library.

10. Harry H. Vaughan, Oral History Interview by Charles T. Morrissey, pp. 104–5.

11. Robert S. Allen and William V. Shannon, *The Truman Merry-Go-Round*, pp. 87–88. Administration sources mentioned are Roger Tubby, Oral History Interview, pp. 138–39; Joseph G. Feeney, Oral History Interview by Jerry N. Hess, p. 71; George E. Allen, Oral History Interview by Jerry N. Hess, p. 39. Vaughan's observation is from Tubby, Oral History Interview, pp. 138–39.

12. Robert L. Dennison, Oral History Interview by Jerry N. Hess, p. 176.

13. Spingarn, Oral History Interview, p. 149.

14. Mara, Oral History Interview, p. 123.

15. Patrick Anderson, *The President's Men: White House Assistants of Franklin D. Roosevelt, Harry S. Truman, Dwight D. Eisenhower, John F. Kennedy, and Lyndon B. Johnson*, p. 98. Other observations in this paragraph are from Dennison, Oral History Interview, p. 176; William M. Rigdon, Oral History Interview, p. 45.

16. Dennison, Oral History Interview, p. 176. Mara's comment is in Mara, Oral History Interview, p. 122. Vaughan's observation, which follows, is from Vaughan, "Whipping Boy First Class," p. 15.

17. Mara, Oral History Interview, p. 38.

18. "Uncensored Dope," *Time* 46 (10 September 1945): 20. The rest of the paragraph is based on this source and "Tut, Tut, General," *Washington Post*, Harry H. Vaughan folder, Eben A. Ayers, Papers, Truman Library; Vaughan, "Whipping Boy First Class," pp. 31–33. At the same gathering, Vaughan made other remarks that provided ammunition for his critics but created less controversy. At one point he called Churchill "a garrulous old gentleman." Later, comparing the Roosevelt administration with that of Truman, he remarked that "after a diet of caviar it is good to get back to ham and eggs."

19. Rt. Rev. Angus Dun to Harry S. Truman, 24 September 1945, and Truman to Dun, 26 September 1945, Harry H. Vaughan folder, PSF Personal File, Truman Papers, Truman Library.

20. Vaughan, "Whipping Boy First Class," p. 33.

21. *New York Times*, 19 October 1945, 2 January 1946.

22. Vaughan, "Whipping Boy First Class," p. 32.

23. Ibid., p. 18. Subsequent statements by General Vaughan in this and the following three paragraphs are drawn from Vaughan, interview by the author; Vaughan, "Whipping Boy First Class," p. 43.

24. Eben A. Ayers, diary, 9 and 10 January 1946, Ayers Papers, Truman Library; Ayers, memo to Charles Ross, 3 August 1949, Harry H. Vaughan folder, Ayers Papers, Truman Library.

25. Ayers, diary, 27 February 1946. The following observation on Vaughan's apparent intervention also is offered in this entry.

26. Vaughan, "Whipping Boy First Class," p. 44.

27. Edward T. Folliard, "Senator's Spilled Gin Started Maragon on Way

to Spotlight," *Washington Post*, 19 August 1949, Five Percenters: the Proceedings, with John F. Maragon folder, Democratic National Committee Clipping File, Truman Library.

28. Ayers, diary, 26 January 1947, 30 November 1946, Ayers Papers, Truman Library.

29. Vaughan, memo, Drew Pearson folder, Vaughan Papers, Truman Library. Vaughan alleged that Pearson obtained the quote by having his legman David Karr telephone and represent himself as Ed Harris, the Washington correspondent for the *St. Louis Post-Dispatch.*

30. Vaughan, "Whipping Boy First Class," pp. 41–42; Westbrook Pegler, "A Fill-in on Events that Evoked Truman's 'S.O.B.,'" Drew Pearson folder, Vaughan Papers, Truman Library; Ayers, diary, 7 February 1947, Ayers Papers, Truman Library. Ayers later did some checking on Maragon's background. He found the old prohibition violation (17 July 1920), three arrests on disorderly conduct charges (none of which had been prosecuted), and an investigation into the shooting death of a police detective, Arthur Scriviner, on 13 October 1926. Maragon had an alibi for the shooting—he was married on that day—and the death was declared a suicide. Handwritten notes, Harry H. Vaughan folder, Ayers Papers, Truman Library.

31. Jack Anderson with James Boyd, *Confessions of a Muckraker*, pp. 21–22.

32. Robert J. Donovan, *Conflict and Crisis: The Presidency of Harry S. Truman, 1945–1948*, p. 165.

33. Drew Pearson, excerpts of radio broadcast, 16 March 1947, Harry H. Vaughan folder, Ayers Papers, Truman Library.

34. "Pearson Columns" summary, Drew Pearson Columns on HHV folder, Vaughan Papers, Truman Library; Ayers, diary, 17–18 March 1947, Ayers Papers, Truman Library.

35. "Pearson Columns" summary, Drew Pearson Columns on HHV folder, Vaughan Papers, Truman Library.

36. Drew Pearson, "The Washington Merry-Go-Round," *Washington Post*, 7 April 1947, News Clippings—Charges of Scandal folder, Victor R. Messall Papers, Truman Library.

37. "Uncensored Dope," *Time* 46 (10 September 1945): 20; Vaughan, "Whipping Boy First Class," p. 26.

38. Vaughan, "Whipping Boy First Class," pp. 16, 46; William H. Neblett to Harry H. Vaughan, 3 April 1947, unlabeled folder, Vaughan Papers, Truman Library.

39. Ayers, diary, 5 August 1947, Ayers Papers, Truman Library.

40. Maragon to Vaughan, 23 May 1947, File 563—Drew Pearson, OF Name File, Truman Papers, Truman Library.

41. Vaughan to Brig. Gen. C. B. Ferenbaugh, 26 May 1947, File 563—Drew Pearson, OF Name File, Truman Papers, Truman Library.

42. Ayers, diary, 5 August 1947, Ayers Papers, Truman Library.

43. Suspected leaks to Pearson continued to plague Vaughan. In August 1949, when Vaughan testified before a committee investigating influence peddling (described in Chapter 4), Secretary of Defense Louis Johnson was suspected of giving information to the columnist. Mara, Oral History Interview, pp. 42–50; Ayers, diary, 12 December 1946, Ayers Paper, Truman Library.

44. Oliver Pilat, *Pegler: Angry Man of the Press*, pp. 16, 237.
45. Ayers, diary, 24 October 1947, 16 November 1947, Ayers Papers, Truman Library.
46. Ibid., 6 February 1948.
47. Vaughan, "Whipping Boy First Class," p. 38; Matthew J. Connelly, Oral History Interview by Jerry N. Hess, p. 238.
48. Connelly, Oral History Interview, pp. 239–41.
49. *New York Times*, 7 February 1948. The background for the initiation of the idea is in Vaughan, "Whipping Boy First Class," p. 38; Ayers, diary, 6 February 1948, Ayers Papers, Truman Library; James Forrestal, *The Forrestal Diaries*, ed. Walter Millis, pp. 324–25.
50. *New York Times*, 7 February 1948; Ayers, diary, 7 February 1948, Ayers Papers, Truman Library.
51. Reverend Cliff R. Johnson to Truman, 9 February 1948, Harry H. Vaughan folder, PSF Personal File, Truman Papers, Truman Library.
52. Truman to Johnson, 13 February 1948, Harry H. Vaughan folder, PSF Personal File, Truman Papers, Truman Library.
53. Herman Klurfeld, *Behind the Lines: The World of Drew Pearson*, pp. 107–8.
54. Truman, diary, 26 March 1946, PSF, Truman Papers, Truman Library.
55. Klurfeld, *Behind the Lines*, pp. 108–9. Vaughan defended his acceptance of the award, saying that it had been cleared by the State Department and approved by the president. Further, an identical award had been made to Gen. Omar N. Bradley and six other World War II generals in August 1948 without any press criticism. Vaughan, "Whipping Boy First Class," p. 51.
56. Drew Pearson, *Diaries: 1949–1959*, ed. Tyler Abell, p. 19.
57. Cited in Klurfeld, *Behind the Lines*, p. 109. Vandenberg's reaction is recorded in Vaughan, "Whipping Boy First Class," p. 53.
58. Pearson, *Diaries*, p. 24. Pearson's reaction, which follows, is from the same source.
59. Anderson with Boyd, *Confessions of a Muckraker*, p. 223.
60. Mara, Oral History Interview, pp. 75–77.
61. Ayers, diary, 8 February 1947, Ayers Papers, Truman Library.
62. Truman to Reverend Cliff R. Johnson, 13 February 1948, Harry H. Vaughan folder, PSF Personal File, Truman Papers, Truman Library.
63. Ayers, diary, 17 March 1947, Ayers Papers, Truman Library.
64. Tubby, Oral History Interview, pp. 65–66.

Notes to Chapter 4
The Five Percenters

1. *New York Times*, 26 June 1949; "Contracts: The 5 Per Centers," *Newsweek* 4 July 1949, p. 20.
2. Bert Andrews, radiogram to Harry H. Vaughan, 20 June 1949; Vaughan radiogram to Andrews, 20 June 1949; 5% Investigation folder, Vaughan Papers, Truman Library.
3. U.S. Congress, Senate, Investigations Subcommittee of the Committee on Expenditures in the Executive Departments, *Influence in Government Procurement: Hearings Pursuant to S. Res. 52*, 81st Cong., 1st sess., 30 Au-

gust 1949, pp. 514–15 (hereinafter *Influence in Government Procurement: Hearings*).

4. *New York Times*, 9 July 1949. The preceding accounts of Republican attacks are in Cornelius J. Mara, Oral History Interview by Jerry N. Hess, p. 76; *New York Times*, 18 July 1949.

5. *New York Times*, 12 August 1949, Five Percenters, General Clips folder, Subject File, Democratic National Committee Clipping File, Truman Library.

6. Representative Paul W. Shafer, press release, 22 July 1949, Harry H. Vaughan folder, PSF, Truman Papers, Truman Library.

7. *Public Papers of the Presidents of the United States, Harry S. Truman, 1949*, pp. 393, 421. Truman stated that Vaughan would be allowed to testify at a press conference on 21 July 1949 and reiterated his statement on 11 August.

8. *New York Times*, 20 July 1949; *Public Papers of the Presidents, Truman, 1949*, p. 392.

9. Eben A. Ayers, diary, 5, 6, 13 August 1949, Ayers Papers, Truman Library.

10. *New York Times*, 23 July 1949; Ayers, diary, 1 August 1949, Ayers Papers, Truman Library; from Diary of Colonel James V. Hunt, Vaughan Papers, Truman Library.

11. Hubert F. Julian, affidavit, 18 July 1949; Frederick S. Weaver, 18 July 1949, 5% Investigation—Affidavits folder, Vaughan Papers, Truman Library; Ayers, diary, 3, 8 August 1949, Ayers Papers, Truman Library.

12. Harry H. Vaughan, "Whipping Boy First Class," pp. 102–3, Vaughan Papers, Truman Library.

13. Eleanora W. Schoenebaum, ed., *Political Profiles: The Truman Years*, p. 231.

14. Ayers, diary, 3 February 1948, Ayers Papers, Truman Library. The other Democrats on the committee were Herbert R. O'Connor of Maryland and James O. Eastland of Mississippi.

15. Vaughan, "Whipping Boy First Class," p. 102.

16. Mara, Oral History Interview, pp. 52–59.

17. Frank McNaughton, "Five Percenters," 8 August 1949, McNaughton Papers, Truman Library.

18. *Influence in Government Procurement: Hearings*, 8 August 1949, p. 1.

19. *Public Papers of the Presidents, Truman, 1949*, pp. 421, 425–26; Ayers, diary, 18 August 1949, Ayers Papers, Truman Library.

20. McNaughton, "Five Percenters," 19 August 1949, McNaughton Papers, Truman Library; Jack Steele, "Secret Inquiry Text Issued in Reply to Truman Criticism," *New York Herald Tribune*, 19 August 1949, Five Percenters folder, Democratic National Committee Clipping File, Truman Library.

21. Vaughan, "Whipping Boy First Class," pp. 16–17. The following discussion is also based on Vaughan, p. 29.

22. Ibid., p. 105. In an oral history interview given several years later, Vaughan recalled that Truman concluded his remarks by saying, "You go up there and tell them to go to hell." Vaughan, Oral History Interview by Charles T. Morrissey, p. 106.

23. *Influence of Government Procurement: Hearings*, pp. 218–19, 694; "Text of Vaughan's Statement," 5% Investigation folder, Vaughan Papers, Truman Library; Vaughan, interview by the author.

24. Mara, Oral History Interview, pp. 80–81. The preceding discussion in this paragraph is based on "Text of Vaughan's Statement," 5% Investigation folder, Vaughan Papers, Truman Library; *Influence in Government Procurement: Hearings*, 30 August 1949, pp. 503, 505; "Home Freezer" record, Home Freezers folder, Vaughan Papers, Truman Library.

25. "Maragon's Boss Tells His Story," Home Freezers folder, Vaughan Papers, Truman Library.

26. "Home Freezer" record, Home Freezers folder, Vaughan Papers, Truman Library; "Text of Vaughan's Statement," 5% Investigation folder, Vaughan Papers, Truman Library; Vaughan, "Whipping Boy First Class," p. 94.

27. *Influence in Government Procurement: Hearings*, pp. 218–20, 235–36, 445–48, 451–54, 463, 524–25, 727–29, 731–32, 734–38; Vaughan, "Whipping Boy First Class," p. 99.

28. McNaughton, "Five Percenters," 26 August 1949, McNaughton Papers, Truman Library; *Influence in Government Procurement: Hearings*, pp. 443–44, 461, 507, 523.

29. *Influence in Government Procurement: Hearings*, pp. 34–36.

30. Ibid., p. 46. The balance of the discussion in this paragraph is based on the hearings, pp. 47–52, 511; Vaughan, "Whipping Boy First Class," p. 72.

31. *Influence in Government Procurement: Hearings*, pp. 57–59, 68, 71–73, 515–17, 631–33; Vaughan, "Whipping Boy First Class," pp. 76–78. During Tighe Woods's testimony, Senator McCarthy claimed the permit was for $150,000 worth of construction material. Woods said he was not sure, but that he would accept the figure. General Vaughan later claimed to have seen the Tanforan application and stated that it was for only $54,000 in material and $132,000 in labor. Vaughan, "Whipping Boy First Class," p. 78; *Influence in Government Procurement: Hearings*, p. 72.

32. *Influence in Government Procurement: Hearings*, pp. 58, 60, 62–63, 514–17, 519. Vaughan had additional information that bolstered his position on the responsibility of the government to the Tanforan owners that did not come out in the hearings. In an unsolicited letter, a San Francisco attorney who was familiar with the ruling against the original owners of Tanforan rendered an opinion: "It is all very well to speak of the critical materials that were involved, to the detriment possibly of the building of some houses for veterans, but had the Tanforan owners not agreed to restoring the property on their own behalf, the Government would certainly have been required to do so and there would have been no issue raised with respect to the use of critical materials." John D. Costello to Vaughan, 12 August 1949, unlabeled folder, Vaughan Papers, Truman Library.

33. Vaughan, "Whipping Boy First Class," p. 77; *Influence in Government Procurement: Hearings*, p 73.

34. Pearson columns that included charges concerning Tanforan appeared on the following dates: 4 August 1949, 5 August 1949, 3 June 1950, 7 November 1953, and 21 October 1954. Considine's column of 16 April 1951 included the Tanforan charges in a shopping list of old charges against Vaughan. "Pearson Columns," Drew Pearson—Columns on HHV folder, Vaughan Papers, Truman Library; "Articles by Bob Considine," 5% Investigation folder, Vaughan Papers, Truman Library.

35. Ayers, diary, 5 August 1949, Ayers Papers, Truman Library.

36. *Influence in Government Procurement: Hearings*, pp. 313–15, 322–27. It also developed during Elvove's testimony that the tank car for which Vaughan had requested release was not inedible blackstrap as represented by Allied but rather a strictly controlled refiner's syrup.

37. *Influence in Government Procurement: Hearings*, pp. 528–40, 582–83; Vaughan, "Whipping Boy First Class," p. 106.

38. *Influence in Government Procurement: Hearings*, p. 583.

39. Ibid., pp. 545–53, 625–27; Drew Pearson, *Diaries: 1949–1959*, ed. Tyler Abell, p. 73; Ayers, diary, 19 November 1953, Ayers Papers, Truman Library; "Whipping Boy First Class," pp. 47–48.

40. *Influence in Government Procurement: Hearings*, pp. 542–43, 547–48, 564–65; Vaughan, "Whipping Boy First Class," pp. 85–86.

41. *Influence in Government Procurement: Hearings*, pp. 567–73. In this case, attorney William Neblett, an old friend of Vaughan from their days in the South Pacific, allegedly had sought a parole for a client named Robert Gould. Neblett's campaign contribution came after his lawyer-client relationship with Gould had been dissolved. Ironically, when Gould did obtain a pardon, he was represented by Thurman Arnold, the father-in-law of Drew Pearson's daughter. The Gould case was never discussed in Pearson's column. "Pearson-Gould" clipping and chronology, Robert Gould Case folder, Vaughan Papers, Truman Library; "Pearson Charges Made Part of Senate Investigation," William Burton Tax Case folder, Vaughan Papers, Truman Library.

42. *Influence in Government Procurement: Hearings*, p. 588.

43. Mara, Oral History Interview, pp. 52–54.

44. McNaughton, "Vaughan—1," 31 August 1949, McNaughton Papers, Truman Library.

45. Years later, Vaughan, still bitter about McCarthy's behavior during the hearings, recalled that each time the senator addressed him as "Mr." Vaughan, he in turn addressed the senator as "Mr." McCarthy, and that when McCarthy addressed him as "General," he in turn called McCarthy "Senator." Vaughan remembered this as bringing an end to the "Mr." appellation. The official record shows no instances of Vaughan calling McCarthy "Mr." but several of McCarthy so addressing Vaughan. Frank McNaughton, who attended the hearings, wrote that Vaughan inititally winced each time he was called "Mr." but later took it in stride. Vaughan, interview by the author; McNaughton, "Vaughan—1," 31 August 1949, McNaughton Papers, Truman Library.

46. *Influence in Government Procurement: Hearings*, p. 544. The discussion in the following paragraph is based on the hearings, pp. 539–40, 544.

47. Mara, Oral History Interview, p. 53; Ayers, diary, 30 August 1949, Ayers Papers, Truman Library.

48. McNaughton, "Vaughan—1," 31 August 1949, McNaughton Papers, Truman Library. For McNaughton's earlier opinion, see McNaughton, "Five Percenters," 19 August 1949, McNaughton Papers, Truman Library.

49. Vaughan, "Whipping Boy First Class," p. 102.

50. *Public Papers of the Presidents, Truman, 1949*, p. 455–56, 512.

51. U.S. Congress, Senate Subcommittee on Investigation of the Committee on Expenditures in the Executive Departments, *The 5-Percenter Investigation pursuant to S. Res. 52*, 81st Cong., 2d sess., 18 January 1950, S. Rept. 1232, pp. 14–15. While Maragon came under the harshest attack in

the report, the phrasing of the condemnation of his actions implied further criticism of Vaughan: "It seems incredible to the subcommittee that over a period of several years a man like Maragon could continue his nefarious activities. This is particularly true because in recent years his activities have received attention in the public press."

52. *Influence in Government Procurement: Hearings*, p. 501.

53. When Senator Hoey was asked about this interpretation of Vaughan's actions on a "Meet the Press" broadcast three days before Vaughan testified, he did an artful job of fence straddling. He concurred that "the whole United States is the constituent of the President," but also agreed with a questioner that "a secretary in the White House [has] to be more restrained and circumspect." "Meet the Press" transcript, 26 August 1949, 5% Investigation, 1949—Hoey Committee folder, Vaughan Papers, Truman Library.

54. Stephen J. Spingarn, Oral History Interview by Jerry N. Hess, pp. 152–53.

55. Senator Hoey concurred with the notion that senators' secretaries have a responsibility to expedite matters for their constituents in his "Meet the Press" appearance on 26 August 1949, but he was not explicit as to whether he considered that Vaughan should have the same function as Truman's military aide. He emphasized the right to *expedite* decisions, not to influence their determination. "Meet the Press" transcript, 26 August 1949, 5% Investigation, 1949—Hoey Committee folder, Vaughan Papers, Truman Library.

56. Truman, Interview, Politics: Cronyism folder, PPF Memoirs File, Truman Papers, Truman Library.

57. *Influence in Government Procurement: Hearings*, pp. 3–4; *New York Herald Tribune*, 25 December 1949, Five Percenters—General Clips folder, Democratic National Committee Clipping File, Truman Library; *Washington Post*, 3 July 1952, Five Percenters—Legislation 82d Congress folder, Democratic National Committee Clipping File, Truman Library.

Notes to Chapter 5
Senator Fulbright and the RFC

1. Jesse H. Jones with Edward Angly, *Fifty Billion Dollars: My Thirteen Years with the RFC (1932–1945)*, pp. ix–x, 8–10; Addison W. Parris, *The Small Business Administration*, p. 8–11; Jules Abels, *The Truman Scandals*, pp. 70–72.

2. Jones with Angly, *Fifty Billion Dollars*, pp. 138–41.

3. Frank McNaughton to Don Bermingham, "RFC," 5 August 1949, McNaughton Papers, Truman Library. The following summary of Tobey's charges is from U.S. Congress, Senate, Committee on Banking and Currency, *Proposed Extension of the Reconstruction Finance Corporation: Hearings of $80,000,000 Loan to the B. & O. Railroad*, 80th Cong., 1st sess., 29 April 1947, pp. 160–61; Charles W. Tobey to Charles B. Henderson, 28 March 1947, R.F.C. 1933–1950 folder, John W. Snyder Papers, Truman Library.

4. Jones with Angly, *Fifty Billion Dollars*, p. 142.

5. "How Temporary Becomes Permanent around Here," Box 23, Record Group 234, Records of the Reconstruction Finance Corporation, National Archives, Washington, D.C.; *New York Times*, 23 April 1947; Charles B. Henderson to Sen. Burton K. Wheeler, 22 August 1945, R.F.C., 1933–

1950 folder, Snyder Papers, Truman Library; Jones with Angly, *Fifty Billion Dollars*, p. 140.

6. T. Coleman Andrews to Board of Directors, RFC, R.F.C. folder, PSF, Truman Papers, Truman Library. The preceding discussion is based on Jones with Angly, *Fifty Billion Dollars*, pp. 277–86; Jones to W. W. Kiplinger, 21 August 1946, R.F.C. folder, PSF, Truman Papers, Truman Library.

7. Cited in Jones with Angly, *Fifty Billion Dollars*, p. 9. For intended life span of the RFC, see "How Temporary Becomes Permanent around Here," Box 23, Record Group 234, Records of the Reconstruction Finance Corporation, National Archives, Washington, D.C.

8. Blair Bolles, *How to Get Rich in Washington: Rich Man's Division of the Welfare State*, p. 129.

9. Parris, *The Small Business Administration*, pp. 13–14.

10. *New York Times*, 20 May 1947, 27 May 1947, 3 June 1947; Bodman to John W. Snyder, 29 May 1947, R.F.C., 1933–1950 folder, Snyder Papers, Truman Library.

11. Cited in Haynes Johnson and Bernard M. Gwertzman, *Fulbright: The Dissenter*, pp. 102–5.

12. Ibid., pp. 119–20; U.S. Congress, Senate, Subcommittee of the Committee on Banking and Currency, *Study of Reconstruction Finance Corporation: Loan to Waltham Watch Co.: Hearings on S. Res. 219*, 81st Cong., 2d sess., 20 July 1950, pp. 1–2.

13. Richard O. Davies, *Housing Reform During the Truman Administration*, pp. 53–57; Leo Nielson to James F. Sheridan, 10 June 1949, Hoey Report folder, Box 26, Congress—Reports in Connection with Fulbright Hearings, Record Group 234, Records of Reconstruction Finance Corporation, National Archives, Washington, D.C.; "Housing: Bathtub Blues," *Time* 54 (4 July 1949): 55; Abels, *The Truman Scandals*, pp. 97–98.

14. Jones to Fulbright, 10 April 1950, OF 210B, Truman Papers, Truman Library.

15. Hise to Fulbright, 5 May 1950, Fulbright Study of R.F.C. folder, Box 24, Record Group 234, Records of the Reconstruction Finance Corporation, National Archives, Washington, D.C. The balance of the discussion of the Texmass loan is based on U.S. Congress, Senate, Subcommittee of the Committee on Banking and Currency, *Study of Reconstruction Finance Corporation: Texmass Loan: Hearings on S. Res. 219*, 81st Cong., 2d sess., 13–27 April 1950, pp. 35–37, 58–64, 144–45, 152, 200–207; U.S. Congress, Senate, Committee on Banking and Currency, *Study of Reconstruction Finance Corporation: Texmass Petroleum Co. Loan: Interim Report pursuant to S. Res. 219*, 81st Cong., 2d sess., 19 May 1950, S. Rept. 1689, pp. 1–19; Fulbright to Sen. Burnet R. Maybank, 26 April 1950, Fulbright Study of R.F.C. folder, Box 24, Record Group 234, Records of the Reconstruction Finance Corporation, National Archives, Washington, D.C.; Franklin N. Parks to Truman, 16 January 1953, R.F.C. folder, PSF Subject File: Agencies, Truman Papers, Truman Library.

16. *Public Papers of the Presidents of the United States, Harry S. Truman, 1950*, pp. 315–19; Harold Seidman, *Politics, Position and Power: The Dynamics of Federal Organization*, pp. 52–53; *New York Herald Tribune*, 7 July 1950; R.F.C.—1950 folder, Democratic National Committee Clipping File, Truman Library; Matthew J. Connelly, memo to Truman, 6 July 1950, Connelly folder, PSF General File, Truman Papers, Truman Library. Truman had opposed transfer to the Treasury Department on the grounds that

both he and Secretary Snyder did not want Treasury to get in the "banking and loan business." Harry S. Truman, *Years of Trial and Hope*, vol. 2 of *Memoirs by Harry S. Truman*, p. 44.

17. The memo was unsigned but was likely written by Donald S. Dawson, the president's administrative assistant for personnel. Memo to Truman, 10 August 1948, R.F.C. folder, PSF Subject File: Agencies, Truman Papers, Truman Library.

18. Dawson, memo to Truman, 18 April 1950, R.F.C. folder, PSF Subject File: Agencies, Truman Papers, Truman Library. Dawson's background is given in Eleanora W. Schoenebaum, ed., *Political Profiles: The Truman Years*, p. 119.

19. "RFC Problems," unsigned memo to Truman, undated (April 1950), R.F.C. folder, PSF Personal File, Truman Papers, Truman Library.

20. Richard E. Neustadt, memo to Stephen J. Spingarn, 6 June 1950, OF 210B, Truman Papers, Truman Library; Spingarn, memo to Dawson, undated (between 6 June 1950 and 16 June 1950), OF 210B, Truman Papers, Truman Library; Notes on Cabinet Meetings, 16 June 1950, Post-Presidential File, Connelly Papers, Truman Library.

21. When Sen. Pat McCarran lobbied on behalf of Hise, Truman replied tersely, "I am sorry that I don't see eye to eye with you on this situation." McCarran, telegram to Truman, 7 August 1950, and Truman to McCarran, 9 August 1950, OF 210B, Truman Papers, Truman Library. There was ill feeling between Hise and Dawson dating back to an incident when Dawson had dropped a Hise-backed candidate from consideration for the RFC board of directors, in part because Hise had not gone through proper channels in forwarding his recommendation. Later, Kansas City Masons challenged Truman regarding the Hise candidacy, claiming he had stolen money from the Masonic lodge. Dawson, interview by the author.

22. *New York Times*, 10 August 1950, 4 October 1950; "RFC Problems," unsigned memo to Truman, undated (April 1950), R.F.C. folder, PSF Personal File, Truman Papers, Truman Library.

23. Johnson and Gwertzman, *Fulbright*, pp. 121–22; Dawson, memos to Truman 9, 11 December 1950, R.F.C. folder, PSF Subject File: Agencies, Truman Papers, Truman Library; Dawson, interview by the author; U.S. Congress, Senate, Committee on Banking and Currency, *Favoritism and Influence: Study of Reconstruction Finance Corporation: Interim Report pursuant to S. Res. 219*, 82d Cong., 1st sess., 5 February 1951, S. Rept. 75, pp. 8–9 (hereinafter *Favoritism and Influence*); *New York Times*, 2 January 1951; Truman to Fulbright, 6 January 1951, OF 285A, Truman Papers, Truman Library.

24. George Meader, Oral History Interview by Charles T. Morrissey, pp. 29–30.

25. *Favoritism and Influence*, p. 7–8. E. Merl Young, an alleged influence peddler, will be examined more explicitly later. Rex Jacobs was the president of F. L. Jacobs Company, which employed Young while he was simultaneously employed by Lustron. Jacobs, through Dunham, was appointed to supervise the survey and reorganization of Lustron. James Windham, treasurer of the F. L. Jacobs Company, had been an aide to RFC Director George Allen when the F. L. Jacobs Company was awarded a $3 million RFC loan. The following paragraph of the discussion is drawn from the same source.

26. *Public Papers of the Presidents of the United States, Harry S. Truman, 1951*, pp. 144–46, 148. Truman's charges and Fulbright's response are discussed in Johnson and Gwertzman, *Fulbright*, p. 122.

27. Truman to Willett, 15 February 1951, R.F.C. folder, PSF Subject File: Agencies, Truman Papers, Truman Library. The preceding discussion is based on an anonymous (likely Dawson) memo to Truman, 12 February 1951, R.F.C. folder, PSF Subject File: Agencies, Truman Papers, Truman Library; *New York Times*, 24 February 1951. Indications that it was Dawson who initiated the congressional letter gambit were strengthened during Dawson's later testimony before the subcommittee. At that time, it was revealed that Dawson had tried to persuade Director Willett to inform the subcommittee of the existence of the letters. Franklin N. Parks, memo to Truman, 16 January 1953, R.F.C. folder, PSF Subject File: Agencies, Truman Papers, Truman Library.

28. Paul H. Douglas, *In the Fullness of Time*, p. 223.

29. *New York Times*, 12 April 1951. When it was revealed by Senator Tobey that he had recorded this and a subsequent telephone conversation with the president, Truman reacted with indignation to the fact that Tobey had recorded the conversation without informing him and without the required warning tone. Truman called the action "outrageous."

30. Parks, memo to Truman, 16 January 1953, R.F.C. folder, PSF Subject File: Agencies, Truman Papers, Truman Library; Douglas, *In the Fullness of Time*, p. 223.

31. Joseph Short, statement, 23 February 1951, Loan Policy Board folder, OF 210B, Truman Papers, Truman Library. Although Truman said he had found no evidence of illegal influence in the letters, there were statements in some of the letters that represented direct attempts to affect RFC policy. Sample statements from some of the letters included the following:

1) "I feel very strongly that R.F.C. should make the loan."

2) "It appears to me that the loan is proper, the security offered is ample, and no reason exists that I can discover for delaying. . . . the loan should be made at once."

3) "I demand reconsideration of the application."

Parks, memo to Truman, 16 January 1953, R.F.C. folder, PSF Subject File: Agencies, Truman Papers, Truman Library.

32. "Reorganization Plan No. 1 of 1951," 19 February 1951, OF 286A, Truman Papers, Truman Library; *New York Times*, 20 February 1951, 4 April 1951.

33. *New York Times*, 11 April 1951. The Fulbright and Douglas grievances are summarized in Johnson and Gwertzman, *Fulbright*, pp. 103–4; Douglas, *In the Fullness of Time*, pp. 223–24.

34. Dawson, memo to Truman, 9 December 1950, R.F.C. folder, PSF Subject File: Agencies, Truman Papers, Truman Library; anonymous (likely Dawson), memo to Truman, 12 February 1951, R.F.C. folder, PSF Subject File: Agencies, Truman Papers, Truman Library.

35. Robert J. Donovan, *Tumultuous Years: The Presidency of Harry S. Truman, 1949–1953*, pp. 335–37.

36. *Philadelphia Enquirer*, 18 March 1951, R.F.C.—Editorials on Probe folder, Democratic National Committee Clipping File, Truman Library.

37. *New York Daily News*, 8 March 1951, R.F.C. Probe, Columnists' Com-

ments folder, Democratic National Committee Clipping File, Truman Library. Other press commentaries on the RFC investigation that made references to the Harding scandals and references to "government by crony" included *St. Louis Post-Dispatch*, 11 March 1951, *Madison Capital Times*, 4 March 1951 and 21 March 1951, *Washington Post*, 7 March 1951 (R.F.C.—Editorials on Probe folder, Democratic National Committee Clipping File, Truman Library); *Washington Post*, 25 March 1951, *Chicago Sun-Times*, 30 March 1951 (R.F.C. Probe—Columnists' Comments folder, Democratic National Committee Clipping File, Truman Library); *Chicago Sun-Times*, 10 March 1951 (Investigation of R.F.C. folder, OF 210B, Truman Papers, Truman Library).

38. *Public Papers of the Presidents, Truman, 1951*, p. 191.

39. Douglas, *In the Fullness of Time*, p. 224.

40. *Philadelphia Enquirer*, 23 March 1951, R.F.C—Editorials on Probe folder, Democratic National Committee Clipping File, Truman Library. Other calls for abolishment included *New York Daily Mirror*, 7 March 1951, *New York Times*, 1 May 1951, R.F.C.—Editorials on Probe folder, Democratic National Committee Clipping File, Truman Library; Raymond Moley, "The Real RFC Lesson," *Newsweek* 26 March 1951, p. 108, R.F.C. Investigtion folder, OF 210B, Truman Papers, Truman Library. A few newspapers, such as the *San Francisco Chronicle*, spoke out in favor of retaining the RFC but urged increasing safeguards against corruption. *San Francisco Chronicle*, 23 March 1951, R.F.C.—Editorials on Probe folder, Democratic National Committee Clipping File, Truman Library.

41. Charles S. Murphy, Oral History Interview by Charles T. Morrissey and Jerry N. Hess, pp. 100–101, 452–53. Other staff members who defended Dawson included Matthew J. Connelly, Stephen J. Spingarn, and Cornelius J. Mara. Matthew J. Connelly, Oral History Interview by Jerry N. Hess, p. 202; Stephen J. Spingarn, Oral History Interview by Jerry N. Hess, pp. 138–40; Cornelius J. Mara, Oral History Interview by Jerry N. Hess, p. 85. Comment on Truman's complaint about the difficulty getting good men is in Raymond P. Brandt, "That 'Washington Mess,'" *St. Louis Post-Dispatch*, 10 March 1951, R.F.C.—Editorials on Probe folder, Democratic National Committee Clipping File, Truman Library.

42. In a note in Dawson's hand dated on the next day, Dawson thanked Murphy for his assistance, though he did not specifically cite help in writing the statement. Dawson, memo to Murphy, 11 May 1951, Donald Dawson folder, Murphy Papers, Truman Library.

43. U.S. Congress, Senate, Subcommittee of the Committee on Banking and Currency, *Study of Reconstruction Finance Corporation: Hearings on S. Res. 219*, 82d Cong., 1st sess., 10–11 May 1951, pp. 1709–1833; "Analysis of 'Favoritism and Influence,'" undated (sent to Senator Moody by Joseph Short, 12 July 1951), Investigation of R.F.C. folder, OF 210B, Truman Papers, Truman Library; Parks, memo to Truman, 16 January 1953, R.F.C. folder, PSF Subject File: Agencies, Truman Papers, Truman Library; Dawson, interview by the author.

44. Douglas, *In the Fullness of Time*, p. 224.

45. U.S. Congress, Senate, Subcommittee of the Committee on Banking and Currency, *Study of Reconstruction Finance Corporation: Hearings on S. Res. 219.* 82d Cong. 1st sess., 11 May 1951, p. 1833. The succeeding quotation is excerpted from this passage, and thus is from the same source. Dawson's response is from Dawson, interview by the author.

46. *New York Times*, 26 February 1951.

47. Johnson and Gwertzman, *Fulbright*, p. 273.

48. Dawson, memo to Murphy, undated, Donald Dawson folder, Murphy Papers, Truman Library.

49. Dawson, interview by the author; Bolles, *How to Get Rich in Washington*, p. 216.

50. Symington press conference summary, 1 June 1951, Loan Policy Board folder, OF 210B, Truman Papers, Truman Library; Ralph G. Martin and Ed Plaut, *Front Runner, Dark Horse*, pp. 309–11; W. Stuart Symington, "The Ethics of Organized Influence," speech, New York, 22 October 1951, R.F.C.—Stuart Symington Administrator folder, PSF Subject File: Agencies, Truman Papers, Truman Library; Paul I. Wellman, *Stuart Symington: Portrait of a Man with a Mission*, pp. 144–47; Bolles, *How to Get Rich in Washington*, pp. 215–16.

51. U.S. Congress, Senate, Committee on Banking and Currency, *Study of Reconstruction Finance Corporation: Report to Accompany S. 515*, 82d Cong., 1st sess., 20 August 1951, S. Rept. 649, p. 39.

52. In one of the ironies of the RFC investigation, Republican National Chairman Guy Gabrielson was accused of improprieties closely paralleling the allegations against Boyle. Gabrielson was accused of representing Carthage Hydrocol before the RFC and continuing to receive a fee from the company after becoming national chairman. The case diffused criticism of Boyle and the Democrats. Gabrielson was cleared by the Hoey committee and continued in his post as national chairman. *Washington Post*, 1 September 1961, William M. Boyle, Jr., folder, PPNF, Truman Papers, Truman Library; Murphy, memo to Truman, 9 August 1951, William Boyle folder, Murphy Papers, Truman Library; Truman, statement, 9 August 1951, OF 210B (1951), Truman Papers, Truman Library; Schoenebaum, ed., *Political Profiles: The Truman Years*, p. 48–49, 183–84.

Notes to Chapter 6
The Bureau of Internal Revenue Scandal

1. James Hill Shelton, "The Tax Scandals of the 1950s," pp 7, 36–37, 330–33; John C. Chommie, *The Internal Revenue Service*, p. 31.

2. Total tax collections grew from $809,393,640 in 1917 to $40,558,913,040 in 1946. The number of BIR employees expanded from 5,053 to 59,693 during the same period. Lillian Doris, ed., *The American Way in Taxation: Internal Revenue, 1862–1963*, p. 285.

3. Chommie, *The Internal Revenue Service*, p. 31.

4. Ayers, memo undated, Corruption, Ethics, etc. folder, Ayers papers, Truman Library.

5. Shelton, "The Tax Scandals of the 1950s," p. 7. The preceding discussion of the problems in the Wilmington collector's office is based on Shelton, "The Tax Scandals of the 1950s"; Lorraine Nelson, "The Trail of the Tax Thieves," p. 11; Jules Abels, *The Truman Scandals*, pp. 11–12.

6. Cited in Shelton, "The Tax Scandals of the 1950s," p. 54. The discussion of Hannegan in this and the following paragraph is based on Shelton, pp. 29–34, 54; Abels, *The Truman Scandals*, pp. 53–54; Helen Fuller, "The Tax Thieves of 1951," p. 9.

7. Frank Pace, Oral History Interview by Jerry N. Hess, p. 24.

8. U.S. Congress, House, Subcommittee of the Committee on Ways and

Means, *Internal Revenue Investigation: Hearings*, 82d Cong., 1st sess., 9 October 1951, pp. 496–501 (hereinafter King Subcommittee Hearings). In addition, the discussion of Finnegan in this paragraph is based on Shelton, "The Tax Scandals of the 1950s," pp. 56–57, 73–87; Abels, *The Truman Scandals*, pp. 218–24; James Kearns, "The Tax Thieves of 1951; The Finnegan Story," pp. 12–14; Blair Bolles, *How to Get Rich in Washington: Rich Man's Division of the Welfare State*, pp. 279–83.

9. *Public Papers of the Presidents of the United States, Harry S. Truman, 1951*, p. 642. Mention of Finnegan as Truman's friend is in Abels, *The Truman Scandals*, p. 4; "President, Scared by Scandal, Discards a Couple of 'Friends,'" *Newsweek*, 22 October 1951, p. 23.

10. King Subcommittee Hearings, 10 October 1951, pp. 514–15, 584–85; *Public Papers of the Presidents, Truman, 1951*, pp. 565, 643; Truman to Finnegan, 4 April 1951, Treasury Department folder, CF, Truman Papers, Truman Library; Truman, interview transcript, p. 5, Domestic Policy—Internal Revenue Department folder, PPF Memoirs File, Truman Papers, Truman Library.

11. Shelton, "The Tax Scandals of the 1950s," pp. 91–96; Abels, *The Truman Scandals*, pp. 210–11. When Delaney's name was forwarded to Secretary of the Treasury Morgenthau, the summary did not mention the bankruptcy or the larceny charge, although it did state, "He has the necessary political support."

12. The committee found $1,911 in March of Dimes contributions from a completed campaign headed by Delaney in a BIR file drawer, which was cited as an example of laxity rather than criminality. A primary piece of evidence of possible Hatch Act violations was a memo to Delaney from a subordinate dated 25 February that read in part: "In considering promotions in the field, I thought you might like to have the list of employees who purchased dinner tickets for the Hannegan reception." John S. Graham, memo to A. L. M. Wiggins, 15 December 1947, Internal Revenue Investigation folder, Secretary E. H. Foley's Files, Box 85, Record Group 56, Records of the Department of the Treasury, National Archives, Washington, D.C.; Shelton, "The Tax Scandals of the 1950s," pp. 96–101; Abels, *The Truman Scandals*, pp. 214–15.

13. Shelton, "The Tax Scandals of the 1950s," pp. 102–27; Abels, *The Truman Scandals*, pp. 215–18; J. Malcolm Barter, "The Tax Thieves of 1951: The Cadillac and the Collector," pp. 12–13.

14. William V. Shannon, "The Tax Thieves of 1951: Business and Pleasure in New York," pp. 12–14; Shelton, "The Tax Scandals of the 1950s," pp. 163–83; Abels, *The Truman Scandals*, pp. 212–14, 224–27; Nelson, "The Trail of the Tax Thieves," pp. 13, 14, 23.

15. King Subcommittee Hearings, 20 February 1952, p. 2665. The discussion of the problems in the San Francisco collector's office in the preceding paragraph is based on "California Investigations," *Internal Revenue Service, 1946–1951* binder, John W. Snyder Papers, Truman Library; Richard Hyer, "The Tax Thieves of 1951: 'Wild Wednesday' in San Francisco," pp. 11–13; Shelton, "The Tax Scandals of the 1950s," pp. 128–62; Abels, *The Truman Scandals*, pp. 227–32.

16. Abels, *The Truman Scandals*, pp. 246–51; Shelton, "The Tax Scandals of the 1950s," pp. 225–27.

17. Bolles, *How to Get Rich in Washington*, pp. 276–77. The preceding paragraph is based on Abels, *The Truman Scandals*, p. 227; Truman, inter-

view transcript, p. 4, Domestic Policy—Internal Revenue Department folder, PPF Memoirs File, Truman Papers, Truman Library; Bolles, *How to Get Rich in Washington*, pp. 275–76; Shelton, "The Tax Scandals of the 1950s," pp. 34–35.
18. Shelton, "The Tax Scandals of the 1950s," pp. 88–89.
19. Truman to Schoeneman, 27 June 1951, Bureau of Internal Revenue (1945–1951) folder, OF 21D, Truman Papers, Truman Library. Schoeneman's letter of resignation is Schoeneman to Truman, 20 June 1951, Bureau of Internal Revenue (1945–1951) folder, OF 21D, Truman Papers, Truman Library.
20. *New York Times*, 20 November 1951; Shelton, "The Tax Scandals of the 1950s," p. 203.
21. U.S. Congress, House, Subcommittee of the Committee on the Judiciary, *Investigation of the Department of Justice: Pursuant to H. Res. 50*, 83d Cong., 1st sess., 1 August 1953, H. Rept. 1079, p. 88 (hereinafter Chelf-Keating Subcommittee Report). The preceding paragraph is based on this source and Charles S. Murphy, Oral History Interview by Jerry N. Hess, p. 511.
22. Chelf-Keating Subcommittee Report, pp. 90–95.
23. Ibid., p. 122; Shelton, "The Tax Scandals of the 1950s," pp. 234–40; "Inquiries: Caudle, Coats and Cars," *Newsweek*, 10 December 1951, p. 21. Caudle claimed that he had cleared acceptance of the commission with Attorney General McGrath, though McGrath denied ever granting such permission.
24. "Inquiries: Caudle, Coats and Cars," *Newsweek*, 10 December 1951, p. 21; King Subcommittee Hearings, 28 November 1951, pp. 1051–54, 1063–64; Shelton, "The Tax Scandals of the 1950s," pp. 248–50; Chelf-Keating Subcommittee Report, pp. 111–12.
25. Shelton, "The Tax Scandals of the 1950s," pp. 240–47; Abels, "The Truman Scandals," pp. 192–95; Chelf-Keating Subcommittee Report, pp. 97–99; King Subcommittee Hearings, 3 December 1951, pp. 1180–99. Interestingly, while the tenor of the King subcommittee inquiry in the Ripps-Mitchell case was accusatory toward Caudle, the Chelf-Keating subcommittee reserved its criticism for others, concluding: "The subcommittee is of the opinion, from the facts available to it, that these charges against Boykin and Caudle and his staff are unwarranted, and that Ford's intervention—as in other instances—was unjustified and improper."
26. Chelf-Keating Subcommittee Report, p. 110. Caudle's letters to Truman referred to in this paragraph are Caudle to Truman, 2 January 1951, File 5624—Caudle, PPF Name File, Truman Papers, Truman Library; Caudle to Truman, 17 October 1951, T. Lamar Caudle folder, PSF, Truman Papers, Truman Library.
27. Chelf-Keating Subcommittee Report, p. 111.
28. Murphy, Oral History Interview, pp. 305–8, 510–14.
29. King Subcommittee Hearings, 4 December 1951, pp. 1306, 1313. The preceding discussion is based further on Eleanora W. Shoenebaum, ed., *Political Profiles: The Truman Years*, pp. 205–6, 423–24; Abels, *The Truman Scandals*, pp. 170–74, 145–57; Shelton, "The Tax Scandals of the 1950s," pp. 220–28.
30. Oliphant to Truman, 5 Decmeber 1951, Bureau of Internal Revenue (1952–1953) folder, OF 21D, Truman Papers, Truman Library.
31. Adrian W. DeWind to Murphy, 14 November 1951, OF 137A, Tru-

man Papers, Truman Library. The preceding discussion is based on *Public Papers of the Presidents, Truman, 1951*, p. 314; Murphy, memo to Truman, between 8 November and 20 November 1951, Memos to and from the President, 1951 folder, Murphy Papers, Truman Library.

32. David E. Bell, memo to Murphy, 30 October 1951, Corruption in Government folder, Murphy Files, Truman Papers, Truman Library.

33. "Action Being Taken to Meet the Bureau's Problems," 19 December 1951, *The Internal Revenue Service, 1946–1951*, p. 2, Snyder Papers, Truman Library. The preceding discussion is based on David D. Lloyd, memo to Dawson and Friedman, 7 November 1951, Bureau of Internal Revenue (1945–1951) folder, of 21D Truman Papers, Truman Library; Bell, memo to Murphy, 30 October 1951, Corruption in Government folder, Murphy Files, Truman Papers, Truman Library; Memo, unsigned and unaddressed, 19 October 1951, Internal Revenue folder, PSF Subject File—Agencies, Truman Papers, Truman Library; William E. Pemberton, *Bureaucratic Politics: Executive Reorganization During the Truman Administration*, p. 164; McKinney to Truman, 1 November 1951, Bureau of Internal Revenue (1945–1951) folder, OF 21D, Truman Papers, Truman Library; *Public Papers of the Presidents, Truman, 1951*, p. 567.

34. "Action Being Taken to Meet the Bureau's Problems," 19 December 1951, *The Internal Revenue Service, 1946–1951*, p. 2, Snyder Papers, Truman Library; "The Historical Development of President Truman's Reorganization Plan No. 1 of 1952 for the Bureau of Internal Revenue," 16, OF 285A, Truman Papers, Truman Library; Treasury Department, press release, 11 December 1951, History of Internal Revenue Reorganization folder, Snyder Papers, Truman Library.

35. Bell, memo to Murphy, 30 October 1951, Corruption in Government folder, Murphy Files, Truman Papers, Truman Library. The preceding discussion is based on an unsigned and unaddressed memo, 19 October 1951, Internal Revenue folder, PSF Subject File—Agencies, Truman Papers, Truman Library.

36. Biddle to Truman, 30 November 1951, Memos to and from the President, 1951 folder, Murphy Papers, Truman Library.

37. *Public Papers of the Presidents, Truman, 1951*, pp. 641–47.

38. Joseph Short, memo to Truman, 3 January 1952, Bureau of Internal Revenue (1952–1953) folder, OF 21D, Truman Papers, Truman Library. The report showed that there had been 39 dismissals for improper actions in relation to tax matters between 1 January 1951 and 2 October 1951 (when public hearings began) for a rate of about 4.3 per month. From 2 October to 28 December there were 28 dismissals of a similar nature, for a monthly rate of over 9.5. Further, critics could argue that the acceleration came in spite of media pressure before the hearings began, pressure that had increased the rate even for the early months of the year.

39. Shannon, "The Tax Thieves of 1951," p. 14.

40. "Program for Completion of Investigation of Tax Administration," memo, unsigned and undated, but attached to explanatory cover memo: Truman, memo to Murphy, 15 December 1951, Charles S. Murphy folder, PSF Chronological File, Truman Papers, Truman Library. The president's memo refers to the "Chairman of the Ways and Means Committee" rather than to King, who was the chairman of the Subcommittee on Administration of the Internal Revenue Laws. Context and a later memo (Bell, memo to Murphy, 17 January 1952, Corruption in Government folder, Murphy

Files, Truman Papers, Truman Library) indicate that the meeting was with King, and surely the memo was King's.
41. Harold F. Reis, memo to Joseph C. Duggan, 11 December 1951, Corruption in Government folder, Murphy Files, Truman Papers, Truman Library; Cabell Phillips, *The Truman Presidency: The History of a Triumphant Succession*, pp. 411–12; *Public Papers of the Presidents of the United States, Harry S. Truman, 1952–53*, pp. 2, 21; Joseph G. Feeney, Oral History Interview by Jerry N. Hess, p. 94. Several other men had been recommended as possible members of such a committee. David Bell suggested Jiggs Donahue and Rudolph Halley. Representative Poage of Texas suggested former Postmaster General James A. Farley, former Secretary of War Robert P. Patterson, and RFC Administrator W. Stuart Symington. Democratic National Chairman Frank E. McKinney seconded Donahue and Patterson and added Burton K. Wheeler, Francis Biddle, Thurmond Arnold, Hugh Dilworth, and Telford Taylor to the list. Bell, memo to Murphy, 30 October 1951, Corruption in Government folder, Murphy Files, Truman Papers, Truman Library; *Public Papers of the Presidents, Truman, 1952–53*, p. 20; McKinney to Truman, 18 January 1952, Charles S. Murphy folder, PSF, Truman Papers, Truman Library.
42. *Public Papers of the Presidents, Truman, 1952–53*, pp. 4, 20; Murphy, memo to Truman, 23 January 1952, Charles S. Murphy folder, PSF, Truman Papers, Truman Library; *Public Papers of the Presidents, Truman, 1951*, p. 644; Bell, memo to Murphy, 30 October 1951, Corruption in Government folder, Murphy Files, Truman Papers, Truman Library; Roger Tubby, Oral History Interview by Jerry N. Hess, p. 142.
43. Frank McNaughton, memo to Don Bermingham, 27 September 1947, Chairman McGrath folder, McNaughton Papers, Truman Library.
44. Schoenebaum, ed., *Political Profiles: The Truman Years*, pp. 351–53.
45. Truman staffers later recalled that McGrath acted on his own, without checking with the president, an assertion denied by McGrath. "Notes on Cabinet Meetings," 11 January 1952, Matthew J. Connelly Files, PPF, Truman Papers, Truman Library; Murphy, memo to Truman, 23 January 1952, Charles S. Murphy Files, Truman Papers, Truman Library; McGrath, statement, 24 March 1955, pp. 24–25, PPF Memoirs File, Truman Papers, Truman Library; Matthew J. Connelly, Oral History Interview by Jerry N. Hess, p. 360; Feeney, Oral History Interview.
46. Schocnebaum, ed., *Political Profiles: The Truman Years*, p. 391; Harold Seidman, Oral History Interview by Jerry N. Hess, pp. 72–73.
47. Seidman, Oral History Interview, p. 73.
48. William F. Finan, memo to Director, Bureau of the Budget, 29 January 1952, Corruption in Government folder, Murphy Files, Truman Library.
49. Newbold Morris in collaboration with Dana Lee Thomas, *Let the Chips Fall: My Battle Against Corruption*, p. 7.
50. Seidman, Oral History Interview, pp. 75–76. The preceding discussion is based on this source and Donald A. Hansen, memo to Murphy, 7 February 1952, Newbold Morris—Message on Subpoena Power folder, Murphy Files, Truman Papers, Truman Library.
51. Hansen, memo to Murphy, 11 February 1952, Newbold Morris—Message on Subpoena Power folder, Murphy Files, Truman Papers, Truman Library. The preceding discussion is based on this source and Seidman, memo to Morris, undated (attached to memo indicating that it was

presented to Morris on 11 February 1952), Newbold Morris—Message on Subpoena Power folder, Murphy Files, Truman Papers, Truman Library.
52. Morris, *Let the Chips Fall*, pp. 11–16; *Public Papers of the Presidents, Truman, 1952–53*, pp. 152–53.
53. Donald A. Hansen, Oral History Interview by Charles T. Morrissey, pp. 45–46.
54. Morris, *Let the Chips Fall*, pp. 19–20. The preceding discussion is based on Hansen, memo to Murphy and Lloyd, 16 February 1952, Newbold Morris—Message on Subpoena Power folder, Murphy Files, Truman Papers, Truman Library.
55. *Public Papers of the Presidents, Truman, 1952–53*, p. 166.
56. Seidman, Oral History Interview, pp. 82–85, 143–56.
57. Hansen, Oral History Interview, p. 48.
58. Seidman, Oral History Interview, p. 98.
59. Ibid., p. 81.
60. Cited in Phillips, *The Truman Presidency*, p. 413. The preceding discussion is based on Schoenebaum, *Political Profiles: The Truman Years*, p. 392.
61. Seidman, Oral History Interview, p. 73.
62. "Meet the Press," transcript, 2 March 1952, Justice Department Investigation folder, Murphy Files, Truman Papers, Truman Library. Col. C. J. Mara, Vaughan's assistant, wrote indignantly to Murphy: "In my estimation this would certainly disqualify Newbold Morris for any position of responsibility. He shows lack of a judicial hand and lack of balance." Mara, note to Murphy, 4 March 1952, Justice Department Investigation folder, Murphy Files, Truman Papers, Truman Library.
63. Seidman, Oral History Interview, p. 88.
64. Morris, *Let the Chips Fall*, pp. 25–26.
65. Seidman, Oral History Interview, pp. 85, 88.
66. U.S. Congress, House, Subcommittee of the Committee on the Judiciary, *Investigation of the Department of Justice: Hearings*, 82d Cong., 2d sess., 31 March 1952, p. 55. The preceding discussion is based on Morris, *Let the Chips Fall*, p. 27; "Notes on Cabinet Meetings," 28 March 1952, Connelly Papers, PPF, Truman Papers, Truman Library.
67. McGrath, statement, 24 March 1955, p. 26, PPF Memoirs File, Truman Papers, Truman Library.
68. Matthew J. Connelly, Oral History Interview by Jerry N. Hess, p. 362; McGrath, statement, 24 March 1955, p. 27, PPF Memoirs File, Truman Papers, Truman Library. Joseph G. Feeney, one of Truman's administrative assistants, recalled that the president's comment regarding the questionnaire was, "The fellow that developed this doesn't belong in Washington; he's out of his mind." Feeney, Oral History Interview, p. 93.
69. Murphy, memo to Truman, 1 April 1952, Newbold Morris folder, Murphy Files, Truman Papers, Truman Library. The preceding discussion is based on Roger Tubby, Oral History Interview by Jerry N. Hess, p. 142.
70. McGrath, statement, 24 March 1955, pp. 27–30, PPF Memoirs File, Truman Papers, Truman Library. The subsequent quotation is from the same source, p. 30.
71. *Public Papers of the Presidents, Truman, 1952–53*, pp. 231–32. The two versions are not irreconcilable, McGrath may not have made it clear he intended to fire Morris immediately, and Truman, who probably was not privy to the Murphy-Short-McGrath confrontation of the night be-

fore, may have accepted McGrath's statement as a decision reached following their previous discussion regarding Morris.

72. McGrath, statement, 24 March 1955, pp. 30–31, PPF Memoirs File, Truman Papers, Truman Library. The preceding discussion is based on Tubby, Oral History Interview, pp. 142–44; Truman, interview, 5 August 1953, Cabinet folder, PPF Memoirs File—Subject File, Truman Papers, Truman Library.

73. Connelly, Oral History Interview, pp. 363–64; Feeney, Oral History Interview, p. 97; *Public Papers of the Presidents, Truman, 1952–53*, p. 230.

74. Truman, interview, 5 August 1953, pp. 2–3, Cabinet folder, PPF Memoirs File—Subject File, Truman Papers, Truman Library. The preceding discussion is based on this source, p.1, and Samuel I. Rosenman, Oral History Interview by Jerry N. Hess, pp. 92–97.

75. Truman to McGrath, 17 April 1952, Cabinet—Attorney General McGrath folder, PSF, Truman Papers, Truman Library.

76. Shelton, "Tax Scandals of the 1950s," p. 106.

77. Chelf-Keating Subcommittee Report, p. 1.

Notes to Chapter 7
The Search for a Positive Response

1. *Public Papers of the Presidents of the United States, Harry S. Truman, 1951*, p. 641.

2. Hechler, memo to Elsey, 1 February 1951, Harry S. Truman 1949–1951 folder, Elsey Papers, Truman Library.

3. "Research Division, Democratic National Committee," unsigned and undated memo (accompanying memo dated 31 May 1951), Truman—Memos to and from the President folder, Alphabetical File, Murphy Papers, Truman Library. Additional background on the research division is in George M. Elsey, Oral History Interview by Charles T. Morrissey, pp. 58–59; Hechler, memo to Murphy, 31 May 1951, Truman—Memos to and from the President folder, Alphabetical File, Murphy Papers, Truman Library.

4. Murphy, memo to Truman, 4 June 1951, Truman—Memos to and from the President folder, Alphabetical File, Murphy Papers, Truman Library.

5. Elsey to Clifford, 28 December 1951, Correspondence 1952 folder, Political File, Clifford Papers, Truman Library.

6. *Chicago Daily Tribune*, 13 February 1951, William M. Boyle folder, PSF, Truman Papers, Truman Library.

7. Truman, memo to Attorney General, 24 February 1951, PSF Subject File, Truman Papers, Truman Library.

8. Truman to Clifford (Personal and Confidential), 27 April 1951, William M. Boyle folder, PSF, Truman Papers, Truman Library. Recommendations against filing suit are in Department of Justice memo, undated, General File, Eben A. Ayers Papers, Truman Library; Siskind and Parks, memo to Boyle, 12 April 1951, William M. Boyle folder, PSF, Truman Papers, Truman Library.

9. Truman to Burrus, 16 April 1951, Rufus Burrus folder, PSF, Personal File, Truman Papers, Truman Library. The preceding discussion is based on Burrus to Huie, 5 April 1951, Rufus Burrus folder, PSF Personal File, Truman Papers, Truman Library.

10. "Is President Truman an Honorable Man?" *The American Mercury* 72 (May 1951): 545. The concluding portion of the paragraph is based on the same source, pp. 546–50.

11. Daniels to Eben A. Ayers, 31 May 1951, Personal—E. Ayers, Trip to Kansas City (June 19–30, 1951) folder, Ayers Papers, Truman Library.

12. Elsey, confidential memo to Short, 14 May 1951, Personal—E. Ayers, Trip to Kansas City (June 19–30, 1951) folder, Ayers Papers, Truman Library. The concluding portion of the paragraph is also drawn from this source.

13. Ayers, diary, 21 May 1951, Ayers Papers, Truman Library.

14. Daniels to Ayers, 31 May 1951, Personal—E. Ayers, Trip to Kansas City (June 19–30, 1951) folder, Ayers Papers, Truman Library. The preceding portion of the paragraph is also drawn from Ayers, diary, 23 May 1951, 7, 8, 16, 18 June 1951, Ayers Papers, Truman Library; Ayers to Daniels, 1 June 1951, Personal—E. Ayers, Trip to Kansas City (June 19–30, 1951) folder, Ayers Papers, Truman Library.

15. Among those with whom Ayers met were Eddie Jacobson, the president's partner in the haberdashery; J. Vivian Truman, the president's brother; George Powell, the cashier at the Twelfth Street Bank, where Harry Truman and Jacobson did business; Judge Caskie Collett, federal judge and friend of the president; Phineas Rosenberg, the lawyer who served Truman and Jacobson in their business failure; George Buecking, president of the Baltimore Bank (formerly the Twelfth Street Bank); Omar Robinson, Vivian Truman's lawyer; Henry Bundschu, referee in the Jacobson bankruptcy; and two men who had sold goods to the haberdashery. Ayers, diary, 23–26 June 1951, Ayers Papers, Truman Library.

16. "Is President Truman an Honorable Man?" *The American Mercury* 72 (May 1951): 547–48. The preceding portion of the paragraph is based on this source, p. 549.

17. "Statements of Omar E. Robinson, attorney, to Mr. Vivian Truman and Eben A. Ayers," 25 June 1951, Personal—E. Ayers, Trip to Kansas City (June 19–30, 1951) folder, Ayers Papers, Truman Library. Truman's reservations concerning Robinson are given in Truman to Jacobson, 22 May 1951, Eddie Jacobson folder, PSF, Truman Papers, Truman Library.

18. Ayers to Daniels, 10 July 1951, Personal—E. Ayers, Trip to Kansas City (June 19–30, 1951) folder, Ayers Papers, Truman Library. The preceding portion of the paragraph is drawn from Ayers, memo to Truman, undated (but forwarded to the president 16 July 1951), pp. 1, 9, Personal—E. Ayers, Trip to Kansas City (June 19–30, 1951) folder, Ayers Papers, Truman Library.

19. Ayers, memo to Truman, undated (but forwarded to the president 16 July 1951), pp. 5–6, Personal—E. Ayers, Trip to Kansas City (June 19–30, 1951) folder, Ayers Papers, Truman Library. Ayers's view on the school fund, which follows, is also drawn from this source, p. 7.

20. Daniels to Ayers, 31 May 1951, Personal—E. Ayers, Trip to Kansas City (June 19–30, 1951) folder, Ayers Papers, Truman Library.

21. Ayers, diary, 16, 26 July 1951, Ayers Papers, Truman Library. Truman returned the cover memorandum for Ayers's report with a note: "Eben: This is O. K. [signed] HST." Ayers, memo to Truman, 16 July 1951, Personal—E. Ayers, Trip to Kansas City (June 19–30, 1951) folder, Ayers Papers, Truman Library.

22. Ayers, diary, 3 August 1951, Ayers Papers, Truman Library. The

new Huie attack on Truman is in William Bradford Huie, "How to Think About Truman."

23. Elsey, memo to Murphy, 11 July 1951, Cabinet—Investigation Reports folder, PSF, Truman Papers, Truman Library.

24. Lloyd, memo to Murphy, 2 November 1951, Chronological File, Lloyd Papers, Truman Library. The concluding portion of the paragraph is drawn from the same memo.

25. Public Opinion News Service, news release, 30 December 1951, 1951 folder, Papers on the Gallup Poll, Truman Library; Edward T. Folliard, "President, Angry, Maps Dramatic Step to be Taken Year End," *Washington Post*, 3 December 1951, Harry S. Truman File, Truman's Defense of Administration—Defense of Aides folder, Democratic National Committee Clipping File, Truman Library; Lloyd to Seymour Harris, 4 December 1951, Chronological File, Lloyd Papers, Truman Library; Nathaniel J. Ely, memo to Jacobson, 13 December 1951, General Correspondence 1937–1955 folder, Correspondence File, Jacobson Papers, Truman Library; *Public Papers of the Presidents, Truman, 1951*, pp. 641–48; Doris Fleeson, "Truman Called Despondent as Scandals Grow," *St. Louis Post-Dispatch*, 14 December 1951, Harry S. Truman File, Truman's Defense of Administration—Criticisms of the Administration folder, Democratic National Committee Clipping File, Truman Library; Elsey, memo to Clifford, 12 December 1951, Political File—Correspondence 1952 folder, Clifford Papers, Truman Library.

26. Carson, memo to Murphy, undated but received 27 December 1951, Corruption in Government folder, Correspondence and General File, Murphy Files, Truman Papers, Truman Library. The preceding comment by Carl V. Rice is in Rice to McKinney, 18 December 1951, Political File—Correspondence 1952 folder, Clifford Papers, Truman Library.

27. Ely, personal memo to Edward Jacobson, 13 December 1951, General Correspondence 1937–1955 folder, Correspondence File, Jacobson Papers, Truman Library.

28. Dawson, memo to Truman, 7 January 1952, Internal Revenue folder, PSF Subject File: Agencies, Truman Papers, Truman Library.

29. Francis H. Heller, ed., *The Truman White House: The Administration of the Presidency, 1945–1953*, p. 103.

30. Ibid., p. 100.

31. The promotion of Lloyd (and of David E. Bell, who received a parallel appointment at the same time) created some hard feeling on the Truman staff. Nobody argued against their abilities, but both Philleo Nash and Eben Ayers believed they were in line for promotions ahead of the younger men. Murphy reportedly wanted to get higher pay for Lloyd and Bell and could not do so under Civil Service regulations. Ayers, diary, 2 January 1952, Ayers Papers, Truman Library.

32. Heller, ed., *The Truman White House*, p. 100.

33. Donald Hansen, Oral History Interview by Charles T. Morrissey, pp. 53–54; William E. Pemberton, *Bureaucratic Politics: Executive Reorganization During the Truman Administration*, p. 166.

34. Harold Seidman, Oral History Interview by Jerry N. Hess, p. 43. The following comment on Truman's strategy in announcing the BIR plan is from Pemberton, *Bureaucratic Politics*, p. 164.

35. *Public Papers of the Presidents of the United States, Harry S. Truman,*

1952–53, p. 1. The concluding sentences of the paragraph describing the plan are from the same source, pp. 1–2.

36. Dawson, memo to Truman, 7 January 1952, Internal Revenue folder, PSF Subject File: Agencies, Truman Papers, Truman Library. Snyder's preceding comments are from Notes on Cabinet Meetings, 4 January 1952, Post-Presidential File, Connelly Papers, Truman Library.

37. *Public Papers of the Presidents, Truman, 1952–53*, p. 28.

38. Hansen, "Outline of Possible Presidential Action on Integrity in Government," 18 January 1952, Corruption in Government folder, Correspondence and General File, Murphy Files, Truman Papers, Truman Library. The rest of the paragraph is baed on this memo and Lloyd, memo to Finan, 28 January 1952, Chronological File, Lloyd Papers, Truman Library; Murphy, memo to Truman, 23 January 1952, Memos to and from the President, 1952 folder, Murphy Papers, Truman Library. Hansen also suggested a permanent, independent federal inspection service, development of a code of ethics for federal employees, approval of a Senate Labor and Public Welfare Committee recommendation for considering a commission on ethics, expansion of disclosure requirements for those doing business with the government, and consideration of several legislative proposals.

39. Finan, memo to Director, Bureau of the Budget, 29 January 1952, Corruption in Government folder, Correspondence and General File, Murphy Files, Truman Papers, Truman Library. Murphy's expectations for the meeting, discussed in the preceding sentences, are from Murphy, memo to Truman, 23 January 1952, Memos to and from the President, 1952 folder, Murphy Papers, Truman Library.

40. Murphy, memo to Truman, 23 January 1952, Memos to and from the President, 1952 folder, Murphy Papers, Truman Library. The Gallup poll results are in Public Opinion News Service, news release, 23 January 1952, 1952 folder, Papers on the Gallup Poll, Truman Library.

41. McCormick, statement, 22 January 1952, Reorganization folder, Frederick J. Lawton Papers, Truman Library; Pemberton, *Bureaucratic Politics*, pp. 113, 165. The CCHR thought the administration was going too slow in implementing Hoover Commission proposals, or distorting them. The administration accused the CCHR of playing politics. Ken Hechler called a CCHR-sponsored television program "ninety-eight percent anti-administration propaganda and two percent discussion of the Hoover Commission" and accused CCHR Chairman Robert L. Johnson of using the committee for partisan purposes. Hechler, memo, 19 June 1950, Reorganization folder, Hechler Files, Truman Papers, Truman Library; Hechler, memo to Elsey, 19 June 1950, Reorganization folder, Hechler Files, Truman Papers, Truman Library.

42. Murphy, memo to Truman, 23 January 1952, Memos to and from the President, 1952 folder, Murphy Papers, Truman Library; Finan, memo to Director, Bureau of the Budget, 29 January 1952, Corruption in Government folder, Correspondence and General File, Murphy Files, Truman Papers, Truman Library; Lloyd memo to Murphy, 5 February 1952, Chronological File, Lloyd Papers, Truman Library.

43. William Hillman, *Mr. President: The First Publication from the Personal Diaries, Private Letters, Papers and Revealing Interviews of Harry S. Truman*, p. 62.

44. Pemberton, *Bureaucratic Politics*, pp. 166–67.
45. Monroney, Moody, Sparkman, and Smathers, press release, 19 January 1952, Corruption in Government folder, Murphy Files, Truman Papers, Truman Library. McClellan's threatened legislation is discussed in Hansen, memo to Murphy, 27 February 1952, Donald Hansen folder, Murphy Papers, Truman Library.
46. Truman to Monroney, fourth draft, undated, Corruption in Government folder, Correspondence and General File, Murphy Files, Truman Papers, Truman Library. The preceding discussion of the Monroney bill is based on "Summary, Re: S. 2484," Corruption in Government folder, Correspondence and General File, Murphy Files, Truman Papers, Truman Library; Pemberton, *Bureaucratic Politics*, p. 168; "Statement of Elmer B. Staats, Assistant Director of the Bureau of the Budget, on S. 2484," draft, 25 February 1952, Corruption in Government folder, Correspondence and General File, Murphy Files, Truman Papers, Truman Library.
47. Pemberton, *Bureaucratic Politics*, p. 167. The battle over the BIR plan is described in this source, pp. 167–68, and in Hansen, memo to Murphy, 27 February 1952, Donald Hansen folder, Murphy Papers, Truman Library.
48. Truman to Barkley, OF 285A (1952–1953) folder, Truman Papers, Truman Library. The preceding mention of Hansen's liaison work with Humphrey is based on Hansen, Oral History Interview by Charles T. Morrissey, pp. 55–56.
49. *New York Times*, 12 March 1952.
50. Hansen, Oral History Interview, p. 56. The preceding discussion of the Senate vote is based on Pemberton, *Bureaucratic Politics*, p. 168.
51. "Excerpts from the Brownlow Committee Report," Reorganization Plans 2, 3, and 4 of 1952 folder, Box 43, Series 39.32, Record Group 51, Records of the Office of Management and the Budget, National Archives, Washington, D.C.; U.S. Commission on Organization of the Executive Branch of the Government, *The Hoover Commission Report on Organization of the Executive Branch of the Government*, p. 266; Murphy, memo to Truman, 23 January 1952, Memos to and from the President, 1952 folder, Murphy Papers, Truman Library; Finan, memo to Lawton, 29 January 1952, Corruption in Government folder, Correspondence and General File, Murphy Files, Truman Papers, Truman Library; Lloyd, memo to Murphy, 14 February 1952, Chronological File, Lloyd Papers, Truman Library; Pemberton, *Bureaucratic Politics*, p. 167.
52. *Public Papers of the Presidents, Truman, 1952–53*, p. 253. The preceding discussion of Reorganization Plans 2, 3, and 4 is based on the same source, pp. 254–55, 257.
53. News Service Report, 11 April 1952, Reorganization Plans 2, 3, and 4 of 1952 (Publicity) folder, Box 43, Series 39.92, Record Group 51, Records of the Office of Management and the Budget, National Archives, Washington, D.C. The preceding discussion is based on Lloyd, memo to Murphy, 14 February 1952, Chronological File, Lloyd Papers, Truman Library; Pemberton, *Bureaucratic Politics*, p. 169.
54. Pemberton, *Bureaucratic Politics*, pp. 169–72.

Notes to Chapter 8
The Corruption Issue in the 1952 Campaign

1. Cited in George Gallup, "G.O.P. County Chairman Call Corruption Issue Top Argument for Beating Democrats in '52," 14 November 1951, 1951 folder, Papers on the Gallup Poll, Truman Library.
2. *Cleveland Plain Dealer*, 7 March 1952, Taft: Politics 1952—Campaigning in New Hampshire folder, Sen. Robert A. Taft File, Democratic National Committee Clipping File, Truman Library.
3. Barton J. Bernstein, "Election of 1952," in Arthur M. Schlesinger, Jr., ed., *History of American Presidential Elections, 1789–1968*, vol. 4, pp. 3242, 3260–61; John Bartlow Martin, *Adlai Stevenson of Illinois: The Life of Adlai E. Stevenson*, p. 762.
4. Truman wrote his decision against running again in a personal memo on 16 April 1950. He informed his staff of the decision in March 1951. Harold F. Gosnell, *Truman's Crises: A Political Biography of Harry S. Truman*, pp. 507–8.
5. *Public Papers of the Presidents of the United States, Harry S. Truman, 1952–53*, p. 224. The following discussion also is based on this source.
6. Dawson suggested that the "Big Steal" was "silently accomplished by the powerful well-heeled lobbies for big business. . . . They are the big business backbone of the Republican Party, who now in an orgy of self-righteousness are trying to smear the Administration because of a few cases of petty wrongdoing." Dawson, memo to Truman, 7 January 1952, Internal Revenue folder, PSF Subject File—Agencies, Truman Papers, Truman Library.
7. *Public Papers of the Presidents, Truman, 1952–53*, p. 224.
8. Harry S. Truman, *Years of Trial and Hope*, vol. 2 of *Memoirs of Harry S. Truman*, pp. 490–96.
9. Truman, personal memo, 25 December 1952, Longhand Personal Memos folder, PSF Longhand Notes File, Truman Papers, Truman Library. Truman's description of Kefauver as "Mr. Cow Fever" is from this source. The preceding discussion is based on Joseph Bruce Gorman, *Kefauver: A Political Biography*, pp. 77, 85, 106, 113, 142.
10. Truman, personal memo, 8 July 1952, Longhand Personal Memos, 1952 folder, PSF Longhand Notes File, Truman Papers, Truman Library.
11. Truman, *Years of Trial and Hope*, pp. 491–93.
12. Cited in Martin, *Adlai Stevenson of Illinois*, p. 445.
13. Cited in "Honesty and Efficiency in Government," Illinois—Adlai Stevenson folder, PSF Political File, Truman Papers, Truman Library.
14. Cited in Martin, *Adlai Stevenson of Illinois*, p. 359. The following discussion is based on this source.
15. Truman, personal memo, Longhand Notes, Undated folder, PSF Longhand Notes File, Truman Papers, Truman Library; Martin *Adlai Stevenson of Illinois*, pp. 522–23; Adlai Stevenson, *Major Campaign Speeches of Adlai E. Stevenson, 1952* with an introduction by the author, pp. xxi–xxii.
16. Martin, *Adlai Stevenson of Illinois*, p. 550. The discussion in the preceding paragraph is based on this source, p. 539–40.
17. Gorman, *Kefauver*, p. 142. The preceding discussion in this and the preceding paragraph is based on this source, p. 113, and Jack Anderson and Fred Blumenthal, *The Kefauver Story*, pp. 168–69.
18. Gorman, *Kefauver*, p. 116.

19. Ibid., p. 145. The preceding discussion is based on this source, pp. 121, 142–45; Bernstein, "Election of 1952," pp. 3235.

20. Elsey to Clifford, 28 December 1951, Correspondence 1952 folder, Political File, Clifford Papers, Truman Library.

21. "Honesty in Government: A Democratic Achievement," 14 April 1952, Research Division Fact Sheets, 1948–1952 folder, David Lloyd Papers, Truman Library. The preceding discussion is based on this source and Gorman, Kefauver, p. 44; Donald Hansen, Oral History Interview by Charles T. Morrissey, pp. 42–43.

22. Bernstein, "Election of 1952," pp. 3228–29; Herbert S. Parmet, Eisenhower and the American Crusades, pp. 4–5.

23. Arthur M. Schlesinger, Jr., ed., History of American Presidential Elections, 1789–1968, vol. 4, pp. 3291–92.

24. Cited in Charles C. Alexander, Holding the Line: The Eisenhower Era, 1952–1961, p. 11.

25. Martin, Adlai Stevenson of Illinois, p. 586.

26. Truman to Stevenson (unsent), undated (mid-August 1952), Longhand Notes, Undated folder, PSF Longhand Notes File, Truman Papers, Truman Library.

27. Stevenson to Alicia Patterson, 28 July 1952, cited in Martin, Adlai Stevenson of Illinois, p. 608.

28. Public Papers of the Presidents, Truman, 1952–53, p. 530.

29. Martin, Adlai Stevenson of Illinois, p. 618. The preceding discussion is based on this source, p. 616–18.

30. Truman, Years of Trial and Hope, p. 498.

31. Martin, Adlai Stevenson of Illinois, p. 644. The following discussion is based on the same source.

32. Public Papers of the Presidents, Truman, 1952–53, p. 530. Truman's acceptance of Stevenson's apology, mentioned in the following sentence, is discussed in Martin, Adlai Stevenson of Illinois, p. 644.

33. Truman to Stevenson (unsent), undated (mid-August 1952), Longhand Notes, Undated folder, PSF Longhand Notes File, Truman Papers, Truman Library. The full text of this letter has been published in Robert H. Ferrell, ed., Off the Record: The Private Papers of Harry S. Truman, pp. 268–69.

34. Truman, personal memo, 22 December 1952, Longhand Personal Memos, 1952 folder, PSF Longhand Notes File, Truman Paper, Truman Library. (Published in full in Ferrell, ed., Off the Record, pp. 279–83).

35. Staff of Senate Minority Policy Committee, "Major Issues of 1952— Background Material," August 1952, Box 9, Robert Humphreys Papers, Eisenhower Library. The report was laden with rhetorical excess. The following three phrases are included within the space of four consecutive sentences on page 55 of the report: "a Niagara of scandal," "the twilight zone between Democratic politics and gangsterism," and "the murky waters of Administration corruption."

36. "Democrats Run on Truman Record," Box 8, Humphreys Papers, Eisenhower Library.

37. "Ike and Dick—They're for You," 1952 Campaign and Election; RNC—Printed Material folder, Box 9, Humphreys Papers, Eisenhower Library.

38. "Want Another Truman?" 1952 Campaign and Election—RNC— Printed Material folder, Box 9, Humphreys Papers, Eisenhower Library.

39. "Campaign Statements of D. D. Eisenhower," Indianapolis, 9 Sep-

tember 1952, p. 94, Corruption File, Box 1, Reference Index, Eisenhower Library.

40. "Campaign Statements of D. D. Eisenhower," Atlanta, 2 September 1952, p. 511, Individuals and Miscellaneous Subjects File, Box 2, Reference Index, Eisenhower Library.

41. "Campaign Statements of D. D. Eisenhower," Philadelphia, 4 September 1952, p. 94, Corruption File, Box 1, Reference Index, Eisenhower Library.

42. Ibid., St. Louis, 20 September 1952, p. 96.

43. Cited in Martin, Adlai Stevenson of Illinois, p. 629.

44. Truman to Stevenson (unsent), undated (probably August 1952), Longhand Notes, Undated folder, PSF Longhand Notes File, Truman Papers, Truman Library.

45. Cited in Gosnell, Truman's Crises, p. 519.

46. Public Papers of the Presidents, Truman, 1952–53, pp. 636, 889, 941.

47. Ibid., p. 694.

48. Ibid., pp. 733–35.

49. Jackson, memo to Hague, 2 October 1952, San Francisco—Corruption, 8 October 1952 folder, Box 3, Benedict Papers, Eisenhower Library.

50. "Senator Nixon's Attacks on the President," 10 October 1952, p. 6, and 3 October 1952, p. 3, Richard Nixon Data folder, PSF Political Campaign Material File, Truman Papers, Truman Library.

51. Ibid., 25 October 1952, p. 8.

52. Eisenhower, speech, 23 October 1952, Buffalo, New York, Buffalo, N.Y. folder, Box 5, Benedict Papers, Eisenhower Library.

53. Martin, Adlai Stevenson of Illinois, p. 761; Bernstein, "Election of 1952," pp. 3260–61; Gosnell, Truman's Crises, p. 529; Hechler, memo to Lloyd, 26 November 1952, Kenneth Hechler folder, Lloyd Files, Truman Papers, Truman Library; Truman, Years of Trial and Hope, p. 499.

54. Truman, personal memo, 22 December 1952, Longhand Personal Memos, 1952 folder, PSF Longhand Notes File, Truman Papers, Truman Library. The following discussion is based on this source and Truman, Years of Trial and Hope, p. 497–500.

Notes to Chapter 9
Postpresidential Years

1. Charles Sawyer, interview, 24 March 1955, p. 14, McGrath and Sawyer folder, PPF Memoirs File, Truman Papers, Truman Library.

2. Tom L. Evans, Oral History Interview by James R. Fuchs, pp. 748–49.

3. Martin Friedman, Oral History Interview by Charles T. Morrissey, p. 21.

4. Frank Pace, Jr., Oral History Interview by Jerry N. Hess, p. 8.

5. George M. Elsey, Oral History Interview by Charles T. Morrissey, p. 35.

6. Truman, "Public Service," July 1954, Longhand Personal Notes, 1954 folder, PSF Longhand Notes Files, Truman Papers, Truman Library.

7. Truman, "Political Ethics," undated, Longhand Notes, Undated folder, PSF Longhand Notes File, Truman Papers, Truman Library.

8. Truman to Pauley, 8 September 1955, Edwin Pauley folder, PPNF, Truman Library. The preceding discussion is based on Pauley to Truman, 30 August 1955, Edwin Pauley folder, PPNF, Truman Library.

9. Jules Abels, *The Truman Scandals*, pp. 40–42; "Brief of Matthew J. Connelly and T. Lamar Caudle in the United States Court of Appeals for the Eighth District" (hereinafter Connelly-Caudle Brief), pp. 1–4, 8–13, Connelly folder, PPNF, Truman Library; Eleanor W. Schoenebaum, ed., *Political Profiles: The Truman Years*, pp. 107–8.

10. Matthew J. Connelly, Oral History Interview by Jerry N. Hess, p. 449. The preceding discussion is based on "Petition for Writ of Certiorari to the United States court of Appeals for the Eighth Circuit in the Supreme Court of the United States, Matthew J. Connelly, Petition" (hereinafter Connelly Petition), October term, 1957, p. 54a, Connelly folder, PPNF, Truman Library.

11. The evidence was a journal entry in Schwimmer's handwriting:

Oct	49
Shu Stile	$10,000
Pd out Oil Royalty M. C.	4,200
held in Escrow to be paid out depending on whether I. Sachs case is dropped	$ 5,800

"M.C." was clearly Connelly, but it was unclear whether Connelly had any knowledge of the so-called escrow account, or whether the money was intended to be paid to Connelly. During the trial, the court expressed ambivalence about whether the evidence should have been admitted in view of Schwimmer's exit from the case. Connelly-Caudle Brief, pp. 17–21.

12. Connelly-Caudle Brief, p. 29. The balance of the discussion in this paragraph is based on this source, p. 27–29, 174–75; "Joint Motion of Defendants Matthew J. Connelly and T. Lamar Caudle for Judgment of Acquittal, or in the Alternative for New Trial, United States District Court, Eastern District of Missouri, Eastern Division," Matthew J. Connelly folder, PPNF, Truman Library.

13. "Decision of the District Court (Successor Judge)," Appendix C. Connelly Petition pp. 62a–63a, Connelly folder, PPNF, Truman Library. The Supreme Court refusal to review the case mentioned in the following sentence is discussed in *Kansas City Times*, 1 April 1958, Matthew J. Connelly folder, PPNF, Truman Library.

14. Truman to Connelly, 6 August 1956, Matthew J. Connelly folder, PPNF, Truman Library.

15. Truman, personal memo, undated, p. 20, Longhand Personal Memos folder, PSF Longhand Notes File, Truman Papers, Truman Library.

16. Donald Dawson, Oral History Interview by James R. Fuchs, p. 88. The preceding discussion of Connelly's character witnesses is based on George E. Allen, Oral History Interview by Jerry N. Hess, pp. 33–34; Moulder to Connelly, 29 June 1956, Matthew J. Connelly folder, PPNF, Truman Library. Among those who commented on Connelly's honesty were former patronage adviser Donald Dawson; Truman's assistant military aide, Cornelius J. Mara; General Trade Commissioner Lowell B. Mason; and John A. Kennedy, who had served with Connelly on the Truman committee. Former special counsel Charles Murphy and former administrative assistant Stephen J. Spingarn, while decrying the verdict, observed that Connelly might have been indiscreet. Mason, handwritten note to Rose Conway, attached to copy of Mason to Connelly, 13 December 1955, Matthew J. Connelly folder, PPNF, Truman Library; and the following

Truman Library oral history interview transcripts: Donald Dawson, by James R. Fuchs, p. 88; Cornelius J. Mara, by Jerry N. Hess, p. 72; Connelly, by Jerry N. Hess, p. 451; John A. Kennedy, p. 27; Charles S. Murphy, by Jerry N. Hess, p. 511; Stephen J. Spingarn, by Jerry N. Hess, p. 124.

17. Mara, Oral History Interview, p. 72.

18. Murphy, Oral History Interview, p. 510.

19. Moulder to Connelly, 29 June 1956, Matthew J. Connelly folder, PPNF, Truman Library.

20. Evans, Oral History Interview, pp. 727, 734.

21. Lashly to Truman, 19 June 1959; Truman to Lashly, 22 June 1959, Matthew J. Connelly—Testimonial Dinner folder, PPNF, Truman Library.

22. Stone to McCormack, 31 August 1959, Matthew J. Connelly—Testimonial Dinner folder, PPNF, Truman Library.

23. *Boston Sunday Globe*, 20 September 1959, Matthew J. Connelly folder, PPNF, Truman Library. The following comment on press coverage of the dinner is from the same source.

24. "Matthew J. Connelly Testimonal Dinner Treasurer's Report," Matthew J. Connelly—Testimonial Dinner folder, PPNF, Truman Library. Among those who did contribute to the dinner were John R. Steelman, Stuart Symington, James McGranery, J. Howard McGrath, Donald S. Dawson, Joseph G. Feeney, John McCormack, and John F. Kennedy, all of whom gave $100; Charles Murphy gave $200, and Dewey Stone, in spite of his criticism, donated $250. The largest contributors were Samuel I. Rosenman ($400), Richard J. Daley ($1,000), and Edwin W. Pauley, ($1,000). List of Contributors, Matthew J. Connelly—Testimonial Dinner folder, PPNF, Truman Library.

25. "Statement of Former President Harry S. Truman," approximately 3 May 1960, Matthew J. Connelly folder, PPNF, Truman Library.

26. *New York Post*, May 1960, Matthew J. Connelly folder, PPNF, Truman Library.

27. Truman to Robert Kennedy, 15 March 1961, Lamar Caudle folder, PPNF, Truman Library.

28. Truman to Samuel I. Rosenman, 13 September 1963; Matthew J. Connelly folder, PPNF, Truman Library.

29. Truman to Robert Kennedy, 10 May 1961, Lamar Caudle folder, PPNF, Truman Library.

30. "Decision of the District Court (Successor Judge)," Appendix C. Connelly Petition, pp. 24a–63a, Matthew J. Connelly folder, PPNF, Truman Library.

31. Robert Kennedy to Truman, undated (May or June 1961), Robert F. Kennedy folder, PPNF, Truman Library. Truman's reply, mentioned in the next sentence, is Truman to Kennedy, 12 June 1961, Lamar Caudle folder, PPNF, Truman Library.

32. Cited in Merle Miller, *Plain Speaking: An Oral Biography of Harry S. Truman*, p. 439. The preceding discussion of previous friction between Truman and Kennedy is based on Arthur M. Schlesinger, Jr., *Robert Kennedy and His Times*, p. 230.

33. Truman to Robert Kennedy, 24 January 1962, Robert F. Kennedy folder, PPF Secretary's Office Files, Truman Papers, Truman Library.

34. Truman to Connelly, 11 May 1962, Matthew J. Connelly folder, PPNF, Truman Library.

35. Truman to John F. Kennedy, 3 December 1962, Matthew J. Connelly folder, PPNF, Truman Library. The preceding discussion is based on *Kansas City Times*, 23 November 1962, Matthew J. Connelly folder, PPNF, Truman Library.

36. Truman, personal memo, 26 December 1951, Longhand Personal Memos, 1951 folder, PSF Longhand Notes File, Truman Papers, Truman Library.

37. Truman to Pearson, 13 September 1954, Drew Pearson folder, PPNF, Truman Library. The preceding discussion is based on Pearson to Truman, 8 September 1954, Drew Pearson folder, PPNF, Truman Library.

38. Drew Pearson, *Diaries, 1949–1959*, ed. Tyler Abell, p. 458.

39. Caudle to Truman, 27 April 1956, Lamar Caudle folder, PPNF, Truman Library; Truman to Robert Kennedy, 15 March, 10 May, 12 June 1961, Lamar Caudle folder, PPNF, Truman Library; Truman to Robert Kennedy, 24 January 1962, Robert F. Kennedy folder, PPF Secretary's Office Files, Truman Papers, Truman Library; Truman to John F. Kennedy, 3 December 1962, Matthew J. Connelly folder, PPNF, Truman Library. Caudle's pardon, mentioned in the last sentence of the paragraph, is discussed in *Kansas City Star*, 2 April 1969, Lamar Caudle folder, PPNF, Truman Library.

40. Vaughan to Truman, 28 January 1954, Harry Vaughan folder, PPNF, Truman Library.

41. Truman to Vaughan, 2 February 1954, Harry Vaughan folder, PPNF, Truman Library.

42. Vaughan to Truman, 17 October 1954, Harry Vaughan folder, PPNF, Truman Library.

43. Truman to Vaughan, 25 October 1954, Harry Vaughan folder, PPNF, Truman Library.

44. Drew Pearson, "Confessions of an S.O.B.," *Saturday Evening Post*, 3 November 1956. The preceding discussion is based on *Kansas City Star*, 15 May 1953, Drew Pearson folder, PPNF, Truman Library; Vaughan to Editor, *Saturday Evening Post*, 20 April 1951, Vaughan to Curtis Publishing Co. folder, Vaughan Papers, Truman Library; Merrick and King to Curtis Publishing Company, 26 April 1955, Material Supplied by Drew Pearson in 5% Investigation 1949—Wm. L. Lee folder, Vaughan Papers, Truman Library.

45. *New York Times*, 1 April 1960.

46. Vaughan to Truman, 5 February 1959, Harry Vaughan folder, PPNF, Truman Library.

47. Mara to Truman, 6 February 1959, Harry Vaughan folder, PPNF, Truman Library.

48. Vaughan to Truman, 6 November 1953, Harry Vaughan folder, PNF, Truman Library; Margaret Vaughan to Truman, 1 November 1954, Harry Vaughan folder, PPNF, Truman Library.

49. Margaret Vaughan to Truman, 1 November 1954, Harry Vaughan folder, PPNF, Truman Library. In a note to Truman a few months later, Vaughan described his motivation for the project: "I would not object making a few thousand dollars out of that thing, as I could see it, but equally important is my wish to get certain things into the record for future reference. I'd hate to think that, in the year 2055, if someone wished to look me up files would contain only the opinions of Pearson, Winchell

and Bob Considine." Vaughan to Truman, 25 February 1955, Harry
Vaughan folder, PPNF, Truman Library.
    50. Truman to Vaughan, 15 November 1955, Harry H. Vaughan folder,
PPF Secretary's Office File, Truman Papers, Truman Library.
    51. Truman to Vaughan, 15 November 1955, Harry H. Vaughan folder,
PPF Secretary's Office File, Truman Papers, Truman Library. The preced-
ing discussion is based on Vaughan to Truman, 17 November 1955, Harry
H. Vaughan folder, PPF Secretary's Office File, Truman Papers, Truman
Library.
    52. David A. Frier, *Conflict of Interest in the Eisenhower Administration*, pp.
9–10.
    53. Miller, *Plain Speaking*, p. 25.

SELECTED BIBLIOGRAPHY ▆▆▆▆▆▆

Manuscript Collections

In the Harry S. Truman Library, Independence, Mo.

Ayers, Eben A. Papers.
Clifford, Clark M. Papers.
Connelly, Matthew J. Papers.
Democratic National Committee Clipping File.
Elsey, George M. Papers.
Gallup Poll. Papers.
Hechler, Kenneth. Files.
Holland, Lou E. Papers.
Jacobson, Edward. Papers.
Lawton, Frederick, J. Papers.
Lloyd, David D. Papers.
————. Files.
McNaughton, Frank. Papers.
Messall, Victor R. Papers.
Murphy, Charles S. Papers.
————. Files.
Snyder, John W. Papers.
Truman, Harry S. Papers as Presiding Judge of the Jackson County (Missouri) Court, 1926–1934.
————.Papers as Senator and Vice-President.
————. Official Files.
————. President's Secretary's Files.
————. Post-Presidential Papers.
Vaughan, Harry H. Papers.

Others

Benedict, Stephen. Papers. Dwight D. Eisenhower Library, Abilene, Kan.
Department of the Navy Records. Record Group 80, National Archives, Washington, D.C.
Department of the Treasury Records. Record Group 56, National Archives, Washington, D.C.
Humphreys, Robert. Papers. Dwight D. Eisenhower Library, Abilene, Kan.
Ickes, Harold L. Papers. Library of Congress, Washington, D.C.
Office of Management and the Budget Records. Record Group 51, National Archives, Washington, D.C.
Reconstruction Finance Corporation Records. Record Group 234, National Archives, Washington, D.C.
Robinson, William E. Papers. Dwight D. Eisenhower Library, Abilene, Kans.

Interviews

Oral History Interviews, conducted at the Harry S. Truman Library, Independence, Mo.

Allen, George E. By Jerry N. Hess, 15 March 1969.
Brandt, Raymond P. By Jerry N. Hess, 28 September 1970.
Connelly, Matthew J. By Jerry N. Hess, 28, 30 November 1967; 21 August 1968.
Dawson, Donald S. By James R. Fuchs, 8 August 1977.
Dennison, Robert L. By Jerry N. Hess, 10 September 1971; 6 October 1971; 2 November 1971.
Elsey, George M. By Charles T. Morrissey and Jerry N. Hess, 10, 17 February 1964; 9 March 1964; 10, 17 July 1969; 9 April 1970; 7, 10 July 1970.
Evans, Tom L. By James R. Fuchs, 8 August 1962; 28 November 1962; 17 April 1963; 13 June 1963; 13 August 1963; 18 September 1963; 10, 19 December 1963.
Feeney, Joseph G. By Jerry N. Hess, 20 September 1966.
Friedman, Martin L. By Charles T. Morrissey, 5 December 1963.
Hansen, Donald. By Charles T. Morrissey, 5 April 1963.
Hehmeyer, Walter. By James R. Fuchs, 16 April 1969.
Irvin, Robert L. By James R. Fuchs, 26 March 1970.
Kennedy, John A. By James R. Fuchs, July 1978.
Mara, Cornelius J. By Jerry N. Hess, 7, 9, June 1971.
Meader, George. By Charles T. Morrissey, 12 June 1963.
Murphy, Charles S. By Charles T. Morrissey and Jerry N. Hess, 2 May 1963; 3 June 1963; 24 July 1963; 21 May 1969; 24 June 1969; 15, 25, July 1969; 19 May 1970.
Pace, Frank, Jr. By Jerry N. Hess, 17 January 1972.
Perlmeter, Irving. By Charles T. Morrissey, 24, 29 May 1963.
Rigdon, William M. By Jerry N. Hess, 16 July 1970.
Rosenman, Samuel I. By Jerry N. Hess, 15 October 1968; 23 April 1969.
Seidman, Harold D. By Jerry N. Hess, 29 July 1970.
Sparks, Wilbur D. By Jerry N. Hess, 5, 19 September 1968.
Spingarn, Stephen J. By Jerry N. Hess, 20, 21, 22, 23, 24, 27, 28, 29 March 1967.
Sundquist, James L. By Charles T. Morrissey, 15 July 1963.
Tubby, Roger. By Jerry N. Hess, 10 February 1970.
Vaughan, Harry H. By Charles T. Morrissey, 14, 16 January 1963.

Interviews by the Author

Dawson, Donald S. Washington, D.C., 26 July 1979.
Vaughan, Harry H. Alexandria, Va., 24 July 1979.

Books

Abels, Jules. *The Truman Scandals*. Chicago: Henry Regnery Company, 1956.

Alexander, Charles C. *Holding the Line: The Eisenhower Era, 1952–1961.* Bloomington: Indiana University Press, 1975.

Allen, Robert S., and William V. Shannon. *The Truman Merry-Go-Round.* New York: The Vanguard Press, 1950.

Anderson, Jack, with James Boyd. *Confessions of a Muckraker: The Inside Story of Life in Washington during the Truman, Eisenhower, Kennedy and Johnson Years.* New York: Random House, 1979.

Anderson, Jack, and Fred Blumenthal. *The Kefauver Story.* New York: Dial Press, 1956.

Anderson, Patrick. *The Presidents' Men: White House Assistants of Franklin D. Roosevelt, Harry S. Truman, Dwight D. Eisenhower, John F. Kennedy and Lyndon B. Johnson.* Garden City, N.Y.: Doubleday & Company, 1968.

Bartley, Ernest R. *The Tidelands Oil Controversy: A Legal and Historical Analysis.* Austin: University of Texas Press, 1953.

Bolles, Blair. *How To Get Rich in Washington: Rich's Man's Division of the Welfare State.* New York: W. W. Norton & Company, 1952.

Chommie, John C. *The Internal Revenue Service.* New York: Praeger Publishers, 1970.

Clemens, Cyril. *The Man from Missouri: A Biography of Harry S. Truman.* Webster Groves, Mo.: International Mark Twain Society, 1945.

Coffin, Tristam. *Missouri Compromise.* Boston: Little, Brown and Company, 1947.

———. *Senator Fulbright: Portrait of a Public Philosopher.* New York: E. P. Dutton & Co., 1966.

Daniels, Jonathan. *The Man of Independence.* Philadelphia: J. B. Lippincott Company, 1950.

Davies, Richard O. *Housing Reform During the Truman Administration.* Columbia: University of Missouri Press, 1966.

Donovan, Robert J. *Conflict and Crisis: The Presidency of Harry S. Truman, 1945–1948.* New York: W. W. Norton & Company, 1977.

———. *Tumultuous Years: The Presidency of Harry S. Truman, 1949–1953.* New York: W. W. Norton & Company, 1982.

Doris, Lillian, ed. *The American Way in Taxation: Internal Revenue, 1862–1963.* Englewood Cliffs, N.J.: Prentice-Hall, 1963.

Dorsett, Lyle W. *The Pendergast Machine.* New York: Oxford University Press, 1968.

Douglas, Paul H. *In the Fullness of Time: The Memoirs of Paul H. Douglas.* New York: Harcourt Brace Jovanovich, 1971.

Engler, Robert. *The Politics of Oil: A Study of Private Power and Democratic Directions.* New York: The Macmillan Company, 1961.

Ferrell, Robert H., ed. *The Autobiography of Harry S. Truman.* Boulder: Colorado Associated University Press, 1980.

———. *Off the Record: The Private Papers of Harry S. Truman.* New York: Harper & Row, 1980.

Forrestal, James. *The Forrestal Diaries.* Edited by Walter Millis with the collaboration of E. S. Duffield. New York: The Viking Press, 1951.

Frier, David A. *Conflict of Interest in the Eisenhower Administration.* Ames: Iowa State University Press, 1969.

Gorman, Joseph Bruce. *Kefauver: A Political Biography.* New York: Oxford University Press, 1971.

Gosnell, Harold F. *Truman's Crises: A Political Biography of Harry S. Truman.* Westport, Conn.: Greenwood Press, 1980.

Heller, Francis H., ed. *The Truman White House: The Administration of the Presidency, 1945–1953.* Lawrence: The Regents Press of Kansas, 1980.

Helm, William P. *Harry Truman: A Political Biography.* New York: Duell, Sloan and Pearce, 1947.

Hillman, William. *Mr. President: The First Publication from the Personal Diaries, Private Letters, Papers and Revealing Interviews of Harry S. Truman.* New York: Farrar, Straus & Young, 1952.

Hoover Commission Report on Organization of the Executive Branch of the Government. New York: McGraw-Hill Book Company, 1949.

Ickes, Harold L. *The Lowering of Clouds, 1939–1941.* Vol. 3 of *The Secret Diary of Harold L. Ickes.* New York: Simon and Schuster, 1954.

Johnson, Haynes, and Bernard M. Gwertzman. *Fulbright: The Dissenter.* Garden City, N.Y.: Doubleday & Company, 1968.

Jones, Jesse H., with Edward Angly. *Fifty Billion Dollars: My Thirteen Years with the R.F.C. (1932–1945).* New York: The Macmillan Company, 1951.

Klurfeld, Herman. *Behind the Lines: The World of Drew Pearson.* Englewood Cliffs, N.J.: Prentice-Hall, 1968.

———. *Winchell: His Life and Times.* New York: Praeger Publishers, 1976.

Lilienthal, David E. *The Atomic Energy Years, 1945–1950.* Vol. 2 of *The Journals of David E. Lilienthal.* New York: Harper & Row, 1964.

McNaughton, Frank, and Walter Hehmeyer. *This Man Truman.* New York: McGraw Hill Book Company, 1945.

Martin, John Bartlow. *Adlai Stevenson of Illinois: The Life of Adlai E. Stevenson.* Garden City, N.Y.: Doubleday & Company, 1976.

Martin, Ralph G., and Ed Plaut. *Front Runner, Dark Horse.* Garden City, N.Y.: Doubleday & Co., 1960.

Mason, Frank. *Truman and the Pendergasts.* Evanston, Ill.: Regency Books, 1963.

Mooney, Booth. *The Politicians: 1945–1950.* Philadelphia: J. B. Lippincott Company, 1970.

Miller, Merle. *Plain Speaking: An Oral Biography of Harry S. Truman.* New York: Berkeley Medallion Books, 1974.

Milligan, Maurice M. *Missouri Waltz: The Inside Story of the Pendergast Machine by the Man Who Smashed It.* New York: Charles Scribner's Sons, 1948.

Morris, Newbold, in collaboration with Dana Lee Thomas. *Let the Chips Fall: My Battle Against Corruption.* New York: Appleton-Century-Crofts, 1955.

Nash, Gerald D. *United States Oil Policy, 1890–1964.* Pittsburgh: University of Pittsburgh Press, 1968.

Parmet, Herbert S. *Eisenhower and the American Crusades.* New York: The Macmillan Company, 1972.

Parris, Addison W. *The Small Business Administration.* New York: Praeger Publishers, 1968.

Pearson, Drew. *Diaries: 1949–1959.* Edited by Tyler Abell. New York: Holt, Rinehart & Winston, 1974.

Pemberton, William E. *Bureaucratic Politics: Executive Reorganization During the Truman Administration.* Columbia: University of Missouri Press, 1979.

Phillips, Cabell. *The Truman Presidency: The History of a Triumphant Succession.* New York: The Macmillan Company, 1966.

Pilat, Oliver. *Drew Pearson: An Unauthorized Biography.* New York: Harper's Magazine Press, 1973.

———. *Pegler: Angry Man of the Press.* Boston: Beacon Press, 1963.

Powell, Gene. *Tom's Boy Harry.* Jefferson City, Mo.: Hawthorne Publishing Company, 1948.

Reddig, William M. *Tom's Town: Kansas City and the Pendergast Legend.* Philadelphia: J. B. Lippincott Company, 1947.

Robbins, Charles. *Last of His Kind: An Informal Portrait of Harry S. Truman.* New York: William Morrow and Company, 1979.

Sawyer, Charles. *Concerns of a Conservative Democrat.* Carbondale: Southern Illinois University Press, 1968.

Schlesinger, Arthur M., Jr. *Robert Kennedy and His Times.* New York: Ballantine Books, 1978.

Schlesinger, Arthur M., Jr., ed. *History of American Presidential Elections, 1789–1968.* Vol. 4. New York: Chelsea House Publishers in association with McGraw-Hill Book Co., 1971.

Schoenebaum, Eleanora W., ed. *Political Profiles: The Truman Years.* New York: Facts on File, 1978.

Seidman, Harold. *Politics, Position and Power: The Dynamics of Federal Organization.* New York: Oxford University Press, 1970.

Steinberg, Alfred. *The Man from Missouri: The Life and Times of Harry S. Truman.* New York: G. P. Putnam's Sons, 1962.

Stevenson, Adlai E. *Major Campaign Speeches of Adlai E. Stevenson, 1952.* New York: Random House, 1953.

Thomas, Bob. *Winchell.* Garden City, N.Y.: Doubleday & Company, 1971.

Truman, Harry S. *Year of Decisions.* Vol. 1 of *Memoirs by Harry S. Truman.* Garden City, N.Y.: Doubleday & Company, 1955.

———. *Years of Trial and Hope.* Vol. 2 of *Memoirs by Harry S. Truman.* Garden City, N.Y.: Doubleday & Company, 1956.

Truman, Margaret. *Harry S. Truman.* New York: William Morrow & Company, 1973.

Wellman, Paul I. *Stuart Symington: Portrait of a Man with a Mission.* Garden City, N.Y.: Doubleday & Company, 1960.

Woodward, C. Vann, ed. *Responses of the Presidents to Charges of Misconduct.* New York: Delcorte Press, 1974.

Articles

Barter, J. Malcolm. "The Tax Thieves of 1951: The Cadillac and the Collector." *New Republic* 125 (10 December 1951): 12–13.

Fuller, Helen. "The Tax Thieves of 1951." *New Republic* 125 (12 November 1951): 9–10.

"Housing: Bathtub Blues." *Time* 54 (4 July 1949): 55.

Huie, William Bradford. "How to Think About Truman." *The American Mercury* 73 (August 1951): 121–28.

"Inquiries: Caudle, Coats and Cars." *Newsweek* 38 (10 December 1951): 21.

"Is President Truman an Honorable Man?" *The American Mercury* 72 (May 1951): 546–50.

Kearns, James. "The Tax Thieves of 1951: The Finnegan Story." *New Republic* 125 (26 September 1951): 12.

Nelson, Lorraine. "The Trail of the Tax Thieves." *New Republic* 125 (12 November 1951): 11–14.

Pearson, Drew. "Confessions of an S.O.B." *Saturday Evening Post* (3 November 1956): 23–25.

"President, Scared by Scandal, Discards a Couple of 'Friends.'" *Newsweek* 38 (22 October 1951): 23.

Shannon, William V. "The Tax Thieves of 1951: Business and Pleasure in New York." *New Republic* 125 (3 December 1951): 14.

"Uncensored Dope." *Time* 46 (10 September 1945): 20.

Newspapers

New York Times

Government Documents

Truman, Harry S. *The Public Papers of the Presidents of the United States, 1945–53.* Washington: U.S. Government Printing Office, 1961–1966.

U.S. Congress. Senate. Banking and Currency Committee. *Proposed Extension of Reconstruction Finance Corporation: Hearings on $80,000,000 Loan to B. & O. Railroad.* 80th. Cong., 1st sess., 28 May 5–6 June 1947.

U.S. Congress. Senate. Subcommittee of the Committee on the Judiciary. *Kansas City Vote Fraud: Hearings on S. Res. 116.* 80th Cong., 1st sess., 28 May 5–6 June 1947.

U.S. Congress. Senate. Investigations Subcommittee of the Committee on Expenditures in the Executive Departments. *Influence in Government Procurement: Hearings pursuant to S. Res. 52.* 81st Cong., 1st sess., 8 August–1 September 1949.

U.S. Congress. Senate. Subcommittee of the Committee on Banking and Currency. *Expansion of R.F.C. Lending Policy: Hearings on S. Res. 2344.* 81st Cong., 1st sess., 2–18 August 1949.

U.S. Congress. Senate. Investigations Subcommittee of the Committee on Expenditures in the Executive Departments. *The 5-Percenter Investigation pursuant to S. Res. 52.* 81st Cong., 2d sess., 18 January 1950. S. Rept. 1232.

U.S. Congress. Senate. Subcommittee of the Committee on Banking and Currency. *Study of Reconstruction Finance Corporation: Texmass*

Loan: Hearings on S. Res. 219. 81st Cong., 2d sess., 13–27 April
1950.

U.S. Congress. Senate. Committee on Banking and Currency. *Study of
Reconstruction Finance Corporation: Texmass Petroleum Co. Loan: Interim
Report pursuant to S. Res. 219.* 81st Cong., 2d sess., 19 May 1950. S.
Rept. 1689.

U.S. Congress. Senate. Subcommittee of the Committee on Banking
and Currency. *Study of Reconstruction Finance Corporation: Loan to
Waltham Watch: Hearings on S. Res. 219.* 81st Cong., 2d sess., 20–21
July 1950.

U.S. Congress. Senate. Subcommittee on Reconstruction Finance Corporation of the Committee on Banking and Currency. *Favoritism
and Influence: Interim Report pursuant to S. Res. 219.* 81st Cong., 1st
sess., 5 February 1951. S. Rept. 76.

U.S. Congress. Senate. Subcommittee of the Committee on Banking
and Currency. *Study of Reconstruction Finance Corporation: Hearings
on S. Rept. 219.* 82d Cong., 1st sess., 2 March–11 May 1951.

U.S. Congress. Senate. Committee on Banking and Currency. *Study of
Reconstruction Finance Corporation and Proposed Amendment of R.F.C.
Act. Report to accompany S. 515 and to serve as a final report pursuant to
S. Res. 219.* 82d Cong., 1st sess., 20 August 1951. S. Rept. 649.

U.S. Congress. House. Subcommittee of the Committee on Ways and
Means. *Internal Revenue Investigation: Hearings.* 82d Cong., 1st sess.,
10 September 1951–29 January 1952.

U.S. Congress. House. Subcommittee of the Committee on the Judiciary. *Investigation of the Department of Justice: Hearings.* 82d Cong.,
2d sess., 26 March 1952–27 June 1952.

U.S. Congress. House. Committee on the Judiciary. *Investigation of the
Department of Justice: Report pursuant to H. Res. 50.* 83d Cong., 1st
sess., 1 August 1953. H. Rept. 1079.

Unpublished Sources

Dorsett, Lyle W. "Truman and the Pendergast Machine." Paper presented at Eighth Missouri Conference on History, University of Missouri, Columbia, Missouri, 25–26 March 1966. Mimeographed.

Maher, Sister M. Patrick Ellen. "The Role of the Chairman of a
Congressional Investigating Committee: A Case Study of the Spe-
cial Committee of the Senate to Investigate the National Defense
Program, 1941–1948." Ph.D. diss., St. Louis University, 1962.

Schmidtlein, Eugene Francis. "Truman the Senator." Ph.D. diss., University of Missouri—Columbia, 1962.

Shelton, James Hill. "The Tax Scandals of the 1950's." Ph.D. diss., The
American University, 1971.

INDEX